I0576249

George Salmon

The Reign of Law

And Other Sermons Preached in the Chapel of Trinity College, Dublin

George Salmon

The Reign of Law
And Other Sermons Preached in the Chapel of Trinity College, Dublin

ISBN/EAN: 9783337160326

Printed in Europe, USA, Canada, Australia, Japan

Cover: Foto ©Lupo / pixelio.de

More available books at **www.hansebooks.com**

THE

REIGN OF LAW:

AND OTHER SERMONS

PREACHED IN

𝕿𝖍𝖊 𝕮𝖍𝖆𝖕𝖊𝖑 𝖔𝖋 𝕿𝖗𝖎𝖓𝖎𝖙𝖞 𝕮𝖔𝖑𝖑𝖊𝖌𝖊,

DUBLIN.

BY

GEORGE SALMON, D.D.

Chancellor of St. Patrick's Cathedral, and Regius Professor of Divinity in the University of Dublin.

𝕷𝖔𝖓𝖉𝖔𝖓:

MACMILLAN AND CO.

1873.

CONTENTS.

SERMON I.

THE REIGN OF LAW.

" Be not deceived ; God is not mocked : for whatsoever a man soweth, that shall he also reap. For he that soweth to his flesh shall of the flesh reap corruption ; but he that soweth to the Spirit shall of the Spirit reap life everlasting."—GALATIANS vi. 7, 8.

THE progress of scientific discovery has now filled the minds of all thinking men with a sense of the universal prevalence of law. If we ascribe events now to chance, the idea we attach to the word is something very different from the signification which it bore in former days. In early times, when the links connecting events were unnoticed, and their sequences believed to be arbitrary, what struck men most was, how short a way human prudence could go in directing the course of affairs. Fortune was then felt to be a divinity—blind, indeed, and capricious, and inconstant, but all-powerful. With malicious joy, she made it her sport to baffle the calculations of the prudent, and chequer with reverses the triumphs of the successful. At her interference, the most deeply-laid schemes of the wise would end in confusion, while she would lavish on some undeserving object riches and honours. Yet no sooner

had he begun to regard them as his own stable possession, than she would snatch them from him, and
shift the uncertain honours to another. It was then
felt to be a rash and foolish thing in any prosperous
man to wound the jealousy of heaven by claiming
for himself the merit of his own success, or by
daring to say of any of his achievements, that in
this fortune had no share. No military skill or civil
ability could enable a public man to inspire such
confidence in his followers, as if he could seem to
be able with truth to proclaim himself the favourite
of fortune, and assume to himself without dispute
the title of Felix. Yet when the facts came to be
soberly looked at, it was seen that life is no such
lottery as some in their moments of disappointment
might proclaim it to be. It is true that occasionally,
carefully sown crops may be blighted by the incle-
mency of heaven, and never come to perfection;
yet on the whole, whatsoever a man soweth, that
he also reaps. As human prudence wrested province
after province from the domain subject to the sway
of fortune, it was felt that it had been after all
nothing but the blind inconsiderateness of men
which had made her a goddess, and enthroned her
in the heaven.

If I were to declare now that nothing takes place
by chance, the statement would be assented to in
different senses by men of two opposite schools.
On the one hand, those events which in common
talk men ascribe to chance, would be referred by a
deeply religious man to the directing providence of
an all-overruling God. Such a man would believe,

that while he himself is blindly groping his way
along the path of life, ignorant whither he is going,
and what he is about to meet, his steps are, never-
theless, watched and governed by One before whom
the whole way lies clear. The very aspect of chance
and confusion which life assumes, when seen from
our very limited range of vision, only serves to
elevate his conceptions of the wisdom of Him who
evolves from the whole His great designs. Just as
to one inspecting the loom in which some gorgeous
tapestry is being wrought, the fact that to his un-
instructed gaze all appears a confused medley of
cards and threads and shuttles, only increases his
admiration for the skill of the contriver who has
disposed all, so that a regular pattern shall emerge
from the seeming disorder. To one who thus looks
on life, the word chance, which implies the absence
of all plan and forethought, seems unmeaning,
since he regards all as exhibiting forethought and
wisdom higher than man's.

But men of a very different school—men, who
either disbelieve in a God, or who set aside the
whole enquiry as to God's existence as beyond man's
powers, and one on which a well-disciplined intellect
would know that it was waste of time to enter—such
men, also, would feel that the word chance, if used
at all, must be employed in a sense very different
from the popular one. Physical science has now
reduced to order a multitude of phenomena, once
supposed to be ungoverned by law. The wandering
stars of heaven are now known to follow no vagrant
course, but return to their predicted places as surely

as the orb of day himself. It were needless to speak
of the triumphs which science has already achieved;
but even those realms which she has not already
taken possession of, we regard as her rightful property. We record the changes of the shifting winds,
and note down all the vicissitudes of our inconstant climate, persuaded that although the key to
their irregularities has not yet been completely
found, yet that undoubtedly order governs all. Nor
do human affairs seem less subject to the operation
of law, than the changes of inanimate nature. The
casualties of life are now made matter of scientific
prediction; not only those which spring from merely
material causes, but those also which arise out of
human volitions. · The likelihood that a confidential
servant will betray his trust, or that a clerk shall
forget to address a letter, can be estimated and provided for as accurately as the probability of the
occurrence of a storm or a shipwreck. What have
seemed to be the happy accidents of the world's
history, are now seen to be less and less under the
dominion of chance. Has a brilliant thought flashed
on the brain of a man of genius, and led him to
some discovery of signal benefit to humanity, ere
he has well secured for himself the glory of the
discovery, there starts up some competitor to dispute
the merit with him; and however the controversy
between them may be decided, it becomes apparent
that the world had been dependent upon neither.
The discovery itself was no matter of chance. It
had come because the times were ripe for it, and
all that chance had to control was, whether it

should make its appearance in one place or another. One who is much in the habit of taking notice of facts of this kind, comes to regard every phenomenon that takes place, as a natural and necessary evolution from the precedent conditions, and is as little inclined to attribute any event to chance, as he would be to say that it is by chance the blossom is succeeded by the fruit. Chance is, with him, but a word to express human ignorance of the laws actually in operation; but he would insist that those things which take place without design or contrivance of ours, are as much the necessary result of causes producing them, as where known causes have been combined by ourselves for the purpose of accomplishing certain foreseen results.

Let us ask, however, is there irreconcilable opposition between the view which sees in all phenomena the operation of law and that which delights to trace in them the working out of the plans of God. Whether we find such opposition or not depends very much on the sources whence we have derived our conceptions of God, The first source of power of which we know anything is our own will; and accordingly in the infancy of the world men ascribed every motion and every change to the operation of some will like our own. The courses of the stars, the running of the streams, the blasts of the winds, they believed to be governed each by some intelligence who made that form of energy his own peculiar care. The actions of their divinities they believed to be directed by completely human motives. Not to speak of those tales which ascribed to the gods some of the

grossest forms of human vice, they supposed them to
be swayed in their conduct by a craving for the
honours paid by men, by jealousy of men's neglect,
by envy of human prosperity, or by mere caprice.
To men with such conceptions of their deities it cost
nothing to believe a miracle. It required little evidence to induce them to believe that the Divine
power had exerted itself in this way or in that, when
they could not find that its interference with human
affairs was regulated by any law, or directed by any
intelligible plan. But if in early times the tendency
was to refer the movements of inanimate nature to
the operations of mind, the study of physical science
has in our days produced the opposite tendency, and
has made men find it difficult to see any other laws
in nature than those which regulate the movements
of inanimate matter. The relation of human volitions to the motives which suggest them, has been
held to be precisely the same as that between any
physical change and the antecedent conditions of
which it is the necessary result. And in systems
which thus recognize the existence only of material
forces, if any room is left for the recognition of a
God at all, He seems to be a mere name to express
the universal order rather than a force capable of
interfering with the working of known secondary
causes.

Perhaps it will help to illustrate the practical bearing of those different conceptions of the nature of
God, if I remind you of the different answers which
have been given to the question, " Can God forgive
sins, and is He likely to do so ?" In the old heathen

conceptions of God's character, no doubt was entertained that indulgence for human frailty could be obtained, and on easy terms. Their divinities were not
conceived as being of such a moral character as to
feel any strong indignation against sin ; and if their
suppliant were careful to pay due honours to the gods
themselves, he could bribe them to connive at sin,
and leave unpunished offences unatoned for, unre-
pented of, and unreformed. Christianity has done
much to elevate men's conceptions of God's moral
character, even among those who reject her claims.
No difficulty, therefore, is felt by any in admitting
that God cannot be reconciled to the hardened and
impenitent sinner ; but the whole Christian doctrine
of atonement has been assailed, because it seems to
represent that there are difficulties which must be
removed before God can fitly forgive even a sinner
who repents. Nay, it is urged, we ourselves think it
unbecoming to retain our anger against one who has
expressed his sorrow for the offence towards us of
which he may have been guilty : can we suppose that
a good and merciful God should be less indulgent
than we ourselves should be towards one who has
wronged us ? Is it not dishonouring to God to imagine that He retains any vindictive feelings which
need to be propitiated by atonement and sacrifice ?
And must we not, therefore, reject the whole Christian account of the efficacy of Christ's sacrifice, and
believe that without any such atonement the way lies
always open for the sinner to return to the favour of
God ? Such was the form of objection to the Christian doctrine of the forgiveness of sin which was at

one time urged with most confidence. But in our time men, whose conceptions of God have been derived from a study of the physical order of the universe, have assailed the Christian scheme, not because it represents that there are difficulties in the way of God's forgiveness of sin, but because it represents the forgiveness of sin as too easy. God, it is said, can no more forgive sin than He can undo the past. "An act of sin" (I quote from one of the ablest champions of modern infidelity*) "ought not to be regarded as an injury done to another party for which atonement and reparation can be made, and satisfaction can be given, but rather as a deed which cannot be undone, eternal in its consequences ; an act which once committed is numbered with the irrevocable past. In a word, sin contains its own retributive penalty as surely and as naturally as the acorn contains the oak. Its consequence is its punishment: it needs no other, and can have no heavier ; and its consequence is involved in its commission, and cannot be separated from it. Punishment (let us fix this in our minds) is not the execution of a sentence, but the occurrence of an effect. It is ordained to follow guilt by God, not as a Judge, but as the Creator and Legislator of the universe." "A sin without its punishment is as impossible, as complete a contradiction in terms as a cause without effect. To pray that God will forgive our sins, is to ask Him to work a miracle in our behalf : to ask Him to violate the eternal and harmonizing order of the universe

* Greg's Creed of Christendom, p. 265.

for the comfort of one out of the infinite myriads of its inhabitants."

"If the foregoing reflections are sound," he adds, "the awful, yet wholesome conviction presses upon our minds, that there can be no forgiveness of sins, that is, no interference with, or remittance of, or protection from their natural effects; that God will not interpose between the cause and its consequence; that whatsoever a man soweth, that shall he also reap. An awful consideration this; yet all reflection, all experience, confirm its truth. The sin which has debased our soul may be repented of, may be turned from, but the injury is done: the debasement may be redeemed by after efforts, the stain may be obliterated by bitterer struggles and severer sufferings, by faith in God's love and communion with His Spirit. But the efforts and the endurance which might have raised the soul to the loftiest heights are now exhausted in merely regaining what it has lost. There must always be a wide difference (as one of our divines has said) between him who only ceases to do evil, and him who has always done well; between the man who began to serve his God as soon as he knew that he had a God to serve, and the man who only turns to heaven after he has exhausted all the indulgences of earth."

"Again, in the case of sin of which you have induced another to partake. You may repent, you may, after agonizing struggles, regain the path of virtue, your spirit may re-achieve its purity through much anguish and after many stripes; but the weaker fellow-creature whom you led astray, whom you made

a sharer in your guilt, but whom you cannot make a
sharer in your repentance and amendment, whose
downward course (the first step of which you taught)
you cannot check, but are compelled to witness, what
forgiveness of sins can avail you there? There is
your perpetual, your inevitable punishment, which
no repentance can alleviate, and no mercy can remit."

" This doctrine, that sin can be forgiven, and its
consequences averted, has been in all ages a fertile
source of mischief. Perhaps few of our intellectual
errors have fructified in a vaster harvest of evil, or
operated more powerfully to impede the moral progress of our race."

" Let anyone look back upon his past career—look
inward on his daily life—and then say what effect
would be produced upon him were the conviction
once fixedly imbedded in his soul that everything
done is done irrevocably ; that even the omnipotence
of God cannot uncommit a deed—cannot make that
undone which has been done : that every act of his
must bear its allotted fruit, according to the everlasting laws—must remain for ever ineffaceably inscribed on the tablets of universal nature ; and then
let him consider what would have been the result
upon the moral condition of our race had all men
ever held this conviction."

I have quoted more fully than I should do if I
were merely laying before you an objection to be
answered ; but what I have read contains a representation of truth, one-sided indeed, and imperfect, yet
truth distinctly taught in Scripture, and in particular
in the text. As far as the objections to Christianity

are concerned, we may safely allow the objectors to reply to each other. If our religion be accused of falsely representing that there are obstacles in the way of God's pardon of sin, for the removal of which an elaborate scheme of redemption was necessary, we may appeal to the testimony I have quoted in proof of the fact that God has written on the laws of nature that it is, indeed, no easy matter to blot out the stain of sin, and restore the transgressor to the place from which he fell. But if the iron and unbending laws of nature be presented in such an aspect as to fill the sinner with despair, we may fitly remember that our first conceptions of God are derived not from the contemplation of the inanimate world without, but from our experience of the powers of our own mind and will. It is no unreasonable inference that the judgments, which the Author of our being has so constituted us that we cannot help forming, indicate His own character, and that the feelings of indignation against wrong, hatred of untruth, pity for human suffering, mercy, forgiveness, loving-kindness, which go to make up the character which is universally recognized as that of a good man, are not alien to the character of God Himself, who has taught us so to feel and so to judge. A scheme which wholly leaves out of account all that may be learned as to God's character from the study of our own moral nature condemns itself as imperfect.

And though it is true that the Christian doctrine of forgiveness of sin has been at times grossly abused; though men despise the long-suffering of God, and wilfully continue in sin, trusting that from His un-wearied mercy pardon can at any time be found ; yet infinitely worse consequences would have followed had no method been provided for the return of the transgressor to the favour of God. If it were taught that each slip we made in treading our course was irrevocable, if our daily accumulating sins were felt to be raising a barrier between us and God, which no strength of ours could surmount, such doctrine would wither up the springs of energy in blank despair. It was by giving hope to the hopeless that the Gospel won its first victories. It sought out the publicans and sinners, whom the contempt of society had deprived of self-respect, and it proclaimed there was hope for them. It gave new life to powers which despair had scared and blighted ; it found its way to hearts frozen up by the scorn of men ; and at its warming touch the seeds of new virtues rapidly blos-somed into fruit. Notwithstanding the fears which many have expressed, lest the Gospel proclamation of free forgiveness through the blood of Christ, should lead to licentiousness, it has been found that greater results have been derived from gratitude and love than could ever have been obtained by the dis-cipline of terror. It might be imagined that the proclamation—" Though your sins be as scarlet, they shall be as white as snow ; though they be red like crimson, they shall be as wool," was nothing else than a license to commit wrong-doing with impunity ; yet, in point of fact, we have no reason to think that any efforts which fear might have urged men to make in order to keep their garments in purity, could have enabled them to rival the purity of those who have washed their robes and made them white in the blood of the Lamb.

The sum, then, of what I have been urging is, that our conceptions of God will be erroneous if we do not base them on a study of all His works. We shall go wrong, if immersed in the study of physical nature, we conceive of God as a machine ruthlessly working on its predestined course, deaf to the cry of human agony, and inaccessible to human entreaty. And we shall go wrong if, not looking beyond our own nature, we conceive of a God altogether such as we are, and attribute to Him human frailty and human caprice. Our conceptions of God must necessarily, to a certain extent, be anthropomorphic; for it is from man that we derive our notions of what is meant by intelligence and design, as well our notions of the moral attributes of justice, goodness, and so forth. But we may purge away all the grosser part of our anthropomorphism, by not only studying the nature with which God has endowed ourselves, but by studying also His other works. We thus learn to exclude from our conceptions of Him all that caprice and inconstancy which so often characterize the actions of man, and to know that there is no inconsistency in tracing in events the working out of the plans of God, while we trace in them also the operation of law. For if it be true that man can only conquer nature by obeying her, it is no less true that the Author of nature Himself obeys the rules which He has prescribed for Himself, and is wont to accomplish His mighty ends without violating any of those laws which He has ordained shall regulate the mutual actions of the creatures which He has made.

I may say that this was the principal merit of Bishop Butler's great work, that He taught us, instead of guessing what, according to our notions, it was likely or fitting that God should do, to study His works, and there learn what in similar cases He had done. Thus new evidence was furnished .for the truth of Revelation, when it was shown that statements written in His Word had been long since written in older characters in the Book of His works. It was shown thus that much which it had been imagined took place by arbitrary appointment resulted naturally from the very constitution that God had given things : that, for example, if there be any future life at all, then, unless a special miracle be wrought to prevent it, the characters formed in us here must remain with us and produce their natural fruit, whether of happiness or misery, throughout eternity. But it cannot be said that the truths to which Butler thus directed attention were *new* truths. So Paul, in the text and elsewhere, appeals to the analogy of nature as exhibiting the rules of God's moral government of the world ; and it is repeatedly taught in the New Testament that future rewards will proceed from the operation of laws of which we may have present experience : that the first fruits of the Spirit enjoyed here are the earnest of the inheritance of which we are hereafter to be put in possession, that "he who believeth on the Son of God *hath* everlasting life ; and that he that believeth not is condemned already, because he hath not believed in the name of the only begotten Son of God."

I have not left myself time to make the practical application I had wished to do of the truths we have been considering. If, indeed, I have at all impressed you with the existence of natural laws which regulate the consequences of our actions, and which cannot be changed without a miracle, it will need but few words to convince you who are in the seed-time of life to take heed now what harvest you prepare for yourselves. Will you leave the fields unsown to be occupied by the weeds which rank and wild spring up in neglected ground, or will you, in the hope of a tardy repentance, sow to the flesh, and of the flesh reap corruption ? The repentance you hope for may come. That is not certain, perhaps not probable, but it may come, and God may graciously accept it ; and yet long afterwards the bitter fruits may continue to spring up of the harvest you have sown in your youth ; and when you strive to dedicate to God powers which have lost their freshness, you will have to mourn over energies exhausted, imagination polluted by sin, influence on others impaired, as you find yourselves unable to win back to the ways of peace those whom your example had tempted into the downward path of sin.

It is true, with regard to the things of this life, that what a man soweth that he also reaps. If you have begun to indulge in the dreams of ambition, and covet a high and honourable place among men, whether these dreams will ever be realized will depend on the exertions you make now ; for God has ordained that persevering and rightly directed labour seldom fails to gain its appropriate reward. Yet it

may fail; for the harvests of this world will occasionally, because of unfertile soil or of unfavourable
seasons, fail to reward the labour of the husbandman.
Or you may obtain the reward you coveted, and find
it wither in your grasp. You have sowed to the
flesh, and have of the flesh reaped corruption. But
if you sow to the Spirit you cannot fail. God's promise is sure. You shall of the Spirit reap life everlasting. Your reward is certain; its work abiding,
its heavenly fruit fadeth not away.

Although I have spoken at some length already, I
must not conclude without at least saying a few words
in reference to the loss we have just sustained in the
removal of one who was officially connected with this
College as its Visitor, and who, though not originally
a member of our University, stands next after the
late Lord Primate in the list of its recent benefactors.*
I shall say nothing as to his public character; it was
well known to you all, and perhaps might be more
fitly estimated by one whose feelings towards him
are more cold than mine. And yet I believe that if I
chose to say all I thought of it, I could speak of it
with more general assent than might have been expected in the case of one who took so active a part
in so many controversies, religious and political. For
it was his fortune to outlive many prejudices; and
in his later years there were few who did not do
justice not only to his ability, but to his thorough
honesty and singleness of purpose. But though

---

* My affectionate regard for the memory of Archbishop Whately
has induced me to include in this collection of Sermons this one
preached on the Sunday after his death.

many knew how much there was in his character deserving of admiration, only those who were intimately
acquainted with him knew how much there was in
him to be loved. They have lost in him one of the
truest of friends, whose confidence, if not lightly given,
was not easily shaken, and whose most common error
of judgment was over-indulgent estimate of the merits
of those whom he loved. And perhaps even they
will own that they had not fully known all his claims
on their affectionate regard until his tedious and
painful illness revealed many a gentler grace, for the
display of which there had not been opportunity before. He had not only to endure severe and long-
continued pain, he had to submit to what was even a
harder trial than pain, when a mind of no ordinary
activity, retaining all its energies, found the body
unable to respond to its wishes, and he was reduced
to a state of utter helplessness peculiarly trying to
one of unusual independence of spirit. Under these
trials his friends found him full of constant thoughtful
consideration for others, present and absent; most
grateful in acknowledgment of services rendered;
supported by a strong sense of Christian duty that
survived his bodily decay; and with pitying admiration they saw him exert all his force of character to
battle down every inclination to murmur, and to sub-
due any expression of petulance or impatience which
could add to the sorrow of those who ministered to
him.

I own I take more pleasure in recalling these
things now than in speaking of the more public and
more prosperous part of his life. From that, indeed,

c

I might illustrate the lesson of the text, " That which a man soweth he shall reap." I might show how in this world God's gifts, conscientiously used, do bear their natural fruit int he honours with which men unsolicited will surround one whom they have learned to esteem, and whom they know they can implicitly trust; and how the good opinion of others, despised, and even defied, for the sake of the steady pursuance of what is believed to be the right course can be won though slowly, yet more surely, than if it had been made the direct object of pursuit. But I rather take pleasure in the thought that the seed which he sowed was not for that corruptible harvest which can be reaped on earth. The time came to him when pain and sickness level alike the artificial distinctions which external rank, and the natural distinctions which high intellectual gifts place between one man and another. Happy for him then that it was not here he had sought his portion, and that the Saviour, in whose merits alone he trusted, and whose example he had sought to imitate, was with him in his sickness, giving him strength to bear the burden which He laid on him, and in the afflictions of his later days ripening those graces which it is His bounty to reward with never-dying fruit.

SERMON II.

THE FIXING OF THE SPIRITUAL STATE.

" Therefore, leaving the principles of the doctrine of Christ, let us go on unto perfection; not laying again the foundation of repentance from dead works, and of faith toward God, of the doctrine of baptisms, and of laying on of hands, and of resurrection of the dead, and of eternal judgment. And this will we do, if God permit. For it is impossible for those who were once enlightened, and have tasted of the heavenly gift, and were made partakers of the Holy Ghost, and have tasted the good word of God, and the powers of the world to come, if they shall fall away, to renew them again unto repentance ; seeing they crucify to themselves the Son of God afresh, and put him to an open shame."—HEBREWS vi. 1-6.

THE verses I have read are commonly reckoned among the difficulties of Scripture ; the difficulty, however, being, not that it seems hard to find the doctrine, which, taken singly, the text appears to teach, but that it seems hard to accept that doctrine, and to reconcile it with the rest of Scripture. There are so many passages of the Bible which speak of God's willingness to forgive sin, and of His readiness to welcome back the returning prodigal, that we are startled when we meet with a verse which seems to declare that there are some against whom the door of mercy is closed ; some in whose case repentance and forgiveness is impossible. Again, there are passages which speak of the well-grounded confidence which a

Christian may entertain, that He who has begun a good work in him will perform it until the day of Jesus Christ ; and hence many have found it difficult to understand how apostacy and final falling away could have been possible in the case of persons whose spiritual condition could be described in the language of the 4th and 5th verses, where we read of them as having been once enlightened, as having tasted of the heavenly gift, having been made partakers of the Holy Ghost, having tasted the good word of God, and the powers of the world to come, and yet, as falling away beyond recovery. In early times the difficulty of these verses was felt ; and some have supposed that the teaching of this part of the Epistle was the cause that its apostolic authority was for a considerable time not acknowledged in the Western Church. It would be gross exaggeration wholly to account in this way for the doubts of which I speak, and which certainly arose from dissatisfaction rather with the external evidence then accessible for the authorship of the Epistle, than with its doctrinal teaching. And yet we cannot help thinking that fears as to the injurious tendency of this part of the Epistle may have prolonged the period of hesitation as to its authority, and made Christians less willing to accept the external evidence offered to them. For it is certain that the doubts lasted longest in the place where the controversy on which these verses bear, raged most warmly.

In our day the questions raised by the verses I have read, may be said in comparison to belong to the department of theoretic and speculative theology ; but

in early times they involved some important practical
points, on which it was necessary that the rulers of
the Church should come to an immediate decision.
It may appear strange to us, that a religion of such
pure morality as ours should ever have seemed to
any immoral in its tendency; and yet it is certain
that many, of decorous and virtuous lives, were
shocked at the freedom of the Gospel promises of
pardon of sins, and at the welcome it gave even to
notorious sinners on their profession of repentance.
You remember how, in our Lord's life-time, the
Pharisees, those careful and precise observers of the
law, were scandalized at seeing Jesus surrounded by
publicans and sinners. Gentile unbelievers learned
to bring the same accusation against the Church
which He founded, and charged her with encouraging
men guilty of the grossest crimes, to think they had
nothing to do but to come to her to be forgiven.
Thus, for example, it was whispered that the attraction which Christianity presented to the first Christian
emperor was, that it promised him absolution for
crimes which pagan morality was too stern to pardon.
And it was true that to souls weighed down by the
consciousness of guilt, the preachers of the Gospel
did offer release from the pressure of unforgiven sin.
Though your sins be as scarlet, they proclaimed, they
shall be white as snow. They permitted their converts to cast oblivion on that part of their life which
had gone by before they had passed through the
waters of baptism. In times past they might have
been fornicators, idolaters, adulterers, thieves, cove-
tous, drunkards, revilers, extortioners; but now they

had been washed, had been sanctified, had been justified, in the name of the Lord Jesus, and by the
Spirit of our God. But no immoral consequences
resulted from the blotting out of those dark memories
of the past. On the contrary, an obstacle was removed
which had kept the soul from approaching to God ;
the sense of His full and free forgiveness, obtained
by the precious blood of His Son, filled the heart
with love and gratitude to Him. And nothing can
secure, not merely purity of outward conduct, but
purity of heart, so well as that love of God, founded
on a sense of His unmerited mercy, which brings
the soul to feel pleasure in habitual thought of the
presence of Him who is of infinite purity.

But the problem, how to deal with sinners who
professed repentance, soon presented itself in a new
form. The reformation worked in the character of
the Christian converts was not in every case permanent. Some, who had escaped the pollutions of the
world through the knowledge of our Lord and Saviour
Jesus Christ, were again entangled therein and overcome. Some, with more or less excuse from terror
of persecution, denied the faith, and blasphemed the
worthy name by which they had been called. What
was to be done with those who had been tried and
had been found wanting, when they came soliciting a
second trial ? The vices of their heathen life had
been forgiven ; they had been trusted, and welcomed
as born anew in Christ ; and if, after this, those professed servants of Christ broke out again into their
heathen vices, was there any ground to hope that a
new forgiveness would not be followed by a new

relapse ? We may bring the matter home to ourselves by an illustration drawn from our own times.
It is not uncommon now to hear of public advocates
of temperance freely owning that in early life they
had themselves been under the dominion of the vice
which they exhort others to forsake ; or to hear of
men engaged in publicly exhorting others to conversion, who do not scruple to acknowledge that, previous to their own conversion, they had been sunk in
ungodliness and utter profligacy. And these confessions are not found to impair the effectiveness of
their preaching. But suppose, after a time, the
preacher to relapse into the vices from which he
boasts that he had escaped, what a scandal such a
fall would be, and how could he expect that any subsequent repentance would enable him to be tried and
trusted again. Now, when the Gospel was first published, every Christian was a preacher of righteousness, and the apostacy or relapse into profligacy of a
private Christian was a scandal to the whole community, such as would be caused among ourselves
by the gross sin of a clergyman, or of some one else
who is counted to have publicly pledged himself to
more than ordinary holiness. There is no difficulty,
then, in understanding the strong feeling entertained
by many Christians against the re-admission of the
lapsed, at least not until after long probation, and
on such terms that their sin should be always held in
remembrance, and never seem to have obtained complete forgiveness. And yet eventually a more merciful
view prevailed in the Church. It may have chanced
that some who had been stern to their fallen brethren,

by their own subsequent fall taught others the full
meaning of the Apostle's admonition, " If a man be
overtaken in a fault, ye which are spiritual restore
such a one in the spirit of meekness, considering
thyself, lest thou also be tempted." And it was
found that not only in the case of sins committed
in the period of heathen darkness, but also in the
case of sins far less excusable, because committed
against clearer light and knowledge, ('deadly sins
wilfully committed after baptism,) it would be wrong
to deny the place of forgiveness to such as truly
repent. Nay, as in the parable of the two debtors,
the recollection how much had been forgiven was
a force constantly urging the pardoned sinner to love
his merciful Saviour more. Those, then, who had
learned by experience the mischievous effects of such
excessive rigour as might drive the sinner to despair,
were naturally cautious in admitting the apostolic
authority of a writing apparently favourable to the
more rigorous view. And when the authority of this
Epistle came to be generally owned, an interpretation
of the text found favour which seemed to lead to no
dangerous consequences. The Apostle, it was said,
did not mean to deny to the fallen the possibility of
repentance ; what he meant to declare was that there
was no possibility of a second baptism. It was not
possible to renew them, or to make them new, by
crucifying for them the Son of God afresh ; words, it
was urged, which pointed to baptism, wherein the
disciple became a new creature, and wherein, as we
learn also from other parts of Scripture, the death
and burial and resurrection of our Lord are repre-

sented, the convert dying unto sin, crucifying the lusts of his earthly members, buried with his Lord in baptism, and rising again to walk in newness of life.

If this interpretation appear strained to you, we may ask ourselves whether we ourselves always resist the temptation of allowing our interpretations of Scripture to be warped by the exigencies of the controversies of our own days ; whether we do not at times turn aside from the obvious meaning of a passage of Scripture, lest it should extort from us a concession of which opponents of ours may make a dangerous use. The remembrance how completely our text has outlived one at least of the controversies on which it seems most directly to bear may remind us that the Bible is a book for all time, whose meaning must not be narrowed down to what we may fancy the requirements of our own day. In striving, then, to draw for our own instruction some of the lessons contained in the verses I have read, I think it safest avoiding all controversial minuteness, to try to fix your minds on some of the great truths which seem clearly taught in the text. And in the first place, if we are to interpret the writer's words according to their natural meaning, he seems plainly to declare that there are some in this world whose spiritual condition may be pronounced hopeless. We are accustomed to think of this life as a scene of constant change—change often modifying the judgments we have formed of the characters of other men, who in some cases disappoint the hopes we have entertained of them ; in others, unexpectedly return to the right

way after we had feared that they had wandered from
it beyond recovery. But we think of death as fixing
a man's condition ; after that there can be no repentance ; where the tree has fallen there it must be. But
we are here taught that it is not in what we call death
that this fixity of condition always first takes place. A
soul may appear to men to live, and yet in God's
sight have assumed the stiffness and rigidity of a
corpse, its capabilities of spiritual life lost irrecover-
ably, save by miracle. This conclusion does not rest on
the text merely : there is another well-known passage
in the tenth chapter of this same Epistle : " If we
sin wilfully after that we have received the knowledge
of the truth, there remaineth no more sacrifice for
sins, but a certain fearful looking for of judgment
and fiery indignation which shall devour the adversaries." And these verses, which speak of the impossibility of repentance under certain circumstances,
connect themselves naturally in our minds with our
Lord's awful warning against that sin against the
Holy Ghost, which hath never forgiveness, neither in
this world nor in that which is to come. The very
unlikeness of these warnings to the general tenor of
the New Testament is a reason, not for rejecting or
turning away our thoughts from them, but for giving
them more earnest attention. The whole Gospel is
a message of forgiveness, free and unmerited. Its
invitations are without restriction or limitation. The
blood of our Lord Jesus Christ, we are told, cleanseth
from all sin. The voice of threatening, then, from
its very rarity, strikes on our ears with awful significance. Our attention is arrested when we hear the

All-merciful declare that there are bounds to His mercy, when He who is all-powerful to redeem tells us of a depth of sin from which there is no return. We should find it hard to believe this, if told us on less weighty authority. Yet now that it has been revealed to us as true, we find on reflection other truths with which it harmonizes.

We are familiar with the operation of the laws of habit. We know how virtuous exertions once only made at the cost of much self-denial, when daily repeated, require less and less effort, and at last become so natural, that it would be a pain to abandon them. We know how temptations once deemed formidable, if manfully resisted, lose their power to entice; and how thus the ways of holiness become more easy and more pleasant the longer they are walked in. And, on the other hand, we know how progress in the downward path of sin becomes with each step accelerated; how habit winds closer and tighter the chains of sin round its votaries; how he who had but intended lightly to taste of sinful pleasures, intoxicated by the draught, loses power to put away the cup from his lips. We may daily see the process of fixing men's spiritual state going on before our eyes. We may see the lines of their characters deepening and hardening; carelessness as to the things of God settling into fixed indifference, and proceeding to contempt and rooted aversion. Now, reason and Scripture lead us to think that death makes no abrupt change in man's state. Rather are our future lives only the development of the fruits of the character formed during our probation time on

earth. The life or death of the soul, which is to last
for ever, begins in this world. "He that believeth
on the Son hath everlasting life; he that believeth
not is condemned already." It is quite credible,
then, that the process of which I speak may go on
so far that the lines of men's characters may have
been deepened and hardened, so as to become,
humanly speaking, unalterable. On the one hand,
we may believe that saints may so grow in grace as
to enjoy on earth the safety of heaven. *They* may
not dare to count themselves to have already attained
the mark they aim at, or to be already perfect; yet
in God's sight they may stand firm, beyond all danger of fall or slip. And on the other hand, men's
hearts may have been so hardened by the deceitful-
ness of sin, that recovery shall have become impossible for them. Observe the nature of the impossibility
of which I speak. The text does not declare that
certain sinners, though truly penitent, and mourning
their offences, shall be unable to find pardon or
atonement for them; the impossibility of which it
speaks is an impossibility of renewing them to repentance. If they remain condemned, it is because
they do not repent; and, as I was saying, there is
nothing which need seem to us incredible in the
statement that sinners may be so hardened in
their sin that their repentance shall have become,
humanly speaking, impossible. We should grievously err if we ventured to pronounce of any sinner
that he is beyond the grace of God. He himself
would grievously err if he were to despair. Nay,
however grievously sunk in sin, as long as he can

mourn his fall, and hate himself for his departure
from God, and sigh after restoration, we have evidence that the seeds of repentance are not yet extinct
in his soul. But yet it may be that a man of whom
God's ministers dare not despair, to whom they are
bound to address their word of exhortation, whether
he will hear, or whether he will forbear, may, in
truth, have so stopped his ears as to be inaccessible
to their warnings; and the stroke of death may not
make him, but find him, insensible to the things of
God.

Thus, I think, we have seen that the doctrine contained in the solemn warning of the text harmonizes
with what we may infer elsewhere from Scripture.
And if we now examine a little more closely into the
text, and enquire in what circumstances arises the
danger of falling into the hopeless condition it describes, the answer also seems plain, that it tells us
that the condition of any is more desperate in proportion to the greatness of the privileges he has
abused, and to the riches of the mercy he has trod-
den under foot. Here, too, we are in sight of the
general law of God's dealings, that privileges involve
responsibility; that from him to whom much is
given, much will be required. Far more hopeless is
the condition of the baptized Christian who despises
the invitation of the Gospel, than that of the heathen
who has never heard the name of Christ. The sufferer under some painful disease may cherish hope
that when his case has been laid before a skilful
physician, a remedy will be found which will restore
him to health; but when all the most skilful physi-

cians have tried their remedies on him in vain, then,
indeed, his state may be pronounced desperate. And
so there is hope of the idolaters of some distant isle,
that when at length the Gospel sound shall have
reached them, they will cast their idols to the moles
and to the bats. But if you, who have heard times
without number the tidings of the infinite love of
God through Christ, hear the wondrous tale un-
moved; the preacher has no message to bring you
but that which has been delivered to you already.
" For those who despise that sacrifice, there remaineth
no more sacrifice for sin." The spotless Lamb of
God has been offered once for all; no new victim can
be slain for those who reject Him, nor can He be
crucified again for those who disdain the offering He
has already made.

But if the condition of the impenitent baptized
Christian is worse than that of the heathen, there is
a further gradation. The condition of the careless
sinner who has scarcely ever attended to the Gospel
message, and in whose ears the preacher's warnings
have sounded but as empty words which convey no
meaning, is less hopeless than that of him who has
heard, and heard with pleasure, whose emotions have
been stirred up, and have subsided again without
ever fastening on the active principles of his nature
and setting them in motion. It may happen, and
often does happen, to the one, that he one day suddenly catches the meaning of words which had often
sounded in his ears without exciting any ideas : that
the message often heard but never understood before
strikes him with all the force of novelty, awaking

new emotions, and touching on new springs of action. But in the case of one who has not only heard all that the Gospel announces, but listened to it, allowed his imagination to dwell on it, and his sensibilities to be excited by it, and yet whose emotions have died away without ever becoming practical principles of action, it is harder far to expect a new awakening of heart. His capabilities of religious emotion have been exhausted: the truths that once had power to stir the liveliest feelings move him but languidly now; and what fruit can we expect in future from appeals and arguments long familiar and long ineffectual?

The connection of the 5th and 6th verses with the beginning of the chapter, may give us a practical lesson as to one of the causes why what seems a promising beginning of the spiritual life is sometimes cut short without leading to any permanent result. To a hasty reader it might seem, when the Apostle declares his intention of not laying again the foundation of repentance from dead works and faith towards God, and of resurrection of the dead, and of eternal judgment, as if he were speaking slightingly of the most fundamental doctrines of the Gospel. But the writer's object in speaking of these fundamental doctrines, plainly is to urge the danger of laying a good foundation, and building nothing on it. And a mistake of an analogous kind seems to me to be committed by those who fix their thoughts too exclusively on the first step in the spiritual life—who care to ask themselves no other question than, Have I been converted?—Have I been born again? and who, if

they can answer Yes, think the Christian minister
has no message to them, but are willing to hear him
exhort others to strive to gain the same privilege.
The truth is, a foundation is important, because a
building is to be reared upon it. We rejoice at a
birth because it is the beginning of a life ; and the
birth of a Christian soul is the beginning of a life of
daily growth under the influence of God's Holy Spirit,
till he attain to the stature of a perfect man in Christ.
To remain in thought and wish always at the first
point of the spiritual life, is, in other words, to be
without growth in grace, that is to say, to be without
any true life at all. And the Apostle would warn us
that if the spiritual life of a man be stationary, always
remaining at the point where it commenced, the
attainments he has made, instead of being a ground
of confidence to him, should fill him with wholesome
fear, lest if, in spite of all these, his soul be in an
unprogressive dead condition, it should only be the
more difficult to renew it again to repentance.

I have spoken of what seem to be the most prominent truths taught in the text, but I have no wish
to evade the question, Does the Apostle here speak of
a fall from grace as possible ? And I do not know
whether the controversies on this subject, as far at
least as they can proceed within the limits of our
Church's teaching, are not theoretical, and perhaps
verbal rather than practical. It is agreed by all that
we learn from this passage that there are workings
of God's Spirit upon the hearts of men who are not
finally saved. Thus Calvin, in his commentary on
this passage, while maintaining that the elect are

without danger of fatal loss, yet says that this hinders
him not from owning that God sprinkles on the reprobate also some taste of His grace, irradiates their
minds with some sparks of His light, affects them
with some sense of His goodness, and in some way
writes His Word in their souls.   And he quotes the
parable of the sower as proving that there may be in
the reprobate some temporary faith and knowledge,
which, however, fail because the roots are not so
deep as they ought to be, or because the seed sown
is choked by the thorns of worldly cares and pleasures.

So, again, the framers of the Lambeth Articles
deliberately rejected the statement that grace fails
not in those to whom it has been once given ; and
adopted the very different one, that it fails not in the
elect ; in other words, admitting, and intending to
admit, that to those not elect there may have been
given a certain grace which does not bring forth fruit
to perfection.   As long, therefore, as both parties
hold to the doctrine of the 17th Article, that the
decrees of God's election are secret to us, the question
whether or not grace may fail in the elect, is less o
a practical one than might have been supposed.   A
man may hear the Word gladly, and do many things
because of it, and give what seem to be evidences of
the work of God's grace in his heart, yet we cannot
predict with absolute certainty that he must abide to
the end.   Only if he fall away we conclude that he
was not one of the elect.   The result, then, if stated
as a theoretical dogma, seems to be—a fall from a
certain kind of grace is possible ; but it is impossible finally to fall away from that particular kind

of grace from which final fall is impossible. And
the result will prove which kind of grace any man
has received.

Some will feel that the explanation I have given converts into a barren truism a doctrine which had been a
source of precious comfort to their souls. A Christian
conscious of much frailty, of frequent coldness of heart,
of repeated wanderings from his Father's ways, and
full, therefore, of distrust in himself, finds comfort
in meditating on the unchanging love of God, which
sought him while yet a stranger, inspired in him
every good thought he can find in himself, and as it
took its origin in no worthiness of his, so he believes
it will not forsake him, notwithstanding his stumbles
on the heavenly road, but will abide with him to the
end. But they who feel thus have already some of
the evidences of election of which the article speaks :
in the working of the Spirit of Christ, mortifying the
works of the flesh and their earthly members, and
drawing up their minds to heavenly things. The
doctrine of the indefectibility of grace may be a most
mischievous one, as held by one full of the spirit of
slavish fear, dreading future punishment, and anxious
for some infallible sign which will enable him to dismiss all apprehension of judgment to come. As the
manna of old, when laid by for the morrow, bred
worms and stank, so the promises which Christ has
given for the daily sustenance of His people are abused,
if it is attempted to support present life on the food
of a former day. A man will trust to a delusion if,
though not living the life with Christ now, he flatters
himself that he must be safe, because he is sure he

was Christ's formerly. But to a soul that loves God, and grieves that it loves Him so imperfectly, and dreading nothing so much as to lose His love, distrusts its own strength, and fears lest it may break away—to such a soul it can do nothing but good to remember that it is not in its own strength it stands ; the Eternal God is its refuge, and underneath are the everlasting arms. The doctrine that man's eternal state may be fixed on earth has not only its awful side, it has an aspect full of comfort. The character that is to abide in heaven, may be fully formed in the discipline of earth, and the white robes of the redeemed worn by men clad in mortal bodies. And every proof of the triumph of God's grace in their souls gives them confidence to say, " Thou, O Lord, will perfect that which concerneth me. Thy mercy, O Lord, endureth for ever. Forsake not, then, the work of Thine Own hands."

I know not whether the precept, " Take no thought for the morrow," has not a spiritual application. We know that in temporal matters our Lord did not mean to forbid forethought and use of means to provide for the future. But if any disquiet himself with the apprehension, I have food and raiment now, shall I always have them ? our Lord would hush all such distracting anxiety with the thought, " Your Heavenly Father knoweth that you have need of these things before ye ask Him." And so I know not whether if any raise the question, I love God now, but shall I always love Him ? the very starting of the question does not imply lack of faith. If you love God, can you not trust Him—trust Him not only for the present, but for the future. Believe assuredly that when you ask for grace to love Him better, and for strength to continue in His love, you ask only what it is His delight to grant. Such a petition He is more ready to grant than you to put forth.

As in temporal matters so in spiritual, the knowledge of God's love is not intended to release us from the use of means or from the need of vigilance. In spiritual matters as in temporal, God would have us under a constant sense of our dependence on Him, and wishes us to put forth petitions for our daily food. But if ever you are a prey to self-torturing anxieties, rebuke them away with the thought that if you love God at all it is because He first loved you with an infinite love. In spiritual matters, even more than in temporal, He knoweth what you have need of before you ask; and if no earthly parent refuses to his child the bread which he asks, so He who loves your souls with a love beyond that of the most affectionate earthly father, will neither now nor at any future time deny His Holy Spirit to you that ask him.

SERMON III.

THE EVIDENTIAL VALUE OF THE EUCHARISTIC RITE.

" And as they were eating, Jesus took bread, and blessed it, and brake it, and gave it to the disciples, and said, Take, eat; this is my body. And he took the cup, and gave thanks, and gave it to them, saying, Drink ye all of it : for this is my blood of the New Testament, which is shed for many for the remission of sins."— MATTHEW xxvi. 26-28.

I DO not know whether it is necessary to offer any explanation of the fact, that of the Gospel history, about one-third part is occupied with the account of the sayings and events of the last week of the Saviour's life on earth. To say nothing of the intrinsic importance of those deeds and words, we feel how natural it is that the thoughts of any, from whom has been taken one whom they loved and valued, should dwell on the memory of all that he said or did immediately before he was parted from them. Parting words live long in the memory; a dying charge has a peculiar sacredness. There were, then, no words of Christ which it was so impossible for any who heard them ever to forget, as those in which, when about to be separated from His disciples, He

appealed to their love, and taught them how it was
His wish that they should keep Him in memory after
He was gone. And for all who love Him, no words,
it might be supposed, are more suggestive of matter
for solemn and peaceful meditation. Yet it has come
to pass now that with us these words are suggestive
of strife; and I doubt not that many of you, as soon
as you heard my text, prepared yourselves to expect a
sermon occupied with controversy. The subject is
certainly one on which it has now become impossible
to escape controversy; and elsewhere it is my duty
this term to enter into a full discussion of it; but,
at present, I intend to speak only of those things,
the truth of which we all agree in admitting; and
though my treatment of the text will be controversial,
the controversy will be directed against those who are
without. I wish, in short, to dwell on the bearings
on Christian evidences of the history recorded in the
text.

On the revival of learning and the birth of modern
critical science, it was discovered that many documents, handed down from previous generations, and
which had met from them with unenquiring acceptance, were unworthy of the reverence which they
had received. At first this process of rejection went
on but slowly. It seemed presumptuous to question
what men in former days, entitled to honour for their
learning, had with one consent admitted. Assaults
were only made on those works which were least
strongly guarded by prescriptive reverence; and even
with respect to these the battle was, for a considerable
time, stoutly contested. But one victory after another

emboldened the assailants. At length nothing was too sacred for attack; the records of our faith have been subjected to the severest scrutiny, and, often on grounds which scarcely warranted a suspicion, sentence of absolute condemnation has been pronounced. There are symptoms now that the era of merely destructive criticism is passing away. The adversaries of Christianity do not content themselves now with scoffs and objections against the faith which we profess ; they acknowledge the necessity of substituting something of their own ; they own themselves bound to answer the question, what *they* think of Christ ? what facts must they admit as certainly proved concerning that real human life on earth, which undoubtedly has had such abiding influence on the history of our whole race ? For writing the history of this life we have scarcely any materials, but those Gospel narratives which some of the historians, to whom I refer, treat with such scant respect ; and it is, therefore, well that we should fully use the few opportunities we have of testing the truth of these narratives by independent evidence. One of these opportunities is afforded in that history which I have taken for my subject to-day, that of the Institution of the Christian Sacred Feast—a history which could be established by satisfactory proof, even if none of the four Gospels had reached us. As far as we can trace back the history of our religion, this solemn feast was an essential part of Christian worship. In early times, indeed, there was some reserve as to stating publicly in the presence of the heathen what the Church believed as to the food which they there received.

"That which the faithful know," was the common
phrase when speaking in the presence of the unin-
itiated. Yet the veil thus used was so transparent,
and those who employ it at one moment, lay it aside
so carelessly at another, that their reserve appears to
be rather that of reverence than of mystery. Certainly Christians of the very earliest times made no
affectation of concealment. In the second century
Justin Martyr, in his Apology addressed to heathen,
gives a full description of the mode in which the
rite was then administered; and goes on to declare
that Christians had been taught that the food over
which thanksgiving has been made is the Flesh and
Blood of the Incarnate Jesus. "For the Apostles in
their memoirs, which are called Gospels, have delivered that Jesus so commanded them, that He having
taken bread and given thanks, said, 'Do this in remembrance of me. This is my body;' and likewise, having taken the cup and given thanks, He said, 'This is
my blood.'"

The account just cited is professedly founded on the
Gospel History. But we can go back a century earlier
for decisive testimony as to the belief of the first generation of Christians; namely, to the account given by
St. Paul in the first Epistle to the Corinthians—an
epistle, the genuineness of which is not contested by
the most sceptical of critics. St. Paul says, "I have
received of the Lord that which I also delivered to
you, that the Lord Jesus, the same night in which
He was betrayed, took bread; and when He had given
thanks, He brake it and said, Take, eat; this is my
body which is broken for you: this do in remem-

brance of me. After the same manner also He took the cup, when He had supped, saying, This cup is the new testament in my blood ; this do ye as oft as ye drink it in remembrance of me." This account is in verbal agreement with that given by St. Luke in his Gospel ; but there is no reason to think that the one was copied from the other. On comparing the history of the appearances of our Lord after His resurrection, given in the fifteenth chapter of the first Epistle to the Corinthians, with that given in the Gospel, we have every reason for believing in the independence of the two accounts. In particular, if St. Luke, when writing the Gospel, had before him the Epistle to the Corinthians, it seems unlikely that he would not have told us something more about the appearance to St. James, or about that to the five hundred brethren at once. It is the more remarkable, then, that St. Luke's account of the institution of the Eucharist should be in close verbal agreement with that of St. Paul, though not so with those of Matthew and Mark. Yet the matter receives a very simple explanation, if we only suppose a liturgical usage to be apostolic which we can otherwise trace back very close to apostolic times, namely, that of reciting the history of our Lord's institution of the rite at the time of consecration. For if this were so, St. Luke, who must have been so often present when St. Paul celebrated this memorial of his Lord, must have re- peatedly heard these words recited by St. Paul, and therefore might be expected to record them in his Gospel in the form in which Paul had delivered them unto him. On the whole, then, there is absolute historical proof that at the time when the majority were alive of those who professed to have seen Jesus of Nazareth after He rose from the dead, it was the universal belief among Christians that their Master, on the night He was betrayed, had given to His disciples bread and wine, had assured them that in partaking of that food they should eat His body and drink His blood, and had commanded them to continue that celebration in remembrance of Him ; and it is certain that they did so continue it in obedience to that alleged command.

The next question is—Is it possible that this belief and this practice could have arisen, if the account which Christians themselves gave of its origin were not the true one ? Reverence forbids me to describe this Christian institution in the language we should employ if we had never heard of it before, and if we came to know it now for the first time as a religious rite practised by some newly-discovered tribe. But the more there is shocking and seemingly absurd in the language used concerning this institution, the less likely is it that Christians would have spontaneously imagined this mode of doing honour to their Master, and showing their love and gratitude towards Him. We could quite understand the Christian society maintaining and ratifying their relations of mutual friendship by the institution of a common meal. The doctrine of the common brotherhood of all, and the duty of mutual love, would be aptly symbolized by all joining on equal terms to partake of a common meal, consisting of bread and wine, the simplest, and in those countries

the most universal articles of food; and while thus
owning their mutual fellowship, acknowledging also
their dependence on God, whose gifts they owned
these blessings to be, to whom they returned thanks
for them, and to whom they dedicated not only their
offerings, but themselves. If the Eucharistic Feast
were nothing more than a simple repast, forcibly expressing the common human wants of all, and their
common dependence on the bounty of the same
Father, it would commend itself to any one as a
reasonable and wise institution, and we should have
no difficulty in understanding how good men might
have imagined it. But it is mysterious that the
disciples should use concerning their rite language
which would imply that theirs was a banquet on
human flesh and blood—not ordinary human flesh,
but the body of Him whom, when alive, they had
most loved, and whom now they worshipped as God.
It was no uncommon charge brought of old against
different secret societies or bands of dark conspirators,
that in order that the members might testify their
readiness to sacrifice every prejudice and disregard
every law, human or divine, which might interfere
with the fulfilment of their duty to the society, they
were compelled on their initiation to taste of human
blood. Such charges were, no doubt, in many cases
as mere calumnies as the accusation of Thyestean
banquets commonly brought by heathens against the
Christian community. In all cases the charges come
to us on the testimony of enemies; but there is no
instance of a society really innocent of such practices
choosing to use language that implied it was guilty

of them. Least of all should we expect to hear such language from the lips of Jews. Not merely was food at which all men revolt abhorrent to them, but it was the peculiar boast of a pious Jew that nothing common or unclean had ever polluted his mouth. To eat swine's flesh was in their eyes as heinous as an offence against the moral law; to taste the blood of any animal was as much forbidden as to drink human blood; the very touch of a dead body was pollution. Now we know for how long a period the obligation of the Mosaic law was insisted on; how many thousands of Judaizing Christians there were who wished to include this law as an essential part of the Christian system, and that it was at least a century after the Apostles' times before these Judaizers were completely separated from the Christian Church. But we can trace the Eucharistic rite as existing from the earliest times, and as common to all parties in these disputes, however strong their attachment to Mosaic ordinances. Again, if the rite were first heard of in a later generation among men to whom Christ was but a mere name, we might explain the language used as some mystical Eastern mode of expressing their desire to enter into most intimate union with Him whom they venerated as their Founder. But St. Paul's testimony makes it certain that Christians spoke of eating our Lord's flesh and drinking His blood, to whom Jesus was not a mere abstract name for typical perfect humanity; but at a time when the majority were still living of those who professed that they had seen Him after He had risen from the dead; while those were still alive who had known and loved Him as a human friend; who had thought no balms or spices too costly to do honour to His mortal remains, and to whom the thought of violating their sanctity would be as revolting as a similar thought in the case of one of our own dead friends would be to any of ourselves. Thus it appears that the origin of the Christian Eucharistic Feast is absolutely inexplicable if we reject the simple account of it given by the sacred writers—that the disciples use no language concerning it except what their Master Himself had taught them to use.

I dare say I shall seem to many of you to have strangely spent time in painfully elaborating a proof that we may accept as literally true what it never occurred to you to doubt—that our Lord on the night He was betrayed took bread and brake it, and gave it to His disciples with the words: " Take, eat, this My body; do this in remembrance of Me." I have done so because of the important consequences which I regard as following when this fact is proved; as to our Lord's Divine foreknowledge, His intention to found a Church, and the relation which He declared that He himself personally bore to the spiritual life of all men—a doctrine involving pretensions extravagant on the part of any merely human teacher, but strange, indeed, when coming from the mouth of One who is supposed at the time to have given up all hope of a successful issue to His enterprise, and to be looking forward to the prospect of an approaching shameful death. On account of the importance of these consequences I have desired, before attempting to draw them, to show that our belief in the fact on which they are based does not depend on our belief concerning the inspiration of the Gospels, nor even on our belief concerning their antiquity and integrity. Just as we could prove by plain historical evidence, if the Gospels had never come down to us, that the original preachers of Christianity hazarded their lives in attestation of the assertion that their Master rose from the dead, so we can prove independently of the Gospels, that it was their belief that He instituted the rite of which I speak to-day, and I have given reasons for holding that the very existence of such a belief among the first generation of Christians is a sufficient proof of its truth.

The importance which I attach to the proof of this fact is justified by the reluctance to admit it exhibited by sceptical writers, who are clear-sighted enough to perceive that the fact, if admitted, would compel them to reconstruct all their theories concerning the life and character of Jesus. In Renan's life of Jesus, for example, the institution of the Lord's Supper finds no place. His excuse is, that this event is not recorded by St. John, whom Renan, differing herein from the majority of writers of his school, accepts as giving the most trustworthy account of the closing scenes of his Master's life. He assumes, without a shadow of proof, that the breaking of bread was a mysterious rite of unknown signification habitually practised by our Lord ; and his theory is, that afterwards when the disciples came to look on our Lord's death as a sacrifice superseding the offerings of the Old Law, then the tendency of legends to gather round the story of the last hours of the life of Jesus referred the breaking of bread to the Last Supper, and made the wine then poured out to symbolize the blood shed for the salvation of the world. But it is needless to say how completely this theory leaves unsolved the problem of the origin of the Christian Eucharistic rite. That the Christians early looked on their Master's death as a sacrifice we readily admit; but there is an immense gulf between such a belief and the doctrine that Christians were bound in some manner to eat of His body and blood. If we could suppose John's Gospel intended for a complete account of all that Jesus said and did, his omission to explain a thing so much requiring explanation would be a sufficient reason for rejecting his authority; and the story, as given by the other Evangelists, would be plainly in preference entitled to credit. But there are numberless proofs on which I have not now time to dwell, that St. John wrote his Gospel for men to whom the main facts of the Gospel history were already known; indeed, there is every reason to believe for men who had the other Gospels in their hands;* and that, as a general rule, this Evangelist studiously avoids repeating what he might assume was already known to his readers: so that his silence concerning any part of the history cannot be regarded as testimony against it. And certainly his silence concerning the institution of the Eucharist cannot be regarded as testimony against it; for, strangely enough, one of the arguments used by other sceptical critics against the genuineness of

---

* See note at the end of this Sermon.

this Gospel is the coincidence of the language of the discourse in the sixth chapter with language used in the second century, when Eucharistic doctrine was highly developed.

Strauss, unlike Renan, prefers the Synoptic Gospels to the fourth, and therefore he cannot lay stress on the silence of John with respect to a fact attested by the other three. He hesitates, then, and seems unable to make up his mind how much to admit. He believes that our Lord, on this last evening, was depressed in spirits, understanding His real position, unrelentingly pursued by the fanaticism of desperate enemies, and feebly supported by followers incapable of understanding Him. He thinks it possible, then, that when Jesus, as master of the household, broke the bread and poured out the wine for distribution among His disciples, the thought may have involuntarily presented itself to Him that even so would His body soon be broken—so would His blood soon be poured forth ; and that He may have expressed some such gloomy foreboding to His disciples. Nay, Strauss will admit it to be possible that, looking on His death as a sacrifice, He may have regarded His blood as the consecration of a new covenant between God and mankind ; and in order to give a living centre to the community which He desired to found, might have commanded the perpetual repetition of this distribution of bread and wine. All this he says is possible, but whether it really took place is another question. If Jesus had expressed any anticipation of the approaching violent death, and if the Church had adopted the custom of distributing bread and

wine in memory of His death, no doubt, the institution of such a custom would be ascribed to Christ
whether he were really the author of it or not ; and
if the Church had come to look on that bread and
wine as the body and blood of Christ, and the blood
as the blood of a new covenant, no doubt, again, the
story would soon obtain belief that Christ had Himself used language to justify such a belief.   But who
can grant the assumption which this " if " requires ?
How was it possible that the Church should come to
give bread and wine the names of Christ's body and
blood, if He Himself had *not* authorized their doing
so ?

Let us see, then, what follows from the reluctant
admission of our adversaries.   On the last night of
his life, Jesus, though not possessing, as we believe,
Divine foreknowledge of the future, had at least
human knowledge that the toils of his enemies were
closing round Him.   He saw that death could no
longer be escaped, and that the career which He had
planned had ended in failure.   Yet even then He
calmly looks forward to the formation of a new
society, which shall own Him as its Founder.   He
foresees that that flock of timorous followers, whose
dispersion on the next day He ventures to predict,
will recover the shock of their disappointment, and
unite again.   And as for this shameful death, the
thoughts of which oppress Him, instead of antici-
pating that His followers will put it from their
thoughts, and blush to remember their credulity, when
they accepted as their Saviour one unable to save
Himself, He commands His disciples to keep that

E

death in perpetual memory. Notwithstanding the apparent failure of His course, He conceives Himself to be a unique person in the world's history, and in Strauss' words, he regards his death as the seal of a new covenant between God and mankind. What other man has ever dared to set such a value on his own life? If such a belief were not true, it would surely be the very frenzy of insanity. More than this—He makes it an ordinance of perpetual obligation to His followers that they shall seek the most intimate union with His body and blood, and holds out to them this closeness of perpetual union with Himself as the source of all spiritual life. One of the principal grounds on which some have urged us to reject St. John's Gospel is the lofty language which in that Gospel our Lord uses concerning His own person and claims ; pressing these claims, it is said, in an exaggerated way, inconsistent with the meekness and humility which characterize his discourses recorded in the other Gospels. But in this narrative recorded by the Synoptic Evangelists, and not by St. John, we find Him making higher pretensions than on any other occasion, and making these claims under the very shadow of the cross. It was no afterthought of His disciples to smooth away the offence of the cross by ascribing to His death some mysterious efficacy; He Himself had taught them to look on His blood as shed for them and for many for the remission of sins. He intimates that the event then taking place was comparable with the first setting apart of the Jewish nation to be God's peculiar people ; and as Moses had then sprinkled the people with blood, saying, Behold the blood of the covenant which God hath made with you, so now He calls His own the blood of the new covenant, This legislation for a future Church was made at a moment when His most attached disciples could not be trusted to remain with Him for an hour, and when He had Himself predicted their desertion and denial. Our adversaries make no difficulty about admitting that our Lord predicted His death; for this, they think, did not exceed the powers of human forecast, so plain were the symptoms of the storm gathering round Him. But no ordinary human foresight could then discern that the infant Church would survive the shock of its Master's death, and instead of being ashamed of the cross would glory in it, and look upon His death as the source of all life. Thus, then, we have not only in the Last Supper a spectacle of faith, calm and unshaken in circumstances the most desperate, but we have a prophecy of success improbable in the highest degree, and yet which received the most complete fulfilment.

We all believe that that prophecy was no random guess: that faith, no blind enthusiasm; we know that Jesus was all He claimed to be; that His death was the great sin-offering, to restore the broken communion between God and man; union with Him the condition of our spiritual life. And we cannot doubt that it was no empty words which He spoke when instituting that sacred rite. If His words have been perverted so as to give rise to error and superstition, there is the more reason for thinking that He who foreknew these consequences, and yet did not refrain from speaking, wished to make known truths more powerful for good than any of their perversions are for harm. We may believe that He then revealed a covenanted means which will enable those who use it in faith, spiritually to eat His flesh and drink His blood, and to receive therein a pledge of all those blessings which His sacrificed body can yield. Not alone in this rite is He present to those who in faith seek for Him. Where two or three are gathered together in His name He is in the midst of them. Even the private lifting up to Him of a single heart is not unmarked by Him. But we may well believe that an especial blessing attends those who in faith obey His commands, and seek Him in the ordinance He has appointed; not bewildering themselves in vain speculations *how* this man shall give us His flesh to eat; not, on the one hand, denying all supernatural grace, and reducing all beneficial effect to the results of the natural operation of laws of our own minds; nor, on the other hand, insisting that men shall believe in the reality of miracles, of which there is no evidence, save that it seems to us that, in order to make our explanation of His words true, it is necessary that God should work them. Such philosophizing shows want of faith in Christ's true presence, as much as the direct denial of it. Just as God's presence in this world was implicitly denied, not only by those who refused to lift their thoughts above His material works, but by those who strove to localize his presence, and could not recognize Him except where there was some figure to represent Him made by hands of men. But, as I have said, my purpose to-day is not to discuss any of those points on which Christians disagree, but to show the place among the evidences of our religion occupied by the fact, that Christians have from the first observed this institution ; a fact of which no other explanation can be given, but that contained in the Gospel account of the origin of the rite ; and a fact which proves that our Lord, in the immediate prospect of approaching death, looked on that death not as the end of His religion, but the beginning of it ; a sacrifice for the sins of the world, the source of all good to mankind. He who spoke of Himself thus was confessedly a wise man, a meek and humble man. Could He have been only man ?

NOTE ON SERMON III.

THE IRONY OF ST. JOHN.*

In the very first sentence of Renan's Life of Jesus, he gives a specimen of his critical sagacity, in detecting and correcting the blunders of the documents on which his history is founded. He begins with the statement, "Jesus was born at Nazareth, a little town of Galilee." On looking to his notes for the proof of this assertion, we find it to consist in the fact that Matthew and Mark speak of Galilee as "Jesus' own country;" an expression which is supposed to show that the legend of Christ's birth at Bethlehem did not exist in the original form of the story. Matthew, or whoever reduced his Gospel to its present form, is supposed to have clumsily left in an expression which gives the lie to his formal statement at the beginning; while Luke, a more cautious and deliberate falsifier of the story, alters this fatal expression into "Nazareth where he was brought up." But Renan's main reliance is on the authority of the fourth Evangelist.

* In justification of the opinion expressed in the preceding Sermon, as to St. John's acquaintance with the other Gospels, I add, by way of note, the following paper written some time ago for a different purpose.

"As for John he knows nothing of the journey to Bethlehem; for him Jesus is simply 'of Nazareth,' or 'of Galilee,' on two occasions when it would have been of the highest importance to make mention of the birth at Bethlehem. (See John i. 45, 46, and vii. 41, 42.)" It is perhaps hardly fair to quarrel with Renan for his use of a formula common to him with all writers of his school; yet I cannot help protesting against the unscientific character of the language he employs. It has been often observed as the difference between the vulgar and the scientific observer, that the latter alone is able to repeat simply the facts that he has observed, while the former always mixes up with his report inferences of his own. Instead of an accurate statement of facts, he substitutes the conclusion of a syllogism, to which his observation contributes only one premiss, while some theory supplies the other. The writers of Renan's school, when they wish to report the fact, that a certain Evangelist makes no mention of this or that incident of our Saviour's life, can seldom avoid mixing up in their report the assumption, that if the Evangelist had known the incident, he would certainly have mentioned it. And so the formula is of constant occurrence. Matthew "knows nothing of the Ascension," John "knows nothing of the institution of the Lord's Supper," and so forth; a loose and inaccurate mode of speaking, which, for the purposes of scientific investigation, must be resolved into two statements, the statement of fact, the Evangelist is silent about such and such events; the statement of opinion he would not have been silent if he had known them.

In the present example the fact to which Renan (or
rather De Wette before him) has called attention, is
perfectly true, and it is one which ordinary readers
of the Gospel fail to notice.   John never mentions
our Saviour's birth at Bethlehem, and on two or three
occasions a contrary statement is made and not contradicted.   In the first chapter Philip tells Nathanael,
" We have found him, of whom Moses in the law,
and the prophets did write, Jesus of Nazareth, the
son of Joseph ;" to which Nathanael answers, " Can
any good thing come out of Nazareth ?" an objection
to which Philip makes no direct reply.   Afterwards,
when Nicodemus takes our Lord's part, his brother
members of the Sanhedrim exclaim, " Art thou also
of Galilee, search and look, for out of Galilee ariseth
no prophet." And again, the difficulty which Christ's
birth put in the way of his reception, is more strongly
stated in the same chapter. (St. John vii.)—" Others
said This is the Christ, but some said, Shall Christ
come out of Galilee ?   Hath not the Scripture said,
that Christ cometh of the seed of David, and out of
the town of Bethlehem where David was ?"   Thus St.
John tells us expressly that there were current objections to the acknowledgment of our Lord's claims
which ran thus—" Jesus is not of David's seed, as
it was foretold the Messiah should be.   Jesus was
born at Nazareth, but the prophet foretold that the
Messiah should be born at Bethlehem ; therefore
Jesus is not the Messiah of whom the prophets
spoke."   The Evangelist does not tell how these objections were to be got over ; and as there is no possibility of denying that the Jews did understand the

prophets to say that the Messiah should be born in
Bethlehem; (in fact the legend that our Lord was
born there can only be conceived to have arisen out
of the universal belief that the Messiah ought to be
born there ;) Renan apparently would have us understand that the Evangelist, in honest simplicity, relates
the objection which our Lord's adversaries were accustomed to use as a triumphant refutation of His claims,
himself being unable to supply any possible answer
to it. But I cannot hesitate to believe that the true
explanation of the matter is that which has been
received by almost every reader of St. John's Gospel
since the time of its composition, namely, that John
gives no answer to the objection, because he knew,
and could take for granted that all his readers knew,
that the true answer was, that Jesus was indeed of
the seed of David, and was born, not at Nazareth,
but at Bethlehem, as the prophets had predicted.
In fact, we must choose between the suppositions that
John did not answer the objection, because he did
not know how to answer it, or because he did not
think it needed any answer. Now the first solution
is disproved by the late date, which critics of all
schools agree in ascribing to St. John's Gospel, a
date certainly later than the prevalence of belief in
Christ's birth at Bethlehem. The second solution,
therefore, alone remains. This inference, which
would be probable, if we found a similar passage
in any Christian writer of the same date, is certain
to any one who bears in mind what I will call the
peculiar irony of St John's style.

It will be perceived that I have borrowed the title of

this note from Bishop Thirlwall's celebrated essay on
" The Irony of Sophocles," (Philological Museum, II.
483.) As is pointed out in that essay, besides that verbal irony, to which we commonly give the name, where
there is opposition between the speaker's thought and
his words, there is a dialectic irony, of which Plato
and Pascal were two of the greatest masters, where
the writer effects his purpose " by placing the opinion
of his adversary in the foreground, saluting it with
every demonstration of respect, while he is busied in
withdrawing, one by one, all the supports on which
it rests, and he never ceases to approach it with an
air of deference until he has completely undermined
it, when he leaves it to sink by the weight of its own
absurdity." And, again—there is a practical irony,
when there is a strong opposition between the position
of any man, as he himself conceives it, and as it
really is. Nothing is more dramatically effective than
the exhibition of such a contrast, when the character
on the stage is ignorant of something known to the
spectators, and in his ignorance uses expressions
which have a reference that the speaker does not
dream of. No finer examples of this kind of irony
can be found than in the *Œdipus Rex* of Sophocles.
The irony, as Thirlwall has remarked, begins with
the opening scene, where the king, himself untouched
by calamity, receives the petitions of the afflicted city.
He who is the object of the wrath of heaven " stands
alone, calm and serene. Unconscious of his own
misery, he can feel pity for the unfortunate ; to him
all look for succour ; and as in the plenitude of
wisdom and power, he undertakes to trace to its

secret source the evil of which he is himself the sole cause." And through the play passages recur in which the king uses, concerning the murderer of Laius, phrases which have a terrible double meaning, of which he who utters them has no suspicion, for what he fancies he is saying of another he is really saying of himself. The same artifice is as effective in comedy as in tragedy. No scenes are more successful than where a speaker is made unconsciously to pronounce his own condemnation in words which, when he utters them, he does not reflect are more applicable to himself than to anybody else. When Terence makes the duped father boast—

> " Primus sentio mala nostra ; primus rescisco omnia,
> Primus porro obnuntio ; "

the spectators at once feel the irony of the contrast between the speaker's fancied knowledge and real ignorance ; and the slave is presently made to put their feelings into words—

> " Rideo hunc ; se primum ait scire, is solus nescit omnia."

Now, passages of the character I have described occur to an unusual amount in St. John's Gospel. I believe that more examples can be found in that Gospel than in all the rest of the New Testament of cases where the characters are introduced as speaking under misapprehensions which the reader knows how to correct. In the second chapter the Jews exclaim, " Forty and six years was this temple in building, and wilt thou rear it up in three days ? " In the third chapter, Nicodemus asks, " How can a man be born when he is old ; can he enter a second time into his mother's

womb, and be born?" In the fourth chapter the
woman of Samaria cries, "Lord, give me this water,
that I thirst not, neither come hither to draw." In
the sixth chapter the Jews contend, "How shall this
man give us His flesh to eat?" About as many
examples of this kind as there are chapters can be
produced out of St. John. In some cases the Evangelist explains and corrects the misapprehensions of
the speakers, and these cases cannot fairly be classed
under the head of irony; for in irony the reader
or spectator is expected to contribute something of
his own, which will establish the contrast between
the seeming meaning of the words and the real—
between the outward appearance of the action and the
true state of things. But there are several of the
passages to which I have referred in which the detec-
tion of the speaker's mistake is left to the intelligence
of the reader, and these cases may fairly be reckoned
under the head of irony.

I ought not to omit to say something of the dramatic
use of what may be called double irony, where the
speaker says something which he intends as ironical,
but which the better informed spectator perceives to
be literal truth. Without delaying to give examples
of this from profane literature, I pass to the signal
instance of it which the Gospels contain, the saluta-
tion of our Lord as King by His enemies at the time
of his crucifixion. The fact is recorded by all the
Evangelists; but St. John in a peculiar manner calls
his readers' attention to the irony of the situation,
and makes them observe that He was indeed a King
who was thus recognized as King. St. John alone

relates that Pilate presented our Lord to the Jews
with the words, "Behold your King;" and that he
insisted on putting over His cross the inscription
"The King of the Jews," in opposition to the wish
of the chief priests, that the inscription should only
state that He had said that He was King of the Jews.
The Evangelist adds no word of comment; but it is
manifest that he intends the thought to rise in the
mind of the reader that what had been said in mockery
was indeed the truth. To the proofs that the fourth
Evangelist had a keen perception of practical irony,
I think I may not unfairly add his account of the
saying of Caiaphas, that it was expedient that one
man should die for the people, in which the Evangelist recognizes a deep truth, of which the speaker was
unconscious.

In connection with the fourth Evangelist's predi-
lection for the ironical form of expression, may be
mentioned his willingness in general to leave un-
spoken what he can trust his readers to supply. He
does not claim to be the unnamed disciple who heard
the testimony of John the Baptist, nor to be the
unnamed disciple through whose interest Peter was
admitted to the high priest's palace; yet there can
be little doubt that in both cases the impression
received by most readers is that which the writer
intended them to receive. There can be as little
doubt that if the fourth Evangelist were not the
Apostle John, he was one who desired to pass for
him; yet so far is the claim from being directly
made, that one whose knowledge was obtained solely
from this Gospel would never learn that there was an

Apostle of the name of John; and the forerunner of our Lord is not called, as in the other Gospels, John the Baptist, but simply John, as if there were no other John from whom it was necessary to distinguish him.

Bearing in mind these peculiarities of the style of the fourth Gospel, we must pronounce a critic guilty of downright stupidity who imagines that because the Evangelist records, without an attempt at reply, the objections that Jesus could not be the Messiah because He was not of the seed of David, and was not born at Bethlehem, he really meant his readers to understand that the facts actually were as these objectors assumed. Rather we have here a forcible example of " dialectic irony," where the adversary's opinion is treated with mock deference, while the reader is expected to know that it is entitled to no real respect. With sympathetic triumph the writer and his readers watch the objectors staking the case against the Messiahship of Jesus, on an issue on which the verdict is sure to go against them.

If this be the true explanation of the passages referred to by Renan—and I really cannot see how any one of common sense, not to say ordinary critical sagacity, can put any other construction on them—the question whether John was acquainted with other Gospels seems almost determined by the fact that he can state what were felt to be fatal objections against the Messiahship of Jesus without saying one word to refute them. How is it that he can venture to take for granted that his readers would know for certain that Jesus was born at Bethlehem, not at Nazareth ?

How is it that he whose duty it was as an Apostle and an Evangelist to testify about Christ, saw no occasion to deliver any testimony on this fundamental point? I confess that the supposition that John relied on the oral tradition current among Christians, seems to me quite insufficient to meet the exigencies of the case. I do not believe that in the case that there was no authentic record of that tradition, St. John could have been satisfied to state so formidable an objection, without at least indicating by a word or a parenthesis that the answer to it which his readers might be expected to give was a true one. To my mind the objection that Christ must, according to the prophets, be of the seed of David and of the town of Bethlehem, is a plain indication that John knew that his readers had in their hands at least one of the Gospels which contain the genealogy tracing our Lord's descent from David, and in which His birth at Bethlehem is related.* I draw the same inference from an objection elsewhere recorded by him, and without any attempt to answer it—" Is not this Jesus the son of Joseph, whose father and mother we know? How is it, then, that he saith, I came down from heaven?"

It is to be observed, that the hypothesis that the writer of the fourth Gospel knew, at least some of

---

* Renan calls attention to many points of contact between Luke's narrative and John's, though he does not venture to draw the conclusion I believe to be true—viz., that John was acquainted with Luke's Gospel. The most striking verbal coincidence with another Gospel is the difficult expression μύρου νάρδου πιστικῆς, common to John and Mark—Mark xiii. 3; John xii. 3.

the others, is intrinsically highly probable. Critics, with general consent, place an interval of, on a low estimate, twenty years between the publication of Matthew's and Luke's Gospel and St. John's. It is hard to believe that St. John all this time lived so completely out of the Christian world that a copy of one of these Gospels should never have made its way to him. On inspection of his work we cannot but be struck by the manner in which he avoids anything that has been related by the other Evangelists. The exception is, when we find in St. John anything that had been recorded by his predecessors ; and when we do, there is usually some obvious reason for its insertion. Thus the miracle of feeding the multitude, though told by all four Evangelists, is used by St. John to introduce a discourse peculiar to himself. Now the feat required in the ancient ordeals of walking blindfold among red-hot ploughshares, without ever touching one of them, is little less miraculous than that the Evangelist should by mere accident thus traverse the entire life of our Lord, without coming into contact with anything which his predecessors had related.

Several orthodox critics have denied that St. John could have seen the works of the preceding Evangelists, because in several places where his matter is common with them, his narrative is an independent one, not influenced or modified by theirs. But this objection rests on the assumption that if John knew of their Gospels he would not have thought it right to make his own narrative an independent one. On the contrary, we may well believe that an Apostle would not write, as a second-hand historian might, with other manuscripts before him, carefully weighing and deciding between the different statements he found in them. An Apostle who depended on no one else for his information would write freely what came within his own knowledge, and his history would be likely to be an independent one; not, indeed, in real contradiction to any other true narrative, but very probably in apparent opposition. This, then, is one of the cases where one's first thoughts and one's third coincide. The first-sight impression produced by the Gospel is that it was intended to be supplemental to the others, and so a respectable array of fathers maintain. And though several modern writers have rejected this first-sight impression as not corresponding to the results of a closer examination, I believe that a still closer examination brings us back . to our first opinion.

I conclude, then, that the silence of John concerning things told by his predecessors is not the silence of ignorance. Neither is it the silence of disparagement. The case already discussed of our Lord's descent from David, and His birth at Bethlehem, is alone sufficient to prove this. The same inference may be drawn from the case of the Ascension, which St. John does not record. It has been often noticed that the Ascension is, however, incidentally referred to by him—vi. 62—" What and if ye shall see the Son of Man ascend up where he was before ?" But the fact is assumed, not in a single verse, but throughout the Gospel. The Evangelist is never weary of teaching that Jesus is a heavenly person, not an earthly; His true home heaven, not earth.

F

What he most frequently declares is, that Jesus had been in heaven before He came to earth. If he does not equally dwell on the fact that Jesus returned to heaven after He left earth, it can only be that he knew that there was no need for him to bear testimony to what was well known to his readers through the attestation of others; for the doctrine of the pre-existence of Christ is made to smooth away all difficulties in admitting the fact of the Ascension—iii. 13—"No man hath ascended up to heaven but he that came down from heaven, even the Son of Man, which is in heaven." John is as silent about the command to baptize all nations as he is about the institution of the Eucharist; yet in the discussions concerning the efficacy of both sacraments, St. John's Gospel occupies the foremost place, and it suggested the name by which in the middle of the second century baptism was known.* Not to discuss one by one John's other omissions, I may mention John's omission of those transactions of which the Synoptic Evangelists relate him to have been one of three selected witnesses; such as the Transfiguration, the raising of Jairus's daughter, and, in particular, the Agony in the Garden. Renan notices John's selection for narration of incidents in which he himself held a prominent place; and he imputes this to vanity, though it would have been more charitable to think that the Evangelist chose to speak of things to which he could give autoptic testimony. But taking

* Nothing seems to me more disingenuous than the special pleading by which it has been attempted to resist the evidence of Justin Martyr's acquaintance with the fourth Gospel.

Renan's view, we ask, had the Evangelist never heard up to the late epoch when his Gospel was written, of those stories in which the cycle of evangelic traditions described him as specially honoured with his Master's confidence? Had he been never interrogated as to the truth or falsity of accounts which purported to rest on his own testimony? Does he mean by his silence to intimate that the honour attributed to him was undeserved? It is not enough to say, for instance, that the agony in the garden did not take place on the *last* night of our Lord's life. If the argument from St. John's silence proves what it is supposed to prove, it proves that no such incident ever occurred, or at least that St. John was not admitted to witness it.

On the whole, if there were no other reasons for distrusting Renan's conclusions, this is enough, that he proceeds by a faulty method, and does not know how to use that one of the documents to which he justly attributes the highest value. There are some writers who never intend to convey any other impression than that which their words express, and who, consequently, are fully intelligible by a perfect stranger to the things related. There are others with whom the impression intended to be produced is the combined result of the writer's words and the reader's previous knowledge; it may be, as in the case of language commonly called ironical, the impression intended being the exact opposite of that expressed in the writer's words. What I have attempted to show is, that St. John distinctly belongs to the latter class of writers, not the former; so that we can never be sure of understanding him, if we do not enquire what is

the knowledge which he assumed his readers to possess. One who, actually having this knowledge, strives
to divest himself of it for the better understanding of
his author, exhibits an uncritical want of perception of
the characteristics of the book he is studying, enough
to account for any amount of blunders in the results
arrived at.

SERMON IV.

UNSUCCESSFUL PRAYER.

"My strength is made perfect in weakness."—2 COR. xii. 9.

IT always strongly affects the imagination, when we see great results brought about by seemingly inade- quate means. In those popular tales which are the delight of childhood, and which are now found to be common to so many different nations, the exaltation of the despised is the favourite theme, and the hero who performs the great achievements is invariably the person who, in previous estimation, had been counted least capable of them. Of sacred story few parts have more charm for the boyish reader than that which tells how the gigantic Philistine, with spear like a weaver's beam, who scared all the cham- pions of Israel, was laid low by the shepherd lad, who encountered him in the name of the Lord his God, with no other arms than a sling and five smooth stones from the brook. So in profane history, ancient or modern, such stories as how the Greeks repelled the Persian invasion, or how a peasant girl drove the English out of France, owe half their fascination to the contrast between the actual result and what any-one might beforehand have expected.

The history of the establishment of Christianity in the world affords a striking instance of such a con-trast as I have been speaking of. The words " un-learned and ignorant men," which in the Acts express the view of the Jewish rulers concerning the Apostles, are, perhaps, rendered somewhat too strongly by our translators; but it is plain from them that the first teachers of the new religion were men who, in the judgment of the highest authorities among their own people, had little claim to fill the office of instructors of others.

The district whence the new teaching emanated was of little estimation with the Jews. " Can any good thing come out of Nazareth ?" was the cry; " Search and look, for out of Galilee ariseth no pro-phet." But whatever might be the likelihood of Galilean fishermen being accepted as teachers of the Jews, still less would have seemed the likelihood of Jews being accepted as teachers of the world. The Romans, in their pride of power, the Greeks, in their pride of culture, could not be expected to submit to the instruction of a race neither feared by strangers for military prowess, nor respected for intellectual achievements. The Epistle from which the text is taken is full of materials to illustrate how great were the obstacles against which Jewish teachers had to struggle, when they went outside the limits of their own nation. Those obstacles might be supposed re-duced to the lowest in the case of St. Paul. He was not one of the original twelve, but an instrument subsequently raised up in God's Providence, with special fitness for the great work of Apostleship to the Gentiles which was peculiarly his own. He could not be despised as unlearned by Jewish rabbis; for he had been brought up at the feet of one of their most distinguished teachers. He had also a tincture of Gentile learning, and had not merely read heathen books, but read them in no narrow Jewish spirit, and was ready to seize on great truths which were there recognized, and to take them as common ground on which to approach those whom he desired to influence. He was a man of no mean intellectual power, and his writings contain passages to which none can refuse the praise of eloquence. On a hasty judgment we might suppose him endowed with such striking advantages as must gain him the respect of his Grecian hearers. Yet, as we study his reception at Athens and Corinth, we see reason to think of him only as a Jew, who laboured under somewhat less disadvantages for preaching to Grecians than others of his countrymen. His attempt to make good a footing in Athens ended in what can only be described as failure. Idle babbler was the name which the first announcement of his doctrines fixed on him, and though their novelty gained him from that inquisitive people a hearing for a more detailed statement, the interview ended in mockery and insult, and on quitting the city he left behind but a small number of real converts. But at Corinth his stay was longer, and his success greater. He founded there a Church, which owned him as its spiritual father; and we might, perhaps, imagine such a conquest was the natural result of his great natural gifts, and, in particular, his fervid eloquence. A little thought might convince us that Grecian hearers would have much prejudice to overcome, before they could be charmed with the eloquence of one of a nation so despised as the Jewish, speaking, not without solecisms, a language which he, who called himself a Hebrew of the Hebrews, could not acknowledge as his own, and whose tastes and habits of thought had been cast in a different mould from theirs. And so, in point of fact, this Epistle to the Church at Corinth shows that the very disciples whom he had won there murmured at the absence of rhetorical skill in his addresses to them. They complained that he was rude in speech; that his bodily presence was weak, his speech contemptible; and Paul himself confessed that he came not with excellency of speech or of wisdom, that his speech and his preaching was not with enticing words of man's wisdom. He repeats, in fact, again and again, that the words which he spoke were not in the words which man's wisdom teacheth. We may well believe that it was the simple truth that Paul was not possessor of those arts by which itching ears are gratified, when we see what befell the Apostle in his own Church of Corinth— that Church which, as he says, he had begotten in the Gospel. There came thither other teachers, who vied with, or surpassed him, in popularity. The whole part of the Epistle from which my text is taken is a struggle to vindicate his authority against these rival pretensions. He was obliged, as he said, to become a fool in glorying; they had compelled him. He was obliged to go over and remind

them of all that he had done and suffered for the
cause of Christ; and all to prevent his Corinthian
converts from forsaking his teaching for the more
specious eloquence of some of these rival teachers.
The whole Epistle shows marks of wounded feelings.
He writes as one hurt that his love had not been returned by his disciples as it ought to be—as one
grieved that claims on their gratitude and affection,
such as none others could have had, should have been
lightly postponed to the attractive novelty of the later
teachers, who made themselves heads of parties in
the Church of Corinth.

We learn from the text and its context that besides
those disadvantages to which any Jewish preacher
would have been subject in Corinth, St. Paul laboured
under some peculiar personal disadvantages. He suffered from some bodily infirmity, which he describes
as a thorn or stake in the flesh, the messenger of
Satan to buffet him. What was its exact nature we
are not informed; but it would seem to be of a kind
very likely to interfere with his ministerial usefulness.
For instance, in Galatians iv. 13, 14, he records it to
the honour of the Galatian Churches that they did
not scorn him or his message, notwithstanding that
there was, as he owned, that about him which *might*
have exposed him to their contempt. "Ye know
how through infirmity of the flesh I preached the
Gospel unto you at the first. And my temptation
which was in my flesh ye despised not, nor rejected,
but received me as an angel of God, even as Christ
Jesus." And very possibly it is the same thing to
which he alludes in the beginning of the first Epistle

to the Corinthians, where he says, "I came not with excellency of speech or of wisdom. I was with you in weakness and fear, and in much trembling." Is it strange that St. Paul, then, should wonder at God's dealings—why it was that He should allow the spreaders of error and schism to triumph in the attraction of eloquence, while he, the apostle of truth, was encompassed with infirmity, unable, as he felt, to do justice to the message with which he had been entrusted; full of the thought that if he could only speak as he ought to speak, that if God would only remove the stumbling-block which now stood in his way, more souls might be won to God?

A Christian man may not unreasonably hesitate before making prayer for temporal blessings. Many things which we think blessings, have in the result proved far otherwise, and heathen as well as Christian moralists have remarked how ruinous to many has been the gaining of the things they longed and prayed for. On this account we feel it to be wisdom as well as piety, in making request for things of earth, not only to express, but to endeavour to cultivate in our minds, absolute submission to the will of Him who knoweth what things we have need of before we ask Him. If, however, prayer for earthly blessings might ever have been urged without reserve, one would suppose that it would be in the case of Paul's prayer that he might be delivered from his thorn in the flesh. He was asking not merely for an increase of ease and comfort to himself. He was asking for the removal of a hindrance to the extension of the Gospel of God. He was asking that he, the ambassador of Christ, might be enabled to deliver his message more freely —that he might be relieved from infirmities which inclined those to whom he came to despise him, and made them less ready to give him a favourable hearing.

Accordingly, St. Paul tells us, "For this thing I besought the Lord thrice that it might depart from me." I do not know whether it may not seem fanciful, but I think I see in this word "thrice" a confirmation of the fact that St. Paul was one whose experience had led him to expect miraculous answers to his prayers. If a pious clergyman of the present day were describing his conduct under a long-continued bodily trial, which he found a great hindrance to his usefulness, he would possibly say, "I made it for some time a subject of prayer that I might be freed from this burden." Nor would it seem to surprise him that his prayers should be continued a long time without result. But it does not appear that Paul made this thorn in the flesh an ordinary or habitual topic of prayer : on three distinct occasions, probably when he felt his trial intolerable, he set himself to face this messenger of Satan, and to endeavour in the power of prayer to put him to flight ; just as if he had resolved to use in his own case the same means which had often proved effectual for the benefit of others, when over those that were sick he had invoked the name of the Lord Jesus, and they had recovered.

However this may be, it is more important to notice to whom Paul's prayers were addressed. For in the invariable usage of Paul's epistles, the Lord is not, as it popularly is with us, a mere synonym for God, but is the special title of Jesus Christ. With Paul, as he tells us, there were not gods many and lords many, but one God the Father, of whom were all things, and we in Him ; and one Lord Jesus Christ, by whom are all things, and we by Him. The context is sufficient to show that the present passage is no exception to Paul's ordinary usage, and that it is one of the proofs that the Apostles practically showed their belief in the Godhead of their risen Master by addressing to Him their prayers. The Lord had answered his prayer—" My grace is sufficient for thee, for my strength is made perfect in weakness." And the Apostle adds, with reference to this answer, " Most gladly, therefore, will I glory in my weaknesses, that Christ's strength may rest upon me ;" showing most distinctly that Christ was the Lord whose strength was made perfect in his weakness. " I rejoice in weaknesses, in insults, in necessities, in persecutions, in distresses ; for when I am weak, then I am strong."

It is plain what a prominent part of Paul's system was his doctrine concerning the person of Christ ; and how accurately an unbeliever summed up his teaching as being concerning " one Jesus, who was dead, whom Paul affirmed to be alive." Paul had, at first, thought of Jesus as one dead, rightly put to death by the rulers of his nation, whose followers in resisting so manifest demonstration of the falsity of his pretensions, were guilty of criminal disobedience to authority and to reason. But after, on his way to Damascus, he had seen and heard Christ, not a shadow of doubt remained on his mind that He is alive ; thenceforward he looks upon Him as a personal living friend, to whom he can seek for help in every difficulty and distress—with whom he can have such close union, that his strength is Christ's strength, and all he is able to accomplish a revelation of the power of Christ.

Looking back now upon the history, we are at no loss to see reasons why Christ should exhibit His power in His servant's weakness. By refusing to remove the hindrances which, in Paul's own opinion, made him a less successful preacher of the Gospel than he otherwise would have been, his Lord would teach him that it needed not this to make him a sufficient instrument in His hands. He can bring about His designs by the feeblest instruments, and very often it is exactly such that He does choose to accomplish His purposes. And so St. Paul elsewhere sums up his experience—that the weakness of God was stronger than man ; that God had chosen the foolish things of the world to confound the wise ; the weak things of the world to bring to nought the things that are mighty, that no flesh should glory in His presence. That Paul should be made to feel this by his own experience was one of the sources of his success. Elsewhere, when he disclaims having made use of such means as rival teachers used, to gain the confidence and admiration of the Corinthians, he declares that he could on other grounds claim submission from them. His preaching, he says, was not with enticing words of man's wisdom, but with demonstration of the Spirit, and with power. In other words, he appeals to the miracles which he had performed among them ; or, as he calls them, to the signs of an Apostle wrought among them in signs and wonders and mighty deeds, that their faith should stand, not in the wisdom of men, but in the power of God. Yet, if the exhibition of miraculous power was likely to impress the spectators with a deep sense of God's power, it might not necessarily have the same effect on him who performed the miracles, and who, we can see, must be subject to peculiar temptations. Accordingly, it is in express connection with the mention of the extent of Paul's supernatural endowments, that he tells us of this thorn in the flesh sent him for the very purpose that he might not be puffed up with the abundance of the revelations vouchsafed to him.

When we think of the miraculous revolution which was effected by the labours of the Apostles—the overthrow of Paganism, the planting of Christianity in its stead ; when we think of the privileges they enjoyed, the personal intercourse they had had with our Lord Jesus Himself in the days of His flesh, the wonderful works which He enabled them to perform, the spiritual insight, the knowledge of the deep things of God which He communicated to them, we are apt to forget that these Apostles were men of like passions with ourselves, subject to the same human frailties, exposed to the same temptations. Look at it from this point of view, and can you conceive any position in which a man would be more likely to lose his balance than one placed on such a pinnacle as St. Paul. Consider that at his prayer the sick were restored to health, the lame made to walk,

devils were cast out; at his word the heathens cast
their idols to the moles and to the bats; nay, he
himself was caught up into heaven, and heard words
unspeakable, which it was not lawful for a man to
utter; and would it be wonderful if one so honoured
had felt that there was some worthiness in himself
which made him peculiarly fitted to receive these
honours, and that when he saw what great things he
had performed he should think that it was his own
power and wisdom which had done all this?

But God chose to keep His servant humble, by
chequering with reverses the career of triumph which
he trod. He was dishonoured among his own converts; put to shame before them, as it would seem,
by the consequences of some painful and distressing
bodily malady; at any rate, strikingly inferior to his
rivals in all that could make his teaching attractive.
But this was exactly the way in which God ruled it,
that the Apostle's own mind should be kept full, not
of the things which he had done, but of the things
in which he was deficient. His intensity of longing
to be freed from his infirmity, his feeling how much
this hindered his usefulness in the Gospel work, kept
constantly alive in his mind the feeling that it was to
no excellency of his that was owing the multitude of
converts who had crowned his labours, but that all was
due to the power of Christ, who had wrought by him.
And here, again, the wisdom of God was manifested;
and, doubtless, God in His own way wrought greater
things by the hand of Paul than if He had, as Paul
himself desired, made him what men would call a
fitter instrument for the preaching of His Word.

Greater fluency of speech, greater harmony of language, a more commanding aspect, a more attractive
exterior—all these would, no doubt, have swelled the
number of the preacher's auditors, would have brought
together greater crowds to hang upon his lips. But
would they have increased the number of his true
converts? His words might have more charmed the
ear; but would they have sunk so deep into the
heart? I have no doubt it was those very dealings
of God with Paul at which he was at times tempted
to rebel—those dealings which made him painfully
conscious of his own feebleness; those instances of
ill-success in his preaching, of which he felt that his
own defects were the cause; these very things were
part of the secrets of Paul's success; they were part
of his training in humility, part of that discipline
which made him know that man was nothing, that
Christ was all in all, so that out of this deep experimental knowledge, speaking from the heart to the
heart, he could win souls to Christ in a way which
all the oratory in the world could never have accomplished.

What I have said would be true, no matter what
had been the scene of Paul's labours; it is especially
true with reference to his work in Corinth. To anyone who studies the condition of the Corinthian Church
as described in the Epistles, and who compares it
with that of other Churches, it will be evident that
its character was highly-stimulated activity of intellect, together with low morality, and little Christian
love. To these causes we may trace the contentions
and party spirit for which the Apostle has to rebuke

them ; to these, the eagerness with which they grasped at the miraculous gifts of the Holy Spirit, exercising them for ostentation, not for edification of the Church. Now if Paul had taken that course which, of set purpose, he abstained from taking, or if he had attempted to vie with his rivals in that Church of Corinth, by using the same ornaments of words and embellishments of oratory for which they were admired, in the first place, according to all human probability, he must have failed in the attempt. Success would have been as hopeless as that of David would have been had he essayed, in unproved armour, and with weapons new to him, to encounter one who had been a man of war from his youth. But supposing Paul's mastery of the arts by which popularity could be gained in Corinth to have been ever so great—supposing him to have beaten his rivals on their own ground, he would have left un-assailed the exaggerated importance which the Corinthians attached to what they counted intellectual achievement, and would have rather confirmed them in the miserable delusion that religion consists in filling the brain with notions instead of filling the heart with Christian motives, and directing the conscience by Christian principles. St. Paul succeeded, not by showing that he could do better than his rivals what they could do well, but by showing that all their fancied knowledge was nothing in comparison of the knowledge of Jesus Christ and Him crucified. All those dealings of God with Paul, which made him a proficient in that knowledge, were the means of forging the only weapon by which he

G

could triumph. And he having experienced what Christ could in this way do, owned that God had judged what was best for him, and said, " Most gladly, therefore, will I glory in my infirmities, that the power of Christ may rest upon me."

I have occupied our time to-day in dwelling on the one particular case to which the text refers, in which Christ's strength was made perfect in weakness. On next Sunday I hope to discuss further this general principle, and some questions which it suggests. For the present I content myself with noticing the lesson of practical consolation, which may be drawn from the history we have been studying.

We have seen how God, by refusing to grant to St. Paul that for which he prayed, did, in truth, give to his prayer a better answer than if He had literally complied with his petition. Let us draw from our study of his history support and consolation for ourselves when our prayers seem to be unheard. When Paul's prayer was set aside, the Lord bestowed on him a revelation declaring to him why He had so dealt with him. We can expect no such special revelation; and in those seasons of repulse we must rest our faith on our knowledge of God's character, and on what has been revealed to us of the manner in which He has formerly dealt with His servants of old. We know, of course, that we are liable to mistake what is good for us; that God is all good and all wise; that He may have reasons for not complying with our wishes which we cannot now penetrate. Yet there are times when it seems to us that the things we desire are so necessary for our happiness, so conducive to our real good, that we cannot understand how it is possible that it can be right that our petitions should be denied us. The case we have been considering was exactly one of this kind. What could seem more a fitting subject for prayer than that of St. Paul ? He was asking not for himself, but for the cause of God. Yet God saw that the weakness of His servant could be made in His hands a more powerful instrument than his strength. If God sees fit, then, to deny us what we ask, it may also be the case that He is working out our real good—our good for time and eternity—in a way far more effectual than that by which we had hoped to effect it.

There may, indeed, be another cause for the failure of our prayers. St. James touches on it in the New Testament—" Ye ask and receive not, because ye ask amiss ;" and David, in the Old Testament—" If I regard iniquity in my heart, the Lord will not hear me." We may ask of God victory over some form of temptation—the conquest of some besetting sin—and we may wonder that our prayers have not been heard by God, when the fact is that we have not heard these prayers ourselves. The prayers have been but the dreamy expression of wishes not carried out by corresponding acts of the will, not followed up by active and energetic resolutions, not productive of increased watchfulness. If these fail, it is because they are not real prayers ; and the remedy is to be sought by increased diligence in prayer—prayer that God would strengthen our desires for good, would make us feel more deeply our need of His grace, and beg for it more earnestly; for when we pray for our growth in grace, we ask only for what He has promised to give us; and such prayers, if made with our hearts in the name of His Son, cannot fail.

But when we ask for other things, our judgments may err. We may ask for what He may see it to be best for us that we should not obtain. It may be our lot, as it was of One greater than we, to see trials approaching from which our human nature shrinks back; to cry, " If it be possible, let this cup pass from me," and yet that that cup may be pressed more closely to our lips. If such should be our lot, may we also learn from that perfect example implicit confidence in our Father's wisdom and His love—entire resignation to His will; may we to lear , with all our hearts to say, " Father, not my will, but thine, be done."

SERMON V.

MAN'S WEAKNESS AND CHRIST'S STRENGTH.

"My strength is made perfect in weakness."—2 CORINTHIANS, xii. 9.

WHEN I last addressed you, I showed how the general principle here enunciated was verified in Paul's own case, and how those things which he counted as weakness, and which apparently made him less fitted to be a successful preacher of the Gospel, afforded, according to the best judgment we can form, an opportunity of more fully exhibiting the power of Christ, and so of obtaining for the Apostle success which he otherwise could not have had.

I remarked also that the whole history of the early progress of Christianity is a history of a triumph of this world's weakness over this world's strength. When Christianity was first promulgated nothing could seem more firmly established than the system of Paganism which it ultimately overthrew. That system dated from immemorial antiquity; it was in one form or another spread over the whole civilized world; and, indeed, it was supposed that everywhere,

without exception, the same divinities, under different
names, were worshipped. It had been adorned by the
noblest works of poetry and art; and so had infinite
attractions for the cultivated, while it had all the terrors of superstition for the vulgar. It is true that
the sceptical few had begun to discern on how little
basis of evidence the received system rested, yet, for
the most part, they refrained from open assault;
and it was not from the philosophers that that system
met its overthrow, but from what they would have
accounted a superstition less venerable than their own
mythology, and quite as irrational. There are sceptical writers in our own country in the present day;
but nothing they have written would do much to
facilitate the enterprise of one who should attempt to
persuade us to exchange our own religion for the
worship of a prophet who might arise in India, or
some other of the nations conquered by England.
It is, indeed, remarkable how little the educated
pagans were alive to the significance of a movement
destined to have such important results. In the
scanty notices of the progress of Christianity which
we can glean from heathen writers, even after the new
religion had had a century of growth or more, it still
appears in Roman eyes only a superstition of the
subject races; but none suspect that the axe had
been already laid to the root of their own ancient
religion, and that the new creed would soon be enthroned in their imperial seat, and rule the world for
ages.

On the last day I compared this victory of Christianity with other triumphs which history records of

the weak over the strong. It is important to observe, however, that, strictly speaking, there is no such thing as a victory of weakness over strength, though it very often happens that before the event men miscalculate on which side the real strength lies. When, for instance, the countless host of the Persian empire advanced to take possession of Greece, it might well seem beforehand that the odds in favour of the invaders were overwhelming. Yet, over and over again, has it been proved—as, for instance, by our own soldiers in India and elsewhere—how little numerical odds avail against courage and discipline. So the Greeks found it in subsequent contests with the barbarians ; and then, taught by experience, they advanced to conflict with far-outnumbering hosts, in full confidence of superiority, knowing that the wolf counts not how many the sheep be. But their first victories they owed to a different cause. Then they did not know that they were the stronger; they believed themselves to be the weaker; but they had a cause on behalf of which they were willing to sacrifice themselves, counting it more glorious to die fighting for country and freedom than to live as slaves ; and so daring to try a contest with, as they believed, all the chances against them, beyond their own expectations, they were victorious.

It is hard to estimate to what accession of strength is equivalent some motive which will induce a man to put forth all the strength he has. Many a time men fail to accomplish great things quite within their reach, from ignorance of their own strength. In many a battle a general has withdrawn his forces

repelled from their object, because he had not mea-
sured the exhaustion of his enemy, and did not know
what one effort more would have given him. Young
men are not supposed to err generally on the side of
forming too modest an estimate of their own powers;
yet there is a great difference between an opinion
which it may please them to entertain in their own
minds, or to express to others, and a conviction on
which they can venture practically to act. And it is
certain that many, not commonly supposed to be
wanting in vanity, might have attained to heights
which they never reached if, at the outset of life, they
had had sufficient knowledge of their powers to en-
courage them to put forth their whole strength on
enterprises which they supposed to be above them.
On the other hand, prudence obviously counsels that
it is folly to dash against the impossible, and that to
waste our powers in striving after the unattainable, is
not merely to prepare for ourselves disappointment,
but to lose all that by a wiser direction of our energies we might have gained.

For the same reason prudence counsels that if the
chances of success are greatly against us, it is better
not to make an attempt more likely than not to end
in failure. On this account men ordinarily very wisely
abstain from testing their powers to the utmost : and
those historical instances to which I have referred, of
unexpected triumphs of what had been supposed to
be weakness over strength, seldom, if ever, occur unless where there is some strong moral inducement
sufficient to embolden men to stake their all upon
the cast, and accept the consequences of the probable

failure, rather than forego their hopes of the possible success. So if· we were estimating the chances of a conflict between two nations, we might go widely astray if we merely balanced the physical resources of each, and did not take into account their difference in moral strength ; the one, perhaps, being willing to employ all its resources without reserve, and so to submit to hardships and sacrifices which would be grudged by the other.

It is very wisely, then, that Gibbon has counted first in his enumeration of the causes that brought about the triumph of Christianity, the zeal of the Christians, however inadequate be his explanation of the origin of that zeal. There is no spring of human action which has greater power to urge men to essay all that they can do, regardless of consequences, than such a martyr spirit as elicited that spirit-stirring "If not," of the Book of Daniel, " Our God whom we serve is able to deliver us from the burning fiery furnace, and He will deliver us from thy hand, O King. But if not, be it known unto thee, O King, that we will not serve thy gods, nor worship the golden image which thou hast set up." Such a spirit animated the preachers of the Gospel· " I know," said one of them, " that the Holy Ghost witnesseth in every city, saying, that bonds and afflictions abide me. But none of these things move me, neither count I my life dear unto myself, so that I might finish my course with joy, and the ministry which I have received of the Lord Jesus, to testify the Gospel of the grace of God." When the Apostles preached there were multitudes who had a languid traditional belief in their hereditary divinities ; multitudes who had a superstitious fear of the injuries which Jupiter, Venus, or Isis had power to inflict on them. But what fraction of them could be said to *love* these deities, to have a real faith in them, to be willing to die for them, as Christians loved the Lord Jesus, and were glad to die for Him.

What wonder, then, that professors of a religion which had but feeble hold on their hearts, and who, if asked, or if they asked themselves why they be- lieved what they professed, could give no satisfactory account of the grounds of their belief, should be easily influenced by men who seemed to speak from thorough knowledge and conviction, whose whole heart evi- dently was in the cause they advocated, and who were ready, if need be, to die for it.   Undoubtedly, then, the zeal of the Christian preachers was one main cause of their success.   But whence came that zeal ? Gibbon summarily accounts for it as a kind of off- shoot of the intolerant zeal of Judaism ; but con- sidering that, after the first generation of Christians, a very small fraction of them were Jews, and that the zeal burned with equal strength in men whose habits and whose national traditions afforded no example of anything similar, this explanation cannot be considered satisfactory.   This much only we must own, that Judaism and Christianity had this in common, that both religions succeeded in inspiring in their disciples intense faith in the truth of their creeds ; and what, if you please, you may call the intolerant conviction that that truth did not reside in the belief of the surrounding peoples, that the gods

of the heathen were but idols, wood and stone, the
work of men's hands, So much the two religions
had in common ; but the Christian did not, like the
ordinary Jew, rest in the conviction of the superiority
of his creed as a matter of pride and rejoicing, but
burned with desire to make known to others those
truths which were the comfort of his own life.
Christianity and Judaism had in common that both
religions taught the existence of a personal God,
willing to hear the prayers of His creatures, to whom
they might pour out their whole souls, and with
whom they might enjoy intimate communion ; and
the experience of both religions informs us of this,
that men, who make experimental trial of that communion, do arrive at as thorough conviction of its
reality, as men have in the reality of the external
objects which they see and handle every day.   But
Christianity further taught its disciples to know
God as revealed in the person of His Son, and to
approach the Father through Him ; and so, as the
vagueness to which the worship of an unseen God is
liable was removed, far stronger love was felt to God
revealed in a character so capable of inspiring love ;
while a desire was also inspired to be like that character, and to imitate Him in whom the Divine
perfections were embodied, in His self-sacrificing love
to men, even to the unthankful and the evil.   The
zeal, then, of the Christian preachers had its root in
experimental knowledge of the love of Christ, obtained by habitual communion with Him ; so that,
if their zeal were a great part of their strength,
that strength was still the strength of Christ.   In

comparison of this strength, both then and since, all differences in intellectual endowments have been insignificant, and he who has lived a life of prayer, whose thoughts have dwelt on Christ, whose heart is penetrated with His love, and who is resolved to endure labours and sacrifices for His sake, though rude in speech, though destitute of the learning the world counts valuable, has been able to win souls to his Master, whom no mere eloquence could have gained over. Thus has God often chosen the foolish things of the world to confound the wise, and the weak things of the world, and base things of the world, and things which are despised, to bring to nought the things that are mighty. Yet if God does in other cases, as He did in St. Paul's, withhold what men might count advantages for the preaching of His Gospel, He does not really work without the use of means; He rather chooses those means which He sees to be most effectual, disregarding what, however highly esteemed among men, He sees to be of less worth for His service. In short, the idea which on this and on the last day I have been trying to work out is, that God works according to general laws, even in those cases which look like a violation of ordinary laws, and that the paradox that Christ's strength is made perfect in weakness, is no exception to this rule; for, as the experience of failure and consciousness of weakness have driven men to Christ, they have derived, from their experience of communion with Him, an assured conviction of the reality of their intercourse with Him, which they now find no difficulty in communicating to others; as well as such love for Him and zeal for His cause, as inspire them with resolution to put forth without reserve all the strength they have.

And now arises the question, If man's weakness is so often in God's hands a more powerful weapon than his strength, is it not better to be weak than to be strong? Shall we not do well to make a voluntary surrender of some of the advantages which God has put within our reach, in order that, unencumbered by them, we may work for Him more effectually? This season of Lent has been a time during which, for centuries, Christians have been accustomed to abstain from indulgences in themselves perfectly innocent, in order that the flesh being thereby subdued to the spirit, they might gain strength to follow God's motions more freely. Others, not content with exhorting, as Scripture sanctions, that their disciples should be willing so to brace their will by temporary abstinence from lawful indulgence, that they should not be enslaved by pleasures from which they knew not how to part, have demanded a permanent surrender of all that this world prizes. They have insisted on life-long vows of chastity and abstinence. They have required that those to whom God has given wealth should cast it away, and live in voluntary poverty. Others, again, both of the same and of quite an opposite school, persuaded that human learning has no power to win souls for Christ, have insisted that the Christian minister ought not to encumber himself with this fleshly weapon, and should determine, in the literal sense, to know nothing but Jesus Christ, and Him crucified.

It must be conceded that much even of this world's greatness has had its root in humiliation. The observation has been frequently in men's mouths during the last two or three months, that the military greatness to which Prussia has now attained had its origin in the crushing defeat which she suffered at the beginning of this century, and in the few years of bitter humiliation which followed, during which illusions of fancied superiority, founded on her past history, having been dispelled, the foundations were laid of a fabric of solid strength. Lately we have seen the parts reversed that were played at the beginning of the century—the conqueror of that day now discovering the emptiness of reliance on a glorious past, and having to suffer at the hands of the then vanquished humiliation no less bitter than he had inflicted. And there are those who augur that now, likewise, the furnace of affliction through which that great nation is passing will but purge away its dross, and prepare it for a nobler future.

Our ideas are often vague when historians tell us of nations being so enervated by luxury as to be unable to make resistance against invasion. We hardly understand that this opprobrious word luxury may mean no more than what we see among ourselves—namely, that a number of people, comfortably well off, and whose time is felt to be valuable, prefer to leave to others the hardship of military service; and it may need calamities, such as to make the life of ease they would have preferred absolutely impossible, before they are capable of deeds of

heroism. Just in the same manner, the obstacle to
deeds of heroism in the cause of religion is not
necessarily sin or vice. Inability to dispense with
ordinary innocent indulgence is quite sufficient.

Our circumstances do not disclose how much of
the martyr spirit is alive among us ; but it is less difficult for us to judge whether the missionary spirit of the
Church in our day comes short of the apostolic standard. In the mere cause of gain, at the present time,
young men are willing enough to leave their home ; to
part with family and friends, and reside for years in a
distant country ; especially provided that the climate
is not unhealthy, and that there is a fair prospect of
ultimate return to their native land. If, therefore,
we had to answer our Lord's question, " What do ye
more than others ?" some deduction should be made
from the actual number—itself not strikingly large—
of missionaries whom we send forth to labour among
the heathen. It is plain that the higher the standard
of comfort that a man may lawfully and innocently
claim, the greater the sacrifice that is made in abandoning it; and so that a time of general prosperity
is adverse to religious as well as to other heroism.
And yet, shall we say that we are unable to work for
God, unless He discipline us to His service by calamities? that none save he, " qui zonam perdidit," is
a fit soldier for Christ's army ? Thinking of it thus,
we see that it is not without reason the duty is commended to us, and especially at this season, of making
acts of self-denial not actually forced on us, and of
so disciplining our wills that we shall not be enslaved
by indulgence, but shall sit loose to the pleasures of

this world, so as to be able to part with them, if need should be. God rewards this victory of the will over the lower part of our nature with a peculiar pleasure of its own—a pleasure so great, that those who have experienced it, often have preferred it to that which the indulgence of appetite affords. And it is a curious example how precisely similar temptations beset us from opposite directions ; that exactly in the same way as many are tempted by the pleasure which attends the satisfying the appetites which our Creator has planted in us, to indulge those appetites for the mere sake of that pleasure to a degree far beyond what is legitimate, and which is really hurtful to them ; so a few have been tempted by the pleasure which attends a victory over appetite to practise asceticisms bordering on lunacy, utterly deranging the healthy constitution of their own nature, and yielding no benefit to their fellow-men.

But what I had chiefly in view when I proposed the question, Is it lawful or prudent to make a voluntary surrender of our strength, in the hope that thereby Christ's strength may be more fully manifested in us, was in order to say a few words on the question, Is human learning a hindrance to the preacher of the Gospel ? Is it a kind of Saul's armour, of which he who would be victorious in Christ's cause will wisely divest himself? Some things I have said may seem to point to that conclusion, and experience would appear to confirm it. It is notorious that profound knowledge and great power to influence others do not necessarily, or even commonly, go together—that some of the soundest

and most learned divines have been persons incapable
of getting a hearing from a popular audience; and
that some most popular and successful preachers have
been men of but slender attainments.   In the history
of opinion, too, it is remarkable how small a part is
played by reason and argument, so that one is tempted
to say that men in general do not form their opinions
by any intellectual process, but catch them like measles
from one another.   Beliefs the most erroneous have
been exposed by thoroughly convincing. arguments,
yet the faith of hardly a single adherent has been
shaken.   Subsequently, the whole fabric falls at a
single trumpet blast.   The strong convictions of one
endowed with a sympathetic nature flash electrically
into the hearts of multitudes, whose heads would
have been impervious to argumentation.   Yet it would
be a mistake to overlook how much such instantaneous
success is often due to the effect of a preparatory
process of argument, fruitless though it may have
seemed at the time; so that such a sudden fall as I
have described has been no miracle, but the ruin of
a structure previously undermined.   Victory is not
always due to those whose efforts are seen to win it;
not to the valiant soldier who perils his life in the
front of the enemy, but to the quiet, silent man who,
some miles away, sits over his maps, with telegraph
wires close at hand.   God's gifts to His creatures
are unequally distributed, and he who is singularly
endowed with one, will not improbably be deficient
in another of a different kind.   So he who has been
gifted with powers of eloquence may or may not possess discretion and erudition; but plainly his words

will have ten-fold weight if they commend themselves not merely to the ear of the multitude, but to the calm judgment of the thoughtful. And our duty is clear, whatever be the talents with which He who has placed us here has entrusted us, to improve them diligently, and use them conscientiously in His service.

As I said before, though Christ's strength is better than man's strength, weakness is not better than strength. Each power our Maker has given us has its own proper and natural fruit, though it will not accomplish results out of its own province. And God, though not dependent on human instrumentality, ordinarily chooses His instruments with reference to the work He has for them to do. True, God is not dependent on your learning. Nay, answered South, God is not dependent on your ignorance. Learning will not win souls to Christ, eloquence will not win souls to Christ; still less will souls be won by the power to pour forth a noisy stream of words. But we shall act the part of the slothful and unprofitable servant, if because we discover how little our one talent can do, we neglect to improve that talent to our best ability. In the case of Paul, on which I dwelt at such length on last Sunday, little as he sought for artifices of human wisdom, there can be no doubt that his peculiar training fitted him to do a work of Apostleship among the Gentiles, which the Apostles of purely Jewish education could not have accomplished without a miracle. We have seen that in Paul's case consciousness of weakness drove him closer to Christ, and kept him humble notwithstanding the abundance of the revelations that had

been vouchsafed to him.   Can any corresponding
result be looked for in the case of him whose de-
ficiencies cause him no shame nor regret; who thinks
that his uncultivated natural powers are' all that is
needed to do Christ's work, and that what has cost him
nothing is good enough for God?   And we may take
a lesson from one higher than Paul.   Who can pre-
tend to be filled with a burning desire such as His to
do His Father's will, and make His ways known
among men?   Yet what candidate for the ministry
now would not murmur if several years were added to
the time which he must spend in silent training, and
if he were condemned to do no public work for his
Master until thirty years of age?   I would, therefore,
exhort every divinity student here to avail himself to
the utmost of the opportunities for instruction he
enjoys.   If, as is most probable, God has given you
no extraordinary power of eloquence, the defect will
not be supplied by your omitting to gain other means
of usefulness which He has put within your reach.
If He has gifted you with such power, your eloquence
will be all the better if it is guided by knowledge.
But no natural gifts or added acquirements can make
up for the absence of that which alone can qualify
Christ's messenger to speak for Him—intimate personal knowledge of Him whose message he bears.
Men's hearts will not be touched by the parrot echoing
of words you have heard from others.   If you hope to
do something better hereafter than merely gratify an
itching ear, or beguile the tedious hour which con-
vention compels men to spend in church, you must
be able to speak of truths that have come home to

your own heart, and have been proved by your own experience. No other preparation for the ministry can take place of this personal knowledge of Christ, of the endeavour to live close to Him, in constant devout communion with Him, in daily endeavour to be like Him. If you have this knowledge, whatever else God may have denied, you need not fear to go forward in His strength ; and though you may speak for Him with feeble lips and stammering tongue, fear not, Christ's strength will be made perfect in your weakness.

SERMON VI.

INFANT BAPTISM.

"And he said unto them, Go ye into all the world, and preach
the Gospel to every creature. He that believeth and is baptized
shall be saved ; but he that believeth not shall be damned."—
MARK xvi. 15, 16.

IT has often happened to mathematical students to
feel temporary perplexity when called on to demon-
strate some well-known elementary principle, just
because, though they have had frequent occasion to
employ it, and to assume its truth, it is long since
they had occasion to examine its proof. And so in
like manner, in general, men find it easier to support
by argument those parts of their belief which they
have been accustomed to hear assailed (even though
complicated reasoning may be necessary for their
defence) than to give good reasons why they hold
principles which they do not expect to hear disputed,
and for the defence of which they are consequently
unprepared. For example, it has often happened
that a man who might be described as a skilful theo-
logian, as far as regards his power to maintain his
doctrines by Scripture proofs, has been silenced on
meeting for the first time one who denied the autho-

rity of the Bible. The arguments on which he had
been accustomed to rely have suddenly become una-
vailing, while he has not been prepared at once to
give reasons for his submission to an authority which
he is surprised and shocked to hear questioned. It
is on this account that a clergyman's education must
embrace the knowledge of some controversies now
extinct, and of others with which it seems unlikely
that he will ever be brought in contact. Else he is
in danger of being taken unawares when he is called
on to maintain principles which he had expected
would have been conceded to him without controversy.

These introductory remarks are intended to suggest my apology if, in bringing before you to-day the
subject of Infant Baptism, I should seem to have
undertaken to defend a position not seriously in
danger. I am about to try to show to you that the
whole Christian world has not been in error—in error,
without an exception, for 1500 years, and, with insignificant exceptions, for the remaining three or four
centuries of the Church's existence—in supposing that
it was permitted them to bring their children to the
Saviour, and from their earliest years to dedicate
them to His service. I am about to try to show that
our fathers, who have fallen asleep in Christ, lacked
nothing essential to their salvation; that they did
not live and die in disregard of their Master's parting
commands. I am about to try to show that the baptism which alone we and they received, conferred on
us when we were helpless infants, was true baptism,
and needs not to be repeated.

Let it be understood that unless our error is alleged

to be deeply grave and important, there is no room
for controversy. It will not be disputed that the
ceremonies of the Church may be altered from time
to time as national customs change, so as better to
supply the wants of each changing age. In matters
of ritual and Church ordinance there is no absolute
right or wrong unless we are tied up by an express
command from God Himself. Even with regard to
the Sacraments, the obligation of which does depend
on Christ's express command, there is no doubt that
the mere details of the form of administration have
changed from time to time, and may be changed.
When anyone, therefore, says that the whole Christian world has been wrong with respect to the sacrament of baptism, we ask in what respect do you
assert that they have been wrong?—wrong with respect to some non-essential detail, or with respect to
something affecting the very essence of the rite?
Now with respect to any non-essential detail, the
whole Christian world cannot be wrong; for there is
no absolute right or wrong in the matter, and the
manner in which the Christian Church has consented
to use the rite must be the right one. But if you
say that the error reaches to the very essence of the
sacrament, (and this is what *is* asserted; for baptism
conferred in infancy is treated as null, and those who
have only received such baptism are baptized anew,)
if, then, this be so, it follows that for hundreds and
hundreds of years there was scarcely a single baptized Christian in the world; that at this moment
their number can be counted only by hundreds; that
whole generations of Christians eager (superstitiously

eager if you will) to fulfil their Master's commands
to baptize all nations, yet misconceived the meaning
of so plain a precept, and, consequently, wholly failed
to obey it. I must, therefore, try to show that when
Christ instituted the sacrament of Baptism, He did
not conceal from His followers anything essential to
the due performance of the rite. I must show that
if He had intended to place any restrictions as to the
manner in which the rite was to be performed, or as
to the persons to whom it was to be administered, He
did not so wholly omit to warn His people of those
restrictions that the knowledge of them perished out
of the world, and was not revived until in quite
recent times. The question, when stated, seems so
to contain its own answer, that I thought it necessary
to begin by showing the importance of occasionally
going over the proof of truths which seem almost
self-evident. In the present instance certainly the
fact that there are multitudes who traditionally accept
Infant Baptism without ever having reflected what
can be said for or against it, is that which alone has
given any chance of success to the assaults which at
the present time have been made on the principles
of our Church.*

These assaults on the lawfulness of Infant Baptism are usually disguised under the form of an
attack on the doctrine of Baptismal Regeneration.
In this form they seem to have the best chance of
meeting with a favourable reception from many, who,

---

* At the time this sermon was preached, some exertions had been
used to circulate in this country a sermon by Mr. Spurgeon on the
same text, assailing the practice of Infant Baptism.

imagining the assault to be directed only against extreme views held by a section of our Church, over- look that the attack is really made on principles held by all in common. In what I have now to say, I think it important not to be led away from the real points at issue, into discussions only introduced in the hope of causing division in our own ranks. In any case, a question about facts ought to take pre- cedence of a question about words. If any one asserts that it is unmeaning superstition to baptize an infant, who they imagine is incapable of deriving any spiritual benefit from such a rite, there is a real intelligible difference between his doctrine and that of the Church of England. On the other hand, if two persons are completely agreed as to the nature of the benefits conferred by baptism, and only differ as to whether the word regeneration is fitly used to de- scribe these benefits, then the controversy is only verbal. There is no point in theology in which it is more necessary to distinguish verbal controversies from real, than the subject now before us. For it may be laid down as a rule, that when two persons differ widely as to the doctrine of baptismal regenera- tion, they will invariably be found to use the word regeneration in two different senses. No doubt the importance of the right use of words must, by no means, be underrated ; but still our wisest order of proceeding is first, if possible, to ascertain what the facts are, and then we shall be most likely to agree as to the words by which these facts can be most fitly described.

I come, then, to the consideration of the text,

which I have selected because it has been supposed,
I know not why, to be antagonistic to the teaching
of our Church. The text consists of two parts, a
promise, and a threat. And it is plain at first sight,
that two conditions are necessary to bring any one
under the class to which the promise is addressed.
He must believe and he must be baptized. The text,
therefore, seems to be rightly used, when employed
to confute any who mutilate our Saviour's message,
and leave out either of the two conditions which He
has named. On the one hand, if, having read this
text, I were to teach you that baptism without faith
could save you, I should be in glaring opposition to
my text. On the other hand, if having read the text,
"He that believeth, and is baptized, shall be saved,"
I were to proceed to say, "Nay, he that believeth is
saved, and none has a right to be baptized *until* he
is saved," it would only require a moment's reflection
to enable you to see that the preacher was saying one
thing, and the text another.

The more fully convinced we are that our salvation
is a free gift bestowed on us for the merits of our
Saviour, and without any works or deserving of our
own, the more willing shall we be humbly to come to
Him, and hear at His own lips the terms on which
He bestows it. We shall then feel that it does
not become us to form our theories first as to
the conditions which He ought to impose, and to
judge of His statements by our theories, instead of
simply hearing His word and obeying it. Thus
we should come to the investigation of the text
in a wrong spirit, if we were to begin by laying

it down, that baptism could form no part of His requirements, because it seemed to us out of character with the spiritual religion which Christ came to teach, that He should make our salvation in any degree dependent on a mere ceremony. This was precisely the spirit in which Naaman came to the prophet Elisha. He began by forming his theory, how it would be in character that the prophet should proceed, and he rejected his command to wash in Jordan, because he could not see how his cleansing should depend on such a ceremony. It is in a very different spirit we ought to come to our Lord; we should come in a spirit of teachable humility; in a spirit of faith and obedience, prepared, if He declare anything, to believe it, if He command anything, to do it.

It being plain, then, from the text that two things are necessary to bring us under the class to which our Lord's promise is addressed, that we should believe, and that we should be baptized; the next question is when, and in what order should these two things be done. It seems to me that there is but one answer, if we really love our Lord, and are anxious to do His will, "Each of those two things at the very first opportunity in our power." We should believe as soon as we are capable of believing; we should be baptized as soon as we are capable of being baptized. Suppose that anyone whom you ardently loved, and whom you were eager to please, asked you to do two things for his sake, and prescribed nothing as to the order in which those things were to be done, when, and in what order would you do them? Plainly you would do each the very first opportunity. If it were quite

in your power with which you would begin, you
would begin with that which seemed the more important; but if the opportunity presented itself first of
doing that which seemed to you the less important,
you would not refuse to do it, merely lest you should
convey to others a false impression as to the relative
importance of the two things asked of you.

When we ask the question why should we *not* baptize infants? our first impression is, that they who
object must hold far higher opinions than we as to
the importance of the rite. We expect them to say,
" This is no ordinary rite, which Christians might use
at one time in one form, at another time in another.
This is a sacrament in which we must not deviate a
hair's breadth from the form in which the Apostles
administered it. In their time the majority of those
who received it were of adult age. We dare not venture, therefore, now to confer it on children; in the
Apostles' days it was ordinarily administered by
immersion, we dare not venture to think that sprink-
ling will suffice. We care not that all Christians may
have baptized for hundreds of years, only in the way
that you think lawful, we cannot admit the smallest
deviation from what we believe to be primitive usage."
When men, I say, treat our baptism as null, and
insist on our repeating it, it is natural to think that
in their estimation baptism is an important thing,
and that they would not endeavour, for any trifling
matter, to revolutionize the practice of Christendom.
But when these men come to explain themselves, we
find that they are actuated, not by an undue sense of
the importance of baptism, but by a fear lest it should

be thought too important. It is said that if a man has been baptized before he believes, he is in danger of lifting baptism into a saving ordinance, and of overlooking that he is saved by believing and not by baptism, and that the only way to prevent this is to maintain that no man has a right to be baptized until he is saved first. Well, in answer to this I would recur to the illustration I have just employed. If a friend has asked us to do two things, we should not show much love to him if we postponed indefinitely the performance of one of them, solely in order to testify our conviction that it was less important than the other. And we shall not do well, if we think compliance with God's commands a less urgent matter than the establishment of man's theories. If our Master, Christ, [has given us two commands, we show little love to Him if we neglect opportunities, and put off the performance of one of them, in order to testify our sense of their relative importance.

You will see, I think, from what has been said that we are not required to bring proofs of the lawfulness of Infant Baptism. Christ having confessedly instituted Baptism, and ordered His Apostles by that rite to make disciples of all people, the burden lies with those who would place restrictions on it, to give the proofs which justify such restrictions. The text is introduced in words of the widest generality, " Go ye into all the'world, and preach the Gospel to every creature." If any say that there are some to whom Baptism cannot fitly be administered, let them give the Scripture proofs that it was our Lord's will that such persons should be excluded. In particular, if it is asserted that our children may not be brought into covenant relation with Him, let the text be produced where He has forbidden children to come to Him. This is what our opponents are in fairness obliged to do ; and if it were the case that they failed to do so because Scripture was completely silent, nothing more would be necessary in order to establish at least the *lawfulness* of Infant Baptism.

But we go further, and maintain that this mode of using the sacrament is most conformed to the mind of our Lord Himself, because He has not only not forbidden us to bring our children unto Him, but encouraged us to do so. In His own lifetime the very question arose about which we now dispute. I think if the Bible had not told us how our Lord dealt with it, we should have been uncertain how He would have acted. Remember how our Lord was pressed by those who thronged to hear the gracious words that proceeded from His lips. We read of the multitude coming together, so that they could not so much as eat bread. We read of our Lord commanding that a small ship should wait on Him, and of His teaching the multitude out of the ship while they stood on the land. We are told that He committed to His disciples the merely ministerial offices of His religion, and that He Himself baptized not, but His disciples. And now does it seem easy to determine how He would act when His teaching was interrupted by parents who brought to Him children of an age incapable of profiting by His instructions ? St. Luke describes these children as babes—βρέφη. The Apostles, we know, concluded that these infants were

unable to benefit by the presence of our Lord, and
rebuked those who brought them to Him. And were
we less familiar with the history, might it not seem
likely to ourselves also, that their Master would rebuke
the superstition of parents who interrupted His teaching by asking Him to put His hands upon these children, and who imagined that these unconscious babes
could profit by His touch? But we are told that
when He saw the disciples repel these children He
was much displeased; and not only did He take
these children in His arms and bless them, as it had
been desired, but He made what was done in their
case into a general rule—" Suffer the little children
to come unto me, and forbid them not, for of such is
the kingdom of God."

Well has this history been chosen as the Gospel
for the service of Infant Baptism, for it contains by
anticipation an answer to every difficulty that can be
raised by any who would repel us from bringing our
children to the same Saviour who received these children then. We cannot doubt that these parents then
did well in bringing their children to Him. We cannot doubt that the children whom He took in His
arms, and whom He blessed, did receive precious
benefit from that blessing, unconscious though they
were. Yet if any were to ask us to define the nature
of that benefit, we should find it quite as hard a
problem as to define the nature of baptismal grace.
We have no warrant for saying that every child who
received that blessing was certain of obtaining eternal salvation, or. that he walked this world, signed
and sealed in the sight of all men, as a certain inhe-

ritor of eternal glory. We cannot say that he enjoyed any special immunity from temptation. We
do not even know for certain that every one of these
children grew up to know the Gospel, and to be admitted into the visible Church of Christ. For these
children disappear out of the Scripture narrative, and
our curiosity as to their subsequent history has been
ungratified. Yet, assuredly, any of these children
who came in after life to know the Saviour's work, and
to believe on Him and love Him, would cherish, as a
privilege of unspeakable value, the knowledge that he
had in infancy been taken into his Master's arms and
received His gracious blessing. And if asked to
name the first beginning of his union with Christ, I
doubt not that he would not so much think of that
time, when with his own conscious intellect and affections, he took hold of the Saviour, as rather think of
that earlier time when hands he knew not took hold
on him, and love, unearned by deserts of his, embraced him ; the love of Him of whom we must all
confess, " We love Him, because He first loved us."
However this may be, from the history of our Lord's
receiving these infants we learn these two things :
first, that infants are not incapable of receiving a
blessing from Him; and secondly, that whatever
difficulties we may have in theorizing as to the
nature of that blessing, it may not the less be a very
real one, and that our duty to seek it for those we
love may be very clear.

But it remains to notice a difficulty which some
have found in the verse chosen for my text. It consists of two parts, a promise and a threat. Now,

while the promise mentions two things, belief and baptism, the threat mentions only one—"He that believeth not shall be damned." Hence it is urged that belief is the one and only indispensable requisite to salvation. And since an infant is incapable of belief, it is impossible that he can be in a state of salvation. But if this be so, what then becomes of those infants who die before they are old enough to learn the Saviour's name? Must Christian parents, mourning over babes untimely snatched away, have the bitterer grief to know that they are eternally separated from their little ones? must they think of their buds of promise as blighted for ever by some cold unfriendly blast, and not as blossoms early culled by a tender Father's hand? But there is no more fruitful source of error than to found a system of doctrine on a single text, without regarding how that text is modified by other statements of Scripture. In the present case few have any difficulty in seeing that the general statement, "He that believeth not shall be damned," is modified by our knowledge that God does not demand impossibilities, and that He does not require belief of those who are incapable of believing. I have the less need to argue the matter, because I believe our opponents have no more fears than ourselves for the safety of those little ones whom God removes in infancy.

But now arises the deeper question, On what grounds can we have good hopes of the safety of such children? Are we to rest our hopes on their innocency? Are we to say, that having committed no actual sin, they have a natural right to salvation;

I

that they have no need of a Saviour, and must be safe independently of anything Christ has done or suffered ? If any maintain this, I can only say such is not the doctrine that the Christian Church has always taught. She has always held that all who enter heaven, even though they may not have sinned after the similitude of Adam's transgression, are saved, not by right of their own innocency, but for the sake of Christ. The doctrine taught in the Ninth Article of our Church is no modern invention of hers, but has been handed down to her from primitive times, and, as we believe, can be proved by Scripture and by experience. We hold that there are in every child of fallen Adam tendencies to evil, which only require time and opportunity to ripen into act ; and that this corruption of nature constitutes him in whom it exists a sinner in God's sight, and does need to be pardoned. For this reason we regard it as no idle ceremony to dedicate our children to Christ, and claim for them a part in that salvation which He has declared His willingness to give. We ground our assured trust for them, not in the innocency of their years, but in the fact that there is no impediment to their being united to Christ, and being thus made inheritors of the kingdom of heaven. As a matter of fact, there is seldom any difficulty in acknowledging the propriety of Infant Baptism wherever the doctrine of Original Sin is strongly held : and it was in the ardour of controversy against the Pelagians, who denied Original Sin, that the absolute necessity of baptism was asserted more strongly than it had ever been before. And I may add, that any one who believes that there are in fallen man tendencies to evil antecedent to their outward manifestation, has no difficulty in admitting it to be possible that tendencies to good, implanted by grace, may also be long antecedent to *their* outward manifestation.

Before I conclude, it remains for me to notice two objections that have been made to the teaching of the Church of England on the subject of baptism. One is, that experience proves that her doctrine is wrong, because all who have been baptized do not turn out well. Much has been said as to the absurdity of supposing that thieves, and drunkards, and harlots are members of Christ and children of God, or of seeking for inheritors of the kingdom of heaven in the jail or at the gallows. Stripped of all rhetorical amplification, the argument is an attempt to prove that all who are baptized are not ultimately saved. But, surely, it is incumbent on every disputant to try to know something of the opinions of his opponents. Who imagines that anyone, Roman Catholic or Protestant, holds the doctrine that every baptized child is saved? No one dreams that baptism confers any privileges incapable of being lost, or which must result in the eternal salvation of him who receives them. The question at issue, then, is merely this : Is it possible that those who are not finally saved ever can have been partakers of any spiritual privileges? Now to this question there can be but one answer. Those who hold most strongly the doctrine of the final perseverance of the elect do also acknowledge that there may be strivings of God's Spirit with those who are not elect, and who do not persevere; strivings which for a time seem to be successful. There are those whom our Lord describes as receiving the Word with joy, and as believing for a while, but yet who do not endure to the end, and in time of temptation fall away. There are those whom His Apostle describes as having been once enlightened, as having tasted of the heavenly gift, and as having been made partakers of the Holy Ghost, and yet as falling away. It has seemed strange to some how it is that St. Augustine and some of our great reformers, who took him for their chief guide, should, on the one hand, have spoken so highly of baptismal privileges as to be claimed with confidence as holding the doctrine of baptismal regeneration; and, on the other hand, have taught doctrines akin to those which in later times were called Calvinistic. And the explanation is, that the holding these latter doctrines is quite compatible with the full recognition of the fact that high privileges may be enjoyed by those who are not elect, and who do not persevere to the end. Those, then, in our Church who rate highest the privileges conferred by baptism are not in the least embarrassed by the fact that all do not retain these privileges to the end; for from the first they warned their people not to imagine that the possession of such privileges must necessarily terminate in their salvation. All the privileges which members of the Christian Church enjoy may be paralleled in the history of the Jewish Church. And so with a special reference to this subject St. Paul has taught us—" All our fathers were under the cloud, and all passed through the sea, and were all baptized unto Moses in the cloud, and in the sea. But with many of them God was not pleased, for they were overthrown in the wilderness. Now these things were our examples, and they are written for our admonition, upon whom the ends of the world are come. Wherefore let him that thinketh he standeth take heed lest he fall."

But in the last place it is objected that the doctrine of the Church of England deprives her clergy of all power to rebuke sin; for how, it is said, can they stand up in their pulpits and say to their congregations, Ye must be born again, when their formularies teach that their hearers have all already been born again in baptism. Now certainly it is evident that the exhortation, "Ye must be born again," is one which, from its nature, cannot be addressed to a congregation indiscriminately; for unless a person can be born again several times we are not justified in saying, ye must be born again, to those who may have been born again already. And we frankly confess that the Church of England disposes her clergy to address their congregations not as still in their natural state, children of wrath, but as those who have some portion in Christ, and have, through Him, become children of God. I need not look to her teaching about baptism to prove this; it is the character of all her services. The clergyman begins her daily service by addressing his people as dearly beloved *brethren*. He goes on to exhort them in deep humility to make confession of their sins, yet he teaches them to address Him from whose ways they have strayed as their Almighty and Most Merciful *Father*. He asks them to join him in the prayer

which our Lord Himself taught His people, in which
He gives us a right to address God as our Father,
and the whole service proceeds in this tone. But
have our clergy on this account less power to warn,
to threaten, and rebuke sinners? What, if we find
a prodigal who has wasted his substance in riotous
living, and whose soul is perishing with hunger in a
country far from his true home, have we lost our
power to rebuke him for his sin, and to warn him of
the ruin that is his certain fate if he remain where
he is; have we lost, I say, this power if we address
to him the exhortation, Arise and go to thy *father?*
Nay, is it not in this word father that our strength
lies? Is 'it not this which banishes despair, and
makes the sinner know that He whom he has abandoned will welcome his return.

Assuredly, brethren, God's way of dealing with
the sinner is different from that which man would
deem prudent. Good men have thought that the
cause of morality would be lost if we taught that God
conferred His pardon on any who had not first earned
it by consistent obedience. Others, less disposed to
insist on outward good works, still suppose that we
must lose all power to deal with a sinner if we allow
him to think that God has conferred on him any
privileges before his inward state of mind is such as
seems to them worthy of those privileges. But God's
method is freely to give to those who are unworthy,
and by His gifts themselves to make them worthy.
And His ministers find that exhortations addressed
to men's gratitude for what they have already received, and pointing out the responsibility which such

gifts involve, are quite as powerful as exhortations
addressed to men's hope of receiving benefits when
they have done something to deserve them. And if
those who are already walking worthy of their vocation, and bringing forth fruits corresponding to union
with Christ, are asked to date the commencement of
their union with Him, though it would gratify the
pride of their nature to name the time when they
had done something for Him, or when, with conscious
intellect and affection, they first took hold of Him;
yet they will find their love to Him drawn out more
fully by thinking rather how before they themselves
had done anything, He who first loved them embraced
them with the arms of His mercy, and made them
heirs of His salvation.

Brethren, I have spoken to you on a subject on
which there is confessedly diversity of opinion among
members of our Church; nor can I suppose that
every one of my statements will be assented to by all
who hear me. But the amount of our disagreements
must not be exaggerated; for on the most essential
points there is a perfect agreement amongst us. We
all believe that it is a lawful thing to bring our children to Christ, and from their earliest years to dedicate them to His service. We believe that He has
not only not forbidden us, but encouraged us to do
so. We believe that when we comply with His ordinance it would be an insult to His promise to suppose that the prayer of faith would not be attended
with a blessing. And if there be any difference
amongst us in defining the nature of that blessing,
or as to the name by which it may be most fitly

described, all agree that baptismal privileges avail nothing to him who is not united to Christ by a lively faith. Brethren, if you, in whose name a profession of faith in Christ was made in infancy, believe not on Him ; if you, for whom it was promised that you should keep His commandments, disregard His will ; if you, for whom it was promised that you should renounce sin are the willing slaves of sin, more tolerable will it be in the Day of Judgment for those who have never heard the Saviour's name.

SERMON VII.

THE PARABLE OF THE TARES.

" The servants said unto him, Wilt thou then that we go and gather them up? But he said, Nay, lest while ye gather up the tares, ye root up also the wheat with them."—MATT. xiii. 28, 29.

WHEN Jesus grieved His disciples by telling them that one of their own number should be His betrayer, He gave as one reason for His warning, " Now I tell you before it come, that when it is come to pass ye may believe that I am He." Shortly after, He proceeded to tell them, in plainer language, that He must be removed from them ; and again He adds, " And now I have told you before it come to pass, that when it is come to pass ye might believe." And then He went on to tell how they too must suffer from the persecutions which had assailed Himself, so that men should even think they did God service by killing them. And a third time He gives this reason for forewarning them, " These things have I told you, that when the time shall come ye may remember that I told you of them."

And no doubt when the time did come, the remembrance of these predictions often held up their faith from sinking. They could not help recalling to mind how in former days, when *they* had dreamed of nothing but success, and immediate establishment of their Master's kingdom, that Master had given them warnings which they then believed not, and scarcely understood, of approaching rejection to Himself, and persecutions to them. Every fresh trial, then, which they encountered did not, as it otherwise might have done, suggest a doubt whether their cause were God's cause, and whether their Master were able to deliver them. It was but a new proof of the exactness of His foreknowledge, and a new pledge of the certainty of their arriving at that reward to which He had promised through much tribulation to bring them. *

If we were making, without a guide, a journey through a country unknown to us, we should suspect that we had gone astray if the road which we had taken, and which had seemed to lead us in the right direction, suddenly appeared to lose itself in a morass, or turned off in a direction opposite to that in which we wished to go. But if we had taken this road by the direction of one well acquainted with it, who had told us, at such a spot you will find the road broken and difficult; some way further on it bends aside, and proceeds for some distance in a different course; why then the very indications which, if we were exploring for ourselves, would have made us suspect that we had gone wrong—if forewarned of them, we recognize as certain marks that we are in the right way.

The times have gone by when the severest trial of the faith of the followers of Jesus was the temporal adversity which His Church must suffer. The days of persecution have passed ; but even if the Church had to endure affliction and encounter opposition, we have learned that temporal prosperity is not the surest sign of God's favour. We know that there are lessons which God is wont to teach His people in the school of affliction ; and we have faith, too, to believe in the ultimate triumph of His cause. We know that though the progress of the Church may be slow and interrupted, it is still gaining ground, and will one day fill the whole earth. But what is really perplexing is, not that the progress of the Church is so slow, but that vice and error have found their way into the Church itself. If the Church were all truth and all purity, we could wait more patiently for the day of her complete victory. But at the very moment that we are tempted to complain that the boundaries of God's vineyard on earth are so slowly enlarged, we look at the ground already included in its limits, and to our perplexity we see the cultivated land so overgrown with weeds as to be scarce distinguishable from the wilderness without. We profess our belief that the Gospel is the means employed by God for the regeneration of the world. How, then, are we to explain that the nations to whom that remedy has been applied seem so little the better of it : full of disunion and contention, fighting about the theory of their religion, and even when they are agreed as to the theory, allowing it to have very little influence on their practice. When such is the aspect of Christ's visible Church, does it not seem as if the remedy, which we have been calling God's

remedy, had been applied, and had failed? Now, one
great support to our faith in this perplexity, is that,
whether we can understand the reason of this state
of things or not, we have at any rate had warning of
it. From the very first our Lord warned His disciples that they were not to form in their minds any
different ideal of His Church. It was not to be a
scene of perfect truth and perfect holiness. The evil
were to be mixed with the good, and no complete
outward separation between them was to be made
before the time of the end had come.

I do not know that there is any chapter in the
Gospels, which, as often as I read it, conveys to my
mind a stronger impression of the Divine foreknowledge of our Lord, than this 13th chapter of St.
Matthew. I think hardly any one can doubt that we
have here a genuine record of His teaching. The
parables are peculiarly His own. The New Testament represents to us none of the Apostles, or first
preachers of Christianity, as imitating their Master
in this form of His teaching; nor do we find any of
the early uninspired Christian teachers having recourse to this method of impressing their doctrines
on the minds of their hearers. The form, then, in
which these lessons are conveyed, is in itself evidence
of the source whence they come. Now it is most
remarkable that, in this very first series of parables
in which our Lord explains the mysteries of the
kingdom of heaven, He announces as the characteristics of the Church which He is founding, those
very peculiarities which have caused so much perplexity to His disciples. He tells us that it is not only

in the natural world that we may find examples of what may be called the waste of the Author of Nature; not only there that we find instances of means which He has appointed failing to produce their effects, such as innumerable seeds perishing without coming to maturity; in the world of grace, too, a similar spectacle presents itself. Among the hearts in which the word of life is sown, many are unbenefited by it; the word has been thrown on the way-side, whence the wicked one carries it away, or cast in stony places, or choked by thorns, and so rendered unfruitful. If it perplexes us now, that the evil in the Church are so intermingled with the good, as to be distinguished from them with difficulty, this also our Saviour foretold in the parable read in the Gospel for to-day, where He clearly intimates that such was the very state of the Church which He contemplated, and that such it was designed to continue to the end. And the same truth is again represented in another parable in the same chapter, that of the draw-net, which, being cast into the sea, gathered of every kind both good and bad, and it is only at the end of the world that He declares the separation shall be effected.

Now, let it be remembered, that the people among whom Jesus came to minister, had been led by their prophets to expect a time when all defilement should be banished from the city of God. " Awake, awake, put on thy strength, O Zion; put on thy beautiful garments, O Jerusalem, the holy city, for henceforth there shall no more come unto thee the uncircumcised and unclean." " Violence shall no more be

heard in thy land, wasting nor destruction within
thy borders, but thou shalt call thy walls salvation
and thy gates praise. Thy people also shall be all
righteous, they shall inherit the land for ever."
" They shall call thee the holy people, the redeemed
of the Lord." " All thy children shall be taught of
the Lord, and great shall be the peace of thy children.
In righteousness shalt thou be established. Thou
shalt be far from oppression, for thou shalt not fear,
and from terror, for it shall not come near thee."
We know that the disciples who joined themselves to
Jesus did expect that He would fully realize all the
predictions of their prophets. We know also that,
from a very early period, the name by which the
members of their society recognized each other was,
the saints or holy ones. If, then, Jesus had been an
enthusiast whose imagination had been fired by the
prophetic delineations of future purity and glory; or
if He had been one who wished to turn to His own
account the state of feeling which such predictions
had engendered ; He would have formed on this model
His account of the kingdom which He was to establish
on earth. At the very first step of His preaching,
we should have heard those promises which were
reserved for the close of the Canon relating to a time
then future : " There shall in no wise enter into it
anything that defileth, neither whatsoever worketh
abomination or maketh a lie, but they which are
written in the Lamb's book of life." Instead of this,
this first series of parables seems all intended to
moderate the expectations of His followers, and to
prepare them for that corruption within the Church

itself of which we have had too melancholy experience. The choice of topics, then, I say, in this 13th chapter of St. Matthew, is so very unlike what a human teacher would have made, as to be in itself no weak proof of its Divine origin; and the confusion and disorder in the Church from being a stumbling-block, thus becomes a support of our faith; if the sight of this confusion ever cause a doubt, we seem to hear our Master say, " Remember that I told you before."

If, then, we were unable to see any reason why Christ should have permitted defilement to enter the Church which He founded, we might still content ourselves with the knowledge that He had foretold that so it must be, and be satisfied in faith in Him to wait for the time when many a thing which now seems to us mysterious shall be cleared up. But I believe that when we examine into the matter, we shall find good reason to think that the very imperfections of the Church do enable her better to fulfil the work which God has appointed for her in the world.

We might, indeed, sufficiently dispose of the objections which infidels have brought against the Church, founded on the imperfect success with which she has fulfilled her mission, by replying that such objections cannot consistently be made by any believer in natural religion. It is a fact which every one must admit, that God has left a multitude of mankind in ignorance of His true nature. It is a fact, also, that moral evil has widely and lamentably overspread the world. Every one who believes in a God, must hold that these facts are, in some way or other, reconcilable with God's power and goodness. There is no greater difficulty, then, in reconciling with the attributes of God, the fact that the process, which God may have employed for removing ignorance and vice from the world, should be slow, gradual, and interrupted. If God has *told* us that the process which He has actually employed is of this kind, there is no difficulty in believing it. Yet we cannot but feel it a support to our faith, if we discover that some of those things which at first appeared to us to be imperfections in the means which God employs, do really make them better fitted to do His work. And, therefore, in dealing with the subject suggested by the parable, namely, the corruptions which have sprung up within the Church, I shall not content myself with the reflection that Christ has foretold us that these must needs be, but I shall try to show that there is good reason to think that the Church works more efficiently by casting her nets into the world, and sweeping in bad as well as good, than if she included in her society none but those who are holy in act as well as in profession.

The imperfections in the Church, which have in different ways been a stumbling-block to the faith of Christians, are of two kinds : failures with respect to truth and with respect to holiness. The deposit of true doctrine which it was her office to preserve has been tainted with an admixture of human error ; and the practice of her members has too often become relaxed and depraved. It is very important to observe that these two kinds of failure are not independent phenomena, but are so connected that the one could not take place without the other. The truths which

our religion teaches have an important practical influence on the conduct of him who embraces them ;
while again we are taught that the desire to do our
Lord's will is the best guide to the perception of the
truth of His doctrine.   The promise to Christians
that their understandings shall be illuminated by the
light of God's Spirit, is connected with the promise
that their hearts shall be sanctified by the washing
of the same Spirit.   And in those Old Testament
descriptions of the glories of the Church, some of
which I cited just now, predictions of purity of life
and of purity of doctrine go together, giving us to
understand that it is the same period of the Church's
history in which it will be true of her that all her
people shall be righteous as that at which it shall be
true that all her children shall be taught of God.   If
there were ever a time at which Christians should
corrupt or cease to hold the doctrines of the Cross of
Christ, then with the loss of the elevating and puri-
fying influence of these doctrines a degeneracy of
morals must be sure to follow.   If there were ever a
time when the morals of Christians should become
relaxed, so that though nominally members of Christ
they should be not truly holy, not truly united to
Him, they would have no promise of Christ's Spirit
of truth to enlighten them, and must be almost certain to corrupt the simplicity of His teaching.

I insist on this close connexion between purity of
morals and purity of doctrine, because, as you know,
Roman Catholic divines have pursued a different course
when dealing with the perplexity caused by the diversity
of religious teaching among Christians from that which

K

they have followed when dealing with the perplexity caused by the unholiness of their lives. They
freely admit the existence of vice in the Church;
they own that there were times when the morals of
Christians were frightfully corrupted, and when even
the highest seats in the Church were occupied by
monsters of iniquity. But they hold it necessary to
maintain that error can find no place in the Church;
they do this by denying that any are true members
of the Church save those who agree in doctrine with
them. They maintain that those promises which
speak of the perfect holiness of the Church must be
understood in some different way, or referred to some
different time from those which speak of its freedom
from error; and they hold that those of its rulers
whose own lives were most scandalous, might still be
infallible guides to others when error is in question.
They act precisely as the servants in the parable
would have done, if they had argued that since the
householder had sown none but good seed in his
ground, it was impossible that tares should spring up
in the portion which he had sown; and if they had
then partitioned off a certain portion of the field,
which was exclusively to be regarded as his planting,
and had asserted that everything which grew within
these limits was necessarily pure corn. If they do
not follow the same course when the question is
about the morality of Christians; that is to say, if
they do not maintain that the practice of their head
is to be regarded the criterion of morality as much
as his teaching is as the standard of religious truth,
it is because there are certain moral truths which

God has written so plainly in the hearts of men, that it is easier to get them to believe an absurdity than to obliterate permanently in their hearts the distinction between right and wrong.

We do not believe that God is so much more solicitous for the correctness of men's notions than He is for the purity of their lives : we do not believe that God hates error so much more than He hates sin, that He has miraculously provided safeguards against the intrusion of error into His Church, while He acquiesces in her being overrun with sin. We think that we should betray the cause of Christianity if we were to concede to unbelievers their principle, that it is incredible that God should give man a revelation, and yet leave it in his power to mistake and abuse its contents ; and if we were to take issue with unbelievers on the matter of fact, whether the revelation in which we profess our belief is protected by infallible safeguards against such mistakes and abuses. When we consider the matter also, we find reason to think that the scheme of Christian truth does influence the heart more powerfully, and does incorporate itself more intimately with a man's whole nature, when his mind has received it by a careful study of God's Word, even though the process be attended with a risk of error or failure, than if he had received the whole system from another without risk and without enquiry.

I do not wish now to enter into any formal discussion of the question of the Church's infallibility. I rather wish to assume, for my present purpose, those results which we have obtained when engaged in another controversy. In arguing with Romanists, we have often contended that since God has not provided any infallible safeguards against the intrusion of sin into His Church, we have no right to assume that He must necessarily have provided infallible safeguards against error. I would now use the same argument conversely. We, as Protestants, admit that error has been allowed by Christ to spring up within His Church. We find that this liability to error forms an important part of the moral discipline of Christians; that the exertions which it calls forth make the man of God more perfect, and confirm him in virtue, which is incompatible with the absence of all temptation. This liability to error in the Church being acknowledged, I have argued that it is a phenomenon intimately connected with this other one—that the Christian Church is not an assemblage of perfectly holy persons, but one in which the evil are inextricably mingled with the good; and I wish now to show that this admixture, like the liability to error, is not without some compensating advantages.

The dream of an infallible Church is not the only delusion into which men have been led by their disregard of Christ's prophecy of tares that must grow up among the wheat. They have been led into other mistakes in their impatience to witness upon earth the spectacle of a glorious Church, not having spot or wrinkle, or any such thing, but altogether holy and without blemish. They could not regard this promise as fulfilled while sinners were tolerated as members of the Church, still less while they officiated as her ministers. Hence when circumstances

revealed, or party-spirit imagined, the existence of
scandals which Church discipline was too lax to era-
dicate, the sight of these tares unweeded out made
men doubt whether this were indeed the Lord's vineyard. It is notorious in Church history how small
sects have arrogated to themselves the exclusive title
of the Church, or have claimed to be recognized as
the pure, the holy; maintaining that other societies
of Christians, into which things unclean and defiled
were allowed to enter, had by this laxity rendered
themselves unfit to be accounted any part of the
Church of God. Such attempts have been renewed
at intervals down to our own time; for even still
there may be found little societies, ludicrously small
in number indeed, but who regard themselves as the
sole representatives of Christian purity, and who
would even refuse to join in prayer with others not of
their society, and of whose holiness, therefore, they
feel they have no assurance. But the predictions of
the growth and extent of the Church being quite as
express as the prophecies of her holiness, none of
these attempts could succeed which tried to appropriate to some narrow section of Christians the title
and prerogatives of the universal Church; and consequently, those who have been scandalized by the
corruptions of the visible Church have tried another
method with more success. It is, while leaving to the
visible Church its empty titles of honour, to form a
Church within the Church; a society that is not perhaps called indeed by the name of Church, but having
all its essential attributes, having under different
names its sacraments of admission, its terms of

communion, its profession of special holiness, its almost exclusive hopes of salvation.

The most remarkable of such attempts is the monastic movement. In the establishment of monastic institutions all appearance of schism was avoided; the utmost respect was paid to those who bore rule in the Church; and yet, I think, what was done cannot be fairly described in any other way than as the foundation of a Church within the Church, the monk being distinguished from ordinary Christians in precisely the same way that the Christian was distinguished from the heathen; all the Scripture language, likewise, which relates to the separation of the Christian from among the heathen world, being freely applied to the separation of the monk from other Christians. The monk was admitted to his profession by a public ceremony and solemn vows. He received a new name. He undertook to hate father and mother, and wife and children, and lands, and to give up all to follow Christ. He entered into a new brotherhood of holy persons, all bound by special ties of love to each other. I need not remind you that the phrase, a " religious person " came to be appropriated to those who had made such vows as these; while the phrase, " the world," which in Scripture is opposed to the Church, came to be applied to those who had not taken monastic vows, such persons being spoken of as still in the world. The possibility of the salvation of such persons was not denied, but it was spoken of in little more hopeful language than we might now use when speaking of the case of virtuous persons not members of the

Christian Church. And now is it the case that by this association of persons striving after the highest holiness the amount of holiness in the entire Church was increased? I think we can scarcely say that it was. By the separation from the general mass of Christian society of many of the most holy and self-denying of its members, I fear that the Christian tone of those who remained was more lowered than that of those who retired was elevated. To recur to the illustration before employed, they partitioned off that portion of the field which seemed to them to be free from the admixture of foreign growth, and a two-fold evil in consequence followed. In the part outside too hastily abandoned as irreclaimable, every noxious plant grew unchecked; while in the part inside, too hastily assumed to be completely pure, tares were growing also unchecked because unsuspected. Some of the most attractive pictures of monastic holiness which the historians of such bodies have depicted, owe their attractiveness to this: that they stand out in bright relief from the dismal background of a nominally Christian world, sunk into utter godlessness by the withdrawal from it of some of the most earnest and pure of its members. While again, within the monastic communities tares of two kinds grew up. They were overrun with the sins against which they were most on their guard, and with others which they were not watching against. Repeatedly must these orders be reformed on account of the increase of the spirit of self-indulgence, verging upon licentiousness, which was most alien to the spirit of their institution. While long before other sins, which they had not watched against, had invaded them—uncharitableness, religious rancour, violent party-spirit. Repeatedly does Church history tell of acts the most unchristian perpetrated by those bound to the highest perfection. Meetings of Christians assembled to discuss questions of theology requiring the calmest deliberation, end in tumult and violence, excited by the irruption of hordes of angry monks. Chrysostom, sick and in banishment, prefers to encounter the certain hardships of a rugged journey, and the probable risk of falling into the hands of barbarian invaders, rather than venture to trust his life to the tender mercy of a company of Christian monks.

I should consider that I was occupying your time very idly, in pointing out the failures of a system which I suppose no one in this congregation has any inclination to make trial of, if it were not that the same mistake, in which that system took its origin, has been repeated often among ourselves. I mean the mistake of impatience with the spectacle of a mixture of tares and wheat, which the visible Church presents; the mistake of trying to be wiser than our Master, and of striving to make a separation between them; not always, indeed, by trying to root out the tares from the wheat, but more commonly by trying to root out the wheat from among the tares, by partitioning off those who are willing to live the higher Christian life into some smaller visible society which may claim that attribute of holiness which the visible Church realizes so imperfectly. In multiplied ways attempts have been made to form two classes of

Christians. In some cases one sacrament has been made to take the place of the other, and the body of "communicants" have recognized each other as a society distinguished from ordinary Christians, by having undertaken higher pledges and made more solemn vows. The Baptists, in closer conformity with Scripture, have made baptism the rite of admission into their society ; but by so doing, they are forced into a schismatical position, like that of the Donatists of old ; they are forced to arrogate to their own little body the titles and privileges of Christ's Church ; they are forced to deny that persons, not members of their communion, have received true baptism, or are members of the visible Church ; and if Christian charity compels them to admit that they may, notwithstanding, be vitally united with Christ, and receive through Him eternal life, they are obliged to suppose that, instead of the visible Church including what we may call the invisible Church within it, it is the latter which includes the former. Instead of being able to compare the visible Church to a tree, containing indeed many barren and withered branches, but still embracing the bulk of those vitally united to the root, we can scarcely see the true vine, surrounded as it is by a multitude of plants preserving a healthy life, although without any visible connection with it. In consequence of the pressure of this difficulty, it has more generally been preferred to leave baptism in its place as the rite of admission into the visible Church of Christ ; but to form some Church within the Church into which admission is to be gained in some other way, as, for

instance, by a profession of having experienced conversion, the members of which inner society are
alone to be regarded as true Christians; all others
being reckoned as the world. Let it not be supposed
that I would, for a moment, teach' that it is enough
for any man to have been received by baptism into
the visible Church. The parable, in fact, teaches
the reverse. It teaches that that Church includes
tares as well as wheat; it includes nominal Christians who are not real Christians; a man may have
received every privilege that the visible Church can
offer, and yet be a castaway. But what the parable
also teaches us is, that Christ does not sanction our
premature attempts to make a separation between
the tares and the wheat. Just as men have craved
after some infallible guide to distinguish true doctrine from false, they have craved after some infallible
marks to distinguish the true professor from the in-
sincere. They have tried to form within the Church
societies more secure against the intrusion of hypocrisy than the society which *He* founded. They
have endeavoured to attain this end by adding to the
professions which are necessary to become a member
of *His* society, other more stringent professions. The
result of such attempts to convey to men some
stronger assurance that they are Christ's than their
membership with the Church can afford them, has
been to prove that our Lord has wisely withheld such
an assurance. The attempt to give it has been always
attended with a two-fold danger—the danger of false
security and self-deceit in the case of those who have
been admitted into the inner society; the danger of

repelling from Christ those who have not. We make
our confession of Christ badly, if we do it in such a
manner as to lead others to deny Him. I find from
American books that it is no uncommon thing there
that one should ask another, " Are you a Christian?"
and should receive the answer, " No, I do not as yet
make any profession of Christianity." Does not this
show that such persons have been taught by the more
pious of their countrymen to regard as absolutely nothing the stipulations and professions by which they
became members of the Christian Church ; and is
not the teaching the majority to acquiesce in a state of
acknowledged separation from Christ, a mischief not
counterbalanced by the closer union with Him, after
which the minority strive. For it seems to me as if
there the truly godly, of whom there are many there
as excellent as can be found in any country, had less
power than here to leaven the mass with their sentiments ; as if, in consequence, the tone of public
morality dropped lower ; and as if there the holiness
of the few were contrasted with more utter lawless-
ness in the case of others. However this may be,
I believe it remains true, that, whether in mediæval
.times, or our own, every attempt to render the invisible Church visible, and to mark off the tares from
the wheat by some easily discerned line of division,
has done more harm than good. Often thus has the
smoking flax been quenched; and the timid, through
fear of having to make a new profession, drawn back
from that which they had made already.

With one word of warning, then, I would conclude.
We have seen that, by God's appointment, the evil

are so mingled with the good, that no external privileges are infallible marks of God's favour. Watch,
then, and examine yourselves, whether you be in
the faith; prove your own selves. For, as what
Christ has told of the state of His Church was fulfilled, unlike as it was to men's expectation at the
time, so that which is still unfulfilled of His predictions will surely be brought to pass. He has
warned us that the tares will not always be mingled
with the wheat. The reapers shall be directed to
gather the tares into bundles and burn them, but
to gather the wheat into the barn. When that day
of separation comes, may you, my brethren, be
found to have been Christ's, not in name only but
in reality, and to have been united here to Him by
ties which neither death nor aught else can dissolve.

SERMON VIII.

SECURUS JUDICAT ORBIS TERRARUM.

"But we desire to hear of thee what thou thinkest : for as concerning this sect, we know that everywhere it is spoken against."—
ACTS xxviii. 22.

THESE words, which we read in the second lesson
for to-day, recall the memory of the time when the
Christian Church did not possess some of those
notes which now strike the imagination of men most
forcibly—antiquity, extent, catholicity.   In those
days, when the Christian advocate found an audience
willing to give him a patient hearing, the text shows
how the words in which his address was invited
implied that he had to encounter a formidable presumption against his case—"May we know what
this *new* doctrine whereof thou speakest is ;" " for
thou bringest certain strange things to our ears."

And the position which the Christian preacher had
to assail was strong in the very points where he was
weak.   He seemed to undertake a hopeless task, when
he proposed that her magnificence should be destroyed
whom all Asia and *the world* worshipped.   He seemed
to undertake a hopeless task, when he endeavoured to
substitute his upstart religion for beliefs whose origin

was lost in immemorial antiquity. It might indeed
be a matter of theoretical belief in the heathen world
that their gods had not always held sway—that there
had been a time when Jupiter was still in private
station, and Juno yet a maiden, and when the infer-
nal shades were ruled by no kings. But these tales
of predecessors to the later dynasty of gods seem
only invented to exalt the prowess of the conquerors
by whom they had been overthrown, and to do greater
honour to the existing deities by recording their
achievements in times past. It is true, that in one
memorable poem the new dynasty is represented as
having dispossessed divinities more venerable, and
more friendly to man—as exercising its triumph in
all the insolence of lawless power—as doomed itself
one day to tremble before a foe who could devise
flame more piercing than the lightning, noise more
terrible than the thunder. But it may be questioned
whether this language is not used because it was so
opposite to the belief of the hearers that, like the language put into the mouth of Satan in the " Paradise
Lost," it could not possibly be taken for a true representation of the facts. Where an English reader
is chiefly struck by the exhibition of the power of an
inflexible will to bid defiance to overpowering physical
force, a Grecian hearer would see only unbridled
insolence overtaken by just punishment. However
this may be, assuredly such were never the popular
conceptions of the gods. With the bulk of the heathen
world, the gods were the supreme, the alway-existing,
whose worship had dated from a period far anterior
to all historical record, and of whose dominion none

could predict an end. But the heathen religion possessed the note of catholicity in a higher degree than that of antiquity. All over the world, it was believed, substantially the same gods were worshipped, although it might be under different names, and although in different places a different order of precedence might be assigned to the divinities. When the Greeks first came into contact with the elder civilization of Egypt, they believed that they found there the same gods, and they persuaded themselves that it was thence they had derived much of their mythology. It is needless to say how completely the gods of Greece and Rome came to be identified, since it is in quite modern times, and with no small effort of thought, that scholars have been able to distinguish Here and Juno, Artemis and Diana, Hermes and Mercurius, Vulcan and Hephæstus. When the Romans came to be acquainted with the northern nations, they still made no question that their gods differed only in name from their own. Thus, Julius Cæsar reports that Mercurius was the god whom he found most in honour among the Gauls ; that next to him were worshipped Apollo and Mars, Jupiter and Minerva ; and that about these the Gauls held nearly the same opinions as all other nations. Tacitus equally finds among the Germans Mercurius, Hercules, Mars, and even Isis. And the traces which our language still exhibits of the times when Woden and Thor were worshipped, may remind us that Wednesday and Thursday were long accepted as the exact equivalent to dies Mercurii and dies Jovis. Thus then, as I said, the first preachers of Christianity

found their opponents urging against them the
argument from the notes of antiquity, extent, and
catholicity, with as much confidence as any body
of Christians has ever pressed the same argument
against a dissentient minority. The heathen might
confidently affirm that that must be true which had
been believed from times prior to all history, and
among all nations : "quod semper, quod ab omni-
bus, quod ubique." If a sect which everywhere was
spoken against dared to condemn the whole world,
it would seem that argument was unnecessary, and
that it would be enough to reply, " Securus judicat
orbis terrarum."

The subject which I wish to discuss to-day is, what
is the exact value of these notes of extent and catholicity of which I have been speaking. Are numbers
any test of truth ? Can the opinion of a minority be
safely rejected, simply because it is the opinion of a
minority ? If my object were merely to repel the
argument from numbers as used against us by Roman
Catholics in controversy, it would be hardly necessary to add anything to what has been said already.
We have seen already that this weapon was once
wielded by Pagans against Christians with infinitely
more effect than it has ever been wielded by one sect
of Christians against the rest ; and we shall presently
show that the very same argument may be urged with
equal force at the present day against the claims of
Christianity to be the religion of the world. The
early preachers of Christianity, in fact, occupied the
same position that was held by the Reformers three
or four hundred years ago, namely, that of assailants

of prevalent and long-standing superstitions. Consequently, it would be easy to quote from writings of
early fathers passages in which they insist on the
right of truth to prevail against any claims whatever
made on the score of antiquity or general acceptance.
They urged (the argument is Augustine's) that if antiquity might prevail against truth, then murderers,
adulterers, and all wicked men might defend their
crimes ; for these are ancient practices, and began at
the beginning of the world : that the Devil himself
is called ὁ ἀρχαῖος ; that ancient serpent, who was a
liar and a murderer from the beginning. " Custom
without truth," says Cyprian, " is but the antiquity of
error." " Nobody," says Tertullian, " can prescribe
against the truth ; neither space of times, nor the
patronage of persons, nor the privileges of countries."
It would seem, then, that both reason and authority
would justify us in dismissing the argument from
antiquity or from consent as utterly worthless. And
yet undoubtedly we should mistake if we were to dismiss thus summarily an argument which has certainly some weight, and which has possessed and will
possess with men higher influence than that to which
it is justly entitled. For our opinions are influenced
even more by our sympathies than by arguments. If
an opinion be held by a number of persons whom we
respect and like, then without any process of reasoning to prove that we are right in deferring to their
authority, that opinion will tend to become ours by
natural assimilation. And we can easily imagine
cases where we should pronounce a minority not
entitled to a hearing, if it presumed to condemn a

I.

vastly larger body. I take as an example the occasion with reference to which the words were written which I have already quoted, " Securus judicat orbis terrarum." These words if severed, as they have been, from their context, and made into a general rule, would lead to the most absurd results ; but taken in their original connection, they are quite rational and consistent with good sense. The Donatists in Africa, as many of you know, had separated themselves from their brethren, on what was originally a merely personal question, namely, whether the conduct in time of persecution of certain priests and bishops had not unfitted them for high office in the Church. And when the Donatist excommunication of the persons alleged to be guilty found no ratification in the rest of the Christian world, these schismatics went on to maintain that the whole Christian world had profaned itself by communion with these unworthy members, whom it had failed to expel from its society. In opposition to such a notion, St. Augustine had no difficulty in showing the unreasonableness of condemning the whole Christian world, because it had not taken a decisive part in a controversy, respecting which it had but scanty information. Were Christians far apart from Africa to be supposed to have forfeited their privileges, because they had not passed condemnation on men of whose crimes many of them had never heard, and of whose guilt they had no proof. If this were just, how could the African separatists tell whether they might not have forfeited their own privileges by a like remissness in not taking part in some controversy, raging perhaps in some distant part of the world, of which the Africans knew as little as the inhabitans of that part of the world knew of Africa. And he argues that the whole Christian world might safely refuse to accept the condemnation passed by the Donatists on their neighbours, when they saw the rashness with which they excommunicated distant nations who had committed no offence at all. It was a fixed principle, that it was better to endure the evil with patience, than to run the risk of condemning the good indiscriminately. And consequently the whole Christian world could decide with confidence, that those were not to be accounted good, whom they saw without reason, excommunicating the rest of the world. This is a fair summary of St. Augustine's argument.* And we do not hesitate to apply the same rule in judging of those little sects, which in modern times have attempted to make in this life a complete separation between the evil and the good, and which maintain the Donatist principle, that that Church has forfeited her privileges which fails to expel unworthy members from her communion. This principle is nearly incompatible with the existence of a Church at all. Such is the infirmity of human nature, that in a body believed to be wholly pure, the course of time invariably discovers impurities; so then, by the operation of the rule that has been laid down, new separations and excommunications become necessary; the Church of the pure reduces its numbers from hundreds to tens, and in some cases to units. In such cases the whole Christian world may surely, without examina-

* Cont. Epist. Parmeniani iii. 24.

tion, smile at the excommunication which has been passed upon it, and may confidently reject those who trust in themselves that they are righteous, and despise others.

And we may carry the same principle further. If St. Augustine was right in refusing to listen to one small sect when it excommunicated the rest of Christendom (though, indeed, the word small can only be used comparatively, for the four hundred Donatist sees formed no inconsiderable fraction of the whole Christian Episcopate) no more is a large sect to be listened to when it excommunicates the rest of Christendom. The Roman Catholic body, though the largest and most united of the sects into which the Christian world has been broken up, is still decidedly less than the half of the whole, and we, like St. Augustine, may refuse to listen to them when they excommunicate a larger body than themselves. Thus I have shown that the argument from numbers is one not to be summarily rejected as wholly worthless, but that it is one to which we ourselves on some occasions appeal.

And certainly this argument is one which practically is found to be most influential. It was through the operation of this argument that Rome gained some of the most distinguished of her recent converts from our Church. Any one who will trace the history of that movement will find that the change in position of the men of whom I speak, was induced far less by processes of argument, than by a change of sympathies which resulted from their being brought into contact, either through the writings of antiquity, or through foreign travel, with Christians differing from the modern Anglican type. It is so much our nature that our opinions should be regulated by our sympathies, that it seems impossible for the assertors of the importance of a great and neglected principle, to preserve sympathy with those who deny it. And hence it would seem to be inevitable that there should be a certain narrowness in the sympathies of every great reformer. The most conspicuous example of this is the Jewish nation, which perhaps never could have fulfilled its mission as the apostle of monotheism in the world, if it had not been fenced off from contact with the surrounding idolatrous nations. It is needless to quote testimonies to the impression produced on heathens by Jewish exclusiveness, when we have St. Peter's acknowledgment—"Ye know how that it is an unlawful thing for a man that is a Jew to keep company, or come unto one of another nation." Now the reaction against Romish errors at the time of the Reformation entailed a similar intolerance on the part of those who cast off the Papal yoke. They felt that the distance between them and Rome could not be made too wide. Rites or institutions, innocent in themselves, and even venerable for their age, were cast off as polluted, if they were identified in their minds with Rome. They were reluctant to acknowledge that Rome retained any fragments of their common Christianity. Their spirit was expressed in the deprecation in the Litany of our first reformed Prayer Book—"From the tyranny of the Bishop of Rome and all his detestable enormities, Good Lord, deliver us." And though, in the process of time, the opposition to Rome lost some of its bitterness, still the questions at issue between us and Rome were felt to be of importance surpassing that of all others. Consequently, those writers who lived before these questions were agitated, and who, therefore, spoke ambiguously on them, or who could be claimed on the wrong side of them, were regarded with distrust. While the champions of our Church never abandoned the attempt to prove that antiquity is really on our side, the feeling of the majority was that "to the martyrs and confessors, to whom we owe the Reformation, greater reverence is due than to any guides which the Church has had since the Apostles ;" and that if we can trace our religious principles to them, " we trace them to the only human parentage we need be very solicitous to establish for them." In this neglect of antiquity, it came to many as a startling novelty, when the publication of Milner's Church History made known to them that Ambrose and Augustine and Chrysostom were Christians who loved the same Bible as themselves, and who had learned from it to feed their spiritual life on the same Gospel truths. Dr. Newman tells us that it was from this work, the product of the Evangelical School, that he himself was early fired with the love of the ancient Church. · Thence he was led to take an interest in studies which familiarized him with a type of Christianity different from that which his boyhood had venerated. And as his acute and sceptical intellect was ever subjugated by his lively and credulous imagination, his views on modern controversies came to be governed by uncertain analogies suggested by the history of the early Church. What, if the iso-

lated religious position of England were but the re-
production of that of the African Donatists of old,
severed from the whole Christian world. More and
more these words haunted his imagination—" Securus judicat orbis terrarum." At length he resolved
to cast off his allegiance to the most venerable names
that were enthroned in honour by a single island, if
it were incompatible with his veneration of those who
were held in honour all over the earth. " Perish,"
he exclaimed, " perish a whole tribe of Cranmers,
Ridleys, Latimers, and Jewels ; perish the names of
Bramhall, Usher, Taylor, Stillingfleet, and Barrow,
from the face of the earth, ere I should do aught but
fall at their feet in love and in worship, whose image
was continually before my eyes, and whose musical
words were ever in my ears and on my tongue."

The same effect that was produced in this case by
the study of antiquity, has been produced in others
by foreign travel. The peculiar circumstances of our
Reformation isolated England as well from the reformed as from the unreformed on the Continent.
And while there was little intercourse with foreign
Christians, the isolation was not felt as a hardship.
We rather prided ourselves on being the only Church
which had combined apostolic order with apostolic
purity of doctrine. But it often happened to those
who were brought into closer contact with Christians
abroad, to be forced to recognize that there were
among them men who sincerely loved Christ, and
devotedly worked for Him, and thus to be more
struck with the points of likeness between us and
them, than by our points of difference. Then it was

felt to be painful and grievous that there should be schism between us; and the mistake was made of imputing the fault of that schism to our rejection of mediæval novelties, and to our resistance to Papal usurpations, and of overlooking that, in truth, the Papal usurpations were the real impediment to unity; and so attempts were made to re-impose on us a yoke, which neither our fathers nor we were able to bear.

However successful the argument from Catholicity may have been in gaining some converts for Rome, it will be found that this is not the use of the argument which is really most formidable. In this case, as in many others, the arguments used by Dr. Newman against Anglicanism are really arguments against Christianity. Exactly in the same way as some have made the comparative smallness of the number of the members of our Church a reason for not examining into her claim to conformity of doctrine with apostolic times, so have the claims of Christianity herself been set aside by those who have been forced to take notice how far it is, even at the present day, from being the religion of the world. Just as in the history of the contest between Anglicanism and Romanism, so in the history of the contest between Christianity and non-Christianity, a change of feeling has taken place, first through the influence of literature, next through that of foreign travel. There was a long time during which Christians, knowing and caring little about all who lay outside their own pale, were content to think of the whole heathen world as lying in unmixed wickedness.

A great change of feeling took place when, in the revival of learning, heathen poets and philosophers came to be the favourite teachers of Christians. Not to speak of many who were half paganized, even the most orthodox could not think harshly of those " whose musical words were ever in their ears and on their tongue."

Thus, though Dante denies to the bulk of the heathen sages admission into heaven, he makes their position in limbo one of such dignity and honour, that one of his commentators exclaims, that his author is more courteous to poets who were not Christians, than he is to saints who were not Ghibellines. He gladly adopts the legend, that the emperor Trajan had found through the prayers of Pope Gregory admission into paradise. On his own authority, he makes the poet Statius to have been a secret convert to Christianity ; and he gives a place in paradise beside David and Hezekiah to that Trojan prince whom his favourite poet had described as "justissimus unus," " et servantissimus æqui."

In our own days, increased intercourse with non-Christian peoples has inclined many to judge of them more favourably. A European lady spends months in the midst of Mahometans, and finds them pious, courteous, and even tolerant. Lessons of genuine piety and faith in God are quoted from the religious works of men who never heard of Pentateuch or Bible. In nations which know not Christ are found men who seem to be fearing God, and working righteousness. Then arises the question, Can the exclusive claims of Christianity be maintained ? Is it more than one

of the forms in which the religious conceptions of
men have embodied themselves? Do we well when
we try to force our European forms of thought on
Oriental minds, to which they are alien? Have we
realized in thought the vast multitudes of millions of
our fellow-creatures, to whom our creeds are unknown,
or who have refused to receive them? The number
of those in communion with Rome does not bear so
high a proportion to the whole of Christendom, as
that of those outside of Christianity does to the entire
population of the world. So that if Rome can silence
opposition by an appeal to the number of her adherents, with far better right can those who reject
Christianity bar her exclusive claims with the maxim,
" Securus judicat orbis terrarum."

The purport of what has been hitherto said has
been but to illustrate the importance of the subject
proposed for discussion. To treat that question fully
would be impossible in the time that now remains to
me, and I can only attempt briefly to indicate the
principles that may guide us in the solution of it.
And in the first place, it must be acknowledged by
all that numbers are no test of truth. Of almost all
the truths that are now accounted most valuable,
there was a time when everywhere they were spoken
against. The greatest discoveries have had to force
their way against long opposition. What we hold to
be most certain truths, must be rejected if their reception is to depend on the length of time for which
they have been admitted, or on the universality of
their acknowledgment. It is our universal belief now
that the apparent motion of the heavenly bodies is

caused by a real motion of the earth, but that belief is only of three or four centuries' standing: the doctrine, when first propounded, encountered violent opposition, and doubtless at the present day the number of those who hold it is but a small fraction of the population of the earth. If it be true that nothing is harder than to resist the sympathetic influence of the opinions of the multitude among which we live, on the other hand, men feel that their highest honours are due to those heroic souls who are able to resist that influence; to an Athanasius contra mundum; to an Elijah maintaining the cause of Jehovah single-handed against an apostate nation; to him with whom, as with Abdiel, "nor number nor example wrought to swerve from truth, nor change his constant mind though single." We find, then, that it is no presumption against the truth of any doctrine that it was long overlooked; that when discovered, it met with violent opposition; that it had to force its way to acceptance by long and severe struggles; that at the present day it is far from being universally admitted by mankind.

But it is a presumption against a doctrine if it shows no *tendency* to gain this victory. We have faith that that which is true will ultimately prevail. If we see what we regard as error now reigning widely, we can believe that its dominion will not be lasting, if we can trace the causes which give it currency; and if we can see that with increase of light the half truths now misapprehended must be discerned in their full proportions.

With respect to Christianity, then, we must own

that the success of her missionary efforts is the criterion of her Divine origin. But the question by which
she must be tested is not what progress has she
already made in the world, but whether her capacities
for progress are exhausted. And surely, if we compare what she is now with what she was at the time
to which the text refers, *then* everywhere spoken
against, the superstition of a handful of despised
men ; *now* triumphant over those parts of the earth
which are foremost in civilization, in expansive power,
and in all the arts of progress, we shall feel it to be
rash to assert that she cannot gain greater victories
now in her mature strength than she formerly did in
her infancy. It is true that much remains to be
done before she can be owned as supreme over all
the earth. Triumphant over Europe, and over those
countries which have been colonized from Europe,
she has still arrayed against her millions of the
eastern world. But we need not think of Christianity
as a product of western forms of thought, alien to
eastern minds. Christianity herself is a daughter of
the East. One of the first things that strikes western
travellers to oriental lands is the existence there, at
the present day, of manners and customs with which
our sacred books have made us familiar ; so that the
victory which our religion has gained on a continent to
which she was a stranger is an argument *a fortiori*
that she is not incapable of gaining a like victory in
the land of her birth.

Nor is it an argument against her that some of the
truths which she comes to teach have been owned
where she has not been ; that heathens should have

spoken of the fatherhood of God, the consciousness of sin, the fear of retribution, the hope of immortality. Nay, rather we ought to hail with gladness and hope those signs of preparedness to receive her lessons. When a conflagration is spreading over some vast prairie, it is no sign that its force is exhausted if tongues of flame are seen to dart forward in advance of the line of fire, and ever and anon patches kindle up where the conflagration has not yet reached. The great Apostle of the Gentiles, when addressing an heathen audience, did not seek to disparage the knowledge they had already attained. He rather sought to make that knowledge a basis for his own instructions: "Certain of your own poets have said, For we also are His offspring ;" " whom ye ignorantly worship, Him declare I unto you." He admits that " that which may be known of God is manifest even in the heathen:" that " the invisible things of Him from the creation of the world are clearly seen, being understood by the things that are made." And it will be our wisdom in like manner to avail ourselves of any ·element of truth or goodness that can be found in the heathen world. These are too few, too scattered, too little able to propagate themselves, to cause any jealousy to the champions of Christianity. The moral and spiritual condition of no pagan land is such as to allow us to imagine that it stands in no need of a Revelation. The patches of light which here and there diversify the general gloom can be no substitutes for the Gospel, but they may be witnesses for it. These symptoms of preparedness to receive the Gospel may strengthen our faith that the time will come when the whole world will be subject to its sway; when all over the earth the anthem shall be raised, " Hallelujah, for the Lord God omnipotent reigneth. The kingdoms of this world are become the kingdoms of our God and of his Christ, and He shall reign for ever and ever."

SERMON IX.

OLD TESTAMENT MORAL DIFFICULTIES.

" And Jacob sod pottage : and Esau came from the field, and he was faint ; and Esau said to Jacob, Feed me, I pray thee, with that same red pottage, for I am faint ; therefore was his name called Edom. And Jacob said, Sell me this day thy birthright. And Esau said, Behold, I am at the point to die ; and what profit shall this birthright do to me ? And Jacob said, Swear to me this day ; and he sware unto him ; and he sold his birthright unto Jacob. Then Jacob gave Esau bread and pottage of lentiles ; and he did eat and drink, and rose up and went his way. Thus Esau despised his birthright."—GENESIS xxv. 29-34.

A RECENT writer on the subject of miracles has observed, that the fact that repugnance to believe in the miraculous stories recorded in the Bible is more general now than in former times, may in part be accounted for by the greater prevalence now of the power of historical imagination. And he defines historical imagination as the habit of realizing past time ; of putting history before ourselves in such a light that the persons and events figuring in it are seen as once living persons and once present events. To the mass of persons the past presents an inanimate image ; a picture in flat, to which no sense of

reality is attached, and where, consequently, the facts
represented do not raise the questioning which similar occurrences taking place now would raise. It
was the great historical novelist of the last generation
who put flesh and blood on the skeletons of the past—
who so peopled the scenes of former time with living,
breathing figures as to bring it home to us that
those scenes were once present, that those characters
formed the then living world. And since his time
the mode of writing history has been revolutionized.
Perhaps few of Dr. Johnson's judgments seem now
to us more extravagant than what appears to have
been not one of his paradoxes, but his real opinion,
that no great abilities are required in a historian ;
that in historical composition all the greatest powers
of the human mind are quiescent ; that the historian
has facts ready to his hand, and has no need of invention ; that imagination is not necessary in any
high degree ; and that all that is wanting is that a
man should give the application which is necessary, and tell his story in a graceful manner. Now,
on the contrary, we are accustomed to think imagination one of the most needful qualities in a great historian. We expect him to make us feel that the men
of former days, however differently circumstanced from
us, were men of like passions with ourselves. We are
pleased when points in their conduct, which former
historians had represented as inexplicable, are made
plain by being read in the light of the present day :
when, for example, the conduct of Athenian dikasts·is
illustrated by that of English jurymen ; when the
panic fury which was caused by the mutilation of the

Hermæ is made intelligible by comparing it with
that which would be raised in an Italian or Spanish
village, by a similar mutilation of their images of
the Blessed Virgin; or when the ingratitude towards
the victors of Arginusæ is explained by the indignation which would be felt in England if an admiral,
after a victory, should return to his moorings without delaying to rescue the crews of any of his
vessels which had been shattered in the conflict, if
we are not making an impossible supposition in imagining that English sailors could thus leave their
comrades to perish. Nor is it secular history only
which is now thus read in the light of the present
day. The venerable man who lately went from us,
and who showed how the youthful cultivation of a
poetical imagination might form part of the training of a great historian, startled and shocked our
fathers by calling Abraham an Arabian sheik or
emir.* His brother dignitary meets with general approval from the present generation, when he uses his
knowledge of the customs of the unchanging East to
bring before us more distinct and life-like pictures of
what Jewish prophets and patriarchs really were.
But now that we no longer look on the characters
recorded in Scripture as invested, by their intercourse
with Deity, with a mysterious sanctity, extending to
all their actions—now that we try to think of them
as real, living beings, moving and acting like ourselves, it inevitably follows that we test their life by
the standards of the present day; and so difficulties

* This Sermon was preached not long after the death of Dean
Milman.

M

start to view which had been unnoticed in the dim religious light in which we had before regarded them.

Mr. Mozley, whose remark I began by quoting, has shown how this modern habit of thought, this vivifying of past time, places obstacles in the way of accepting testimony to miraculous occurrences. It does practically what Hume's celebrated argument undertook to do theoretically : it makes our present experience the standard of all past time, and disposes us to refuse to admit all that it will not justify. And the same habit of thought explains why we hear so much more now than formerly of the moral difficulties of Scripture. We see those whose history the sacred page records as if they were living before our eyes, and we ask ourselves what we should think of men who should now act as those who were said to be specially beloved of God acted ? And when the verdict is unfavourable, difficulties arise, not by any means new, but far more widely and more vividly felt ; not, as in former days, only to be met with in the pages of cavillers against our religion, but distressing earnest and sincere believers in it.

It will be generally owned that Scripture does not stamp with its approval everything which it records, not even though the things were done by men who had been favoured with supernatural help from God, and other parts of whose conduct were commended by Him ; and we can see that apologists in former days gave themselves needless trouble, when they thought themselves bound to find excuses for bad acts of good men. It will be owned also, that it is unfair to apply the moral standards of the nineteenth

century after Christ, to the acts of men who lived
several centuries before Him ; but the habit of
thought of which I spoke makes it difficult to bear
this rule in mind, and the more distinctly we conceive
the reality of the life of past times, the more we are
tempted to apply to it our own rules and measures.
This remark of course assumes that in morals, as in
other things, God's method of teaching the world
has been gradual, and that those who received His
earlier revelations, are on a lower level than those
who have been taught by Christ.   It would be out of
place if I were to attempt now to remove the difficulties suggested by the fact, that God did not from
the first make His revelation as full and complete
as we might have thought desirable.   Butler, in his
Analogy, has suggested several considerations to'
solve or mitigate these difficulties.   But as to the
matter of fact, that God's method of revelation has
been thus progressive we need not doubt, since we
find our Blessed Lord applying this principle to the
morality of the Old Testament.   He declares that a
lower morality was necessarily tolerated, on account
of the imperfect moral training of those for whom
Moses legislated, and in this way explains why
divorce was permitted by the Mosaic law.   When the
Puritans two centuries ago assumed that everything
recorded without disapproval in the Old Testament,
might be taken as a model for Christian conduct,
they thought to do honour to the Bible, but was it
not really to do dishonour to Christ?   He came as
Prophet as well as Priest and King, and in this
capacity taught lessons of the purest morality.   But

should we have a right to reverence Him as a great
moral teacher, if they who have thoroughly imbibed
His lessons, stand on no higher level than those who
lived before His precepts were delivered. When we
admit that God's method of training the world has
been gradual, we need not wonder that when men
had more lessons than one to learn, He often taught
them but one at a time; first impressed that which was
most needful to be learned, and waited till later to
instruct them in the second. One great lesson He
taught the world through the instrumentality of the
Jewish people, the fundamental principle of monotheism—a sublime doctrine, which history shows not
to have been the product of advancing civilization,
reducing by a process of generalization the many
gods which had been worshipped to one. Monotheism was the doctrine of the Jews as far as we can
trace their history back, and they declared that their
ancestors had received it by Revelation, while their
much more civilized conquerors continued to worship
an ever-increasing number of gods; and even after
Christ's coming men looked back to the belief of
those simple days, when "there was no such crowd
of gods as then, and the heavens were content with
fewer deities." Yet this early belief of the Jews was
a tradition maintained with difficulty, in opposition
to a constant tendency of the nation to assimilate
their practices to those of their idolatrous neighbours.
God's dealing with this people for a series of years
was directed to the end of fencing them off from
other nations, so that the sacred deposit entrusted
to them might be preserved free from corruption.

We have no right to complain that, while the Jews were busy in being taught those fundamental principles on which Christianity, with all its beneficial consequences to the world, is based, they were not taught, at the same time, those lessons of tenderness, humanity, regard to the sacredness of life, in which our modern western world differs so much from our own ancestors a hundred years ago, not to say from the ancients. In this respect the Jews of old ranked low as we should count it, but not lower than other eastern nations of the same time, but rather higher. You may ask, if you will, why God did not teach, through the instrumentality of Moses, all that was afterwards taught by Christ, or rather why the same lessons were not taught long before Moses. But once admit that there may be anything gradual in God's mode of instruction, and it seems plain that lessons on the universal brotherhood of men were not suited to the time, when the great object was to keep the Jews distinct from other people, and when, if the Jews were to be brothers to the surrounding heathen, they must be brothers to them in wickedness and in abominable idolatry.

St. Chrysostom furnishes an example which enables us to compare two methods of solving Old Testament moral difficulties, and which exhibits how defective is that which applies Christian measures to the conduct of Old Testament saints, and tries to persuade us that they satisfy it, but omits to take into account the elevation which Christ's doctrines have given to the moral tone of His disciples. He undertakes to defend Abraham for having allowed his wife to be

taken from him by the king of Egypt, and he admits
that he ought not to have done so, if by the sacrifice
of his life he could have saved her. But he argues
that the sacrifice would have been useless, since
Abraham's fear was that they would kill him, *and*
take her. The two crimes then, murder and adultery,
being threatened, Abraham showed his wisdom, when
he could not avert both, in at least averting one of
them ; and further, in diminishing as far as he could
the Egyptians' guilt in that adultery, by concealing
from them the fact that Sarah was his wife, and only
owning that she was his sister. Such a defence,
which we can scarcely read without a smile, must
have given to any thoughtful man who heard it the
pain which is felt when difficulties are forcibly stated,
and met by unsatisfactory solutions. But we can
hear him with pleasure when, taking different ground,
he owns the inferiority of those who lived before
Christ's revelation :—" Do not blame the righteous
man's pusillanimous spirit, but rather admire the
goodness of God, who, through Christ, has made
death, which was then so terrible, now so easily despised. With Abraham the fear of death could master
the tyrannical passion of jealousy, which is strong as
death, ' cruel as the grave ;' which is ' the very rage
of a man,' and will not regard any ransom, nor be
pacified with gifts. Under the old dispensation,
Jacob trembled when death was threatened him by
Esau, and Elijah fled in terror before the threats of
Jezebel. But Christ has opened to us the hope of
immortality. He has taught us that death is a
passage from the worse to the better. He Himself

descended to the prison-house, and broke the gates of brass; and now, since He has stripped death of his terrors, not only will Paul exclaim, 'I long to depart and be with Christ, which is far better,' but even youths and tender maidens will smile at meeting that which the greatest saints of the old dispensation trembled to encounter."

I have not thought it necessary to explain the connection with the text of the remarks I have made on the moral difficulties of the Old Testament. The course of our Sunday lessons brought before us to-day a chapter containing what cannot be called a very perplexing moral difficulty, but still matter in which most persons feel themselves somewhat out of sympathy with the narrative. Just as when David and his brethren passed before Samuel, those whom man had chosen were rejected by Him who seeth not as man seeth; so now, too, we feel that had we been judges we should have decided differently between Jacob and Esau, and our sympathies are with the brother whom the Lord rejected. And when we read the narrative which I have coupled with that read for the lesson—a story of two brothers, of whom when the elder returned from hunting, the younger refused to give him the food he desired until he had bartered away his birth-right as its price, our condemnation is ready for that unnatural brother, who could turn his brother's necessities to his own advantage, make a hard bargain with him, and wring from him a price out of all proportion to what he was receiving in its stead. But the Bible has no word of censure for Jacob. It is against Esau that the historian cannot suppress his indignation : " Thus Esau despised his birth-right." And his name passes into a by-word : " A profane person, as Esau, who for one morsel of meat sold his birth-right."

It must be owned that of the two great virtues of uncivilized life, bravery and craft, in one of which Esau excelled and in the other Jacob, the former is that which most readily enlists our sympathies; and the bold, daring hunter excites a more romantic interest than the quiet, thoughtful herdsman. Yet it is not only the God of Scripture, but the God of Nature, who gives a triumph to the qualities which we are slowest to admire. The wild beast which the hunter pursues may be his superior in courage and strength, but is conquered by the hunter's patient cunning. And a recent writer has well pointed out what a step in civilization is gained when the hunter gives way to the herdsman :—" The hunter's habits are those of a beast of prey, every beast on the earth, every bird in the air, being an enemy against which his club will be raised or his arrow drawn. On passing into the state of a herdsman, he finds himself surrounded by a number of animals of tender breed, whom he must pity and tend, bearing with their humours under pain of their loss. If he would feed on their milk and eggs, if he would clothe himself in their wool and skins, he must make it his business to save and guard them, must seek out herbage and water for them, consider their times and seasons, and prepare for them a shelter from the heats of noon and the frosts of night. Thus the man's relations to the lower world undergo a change. Where,

in his hunter state, he sharpened his knife against
every living thing, he has now become a student of
nature, a nursing-father to an ever-increasing family
of beasts and birds."

But to come to the Scripture narrative, there is no
reason for thinking that the birthright which Esau
despised had any reference to the possession of this
world's goods. It would seem that Esau inherited his
father's wealth, and that Jacob's riches were all his
own hard earnings in a foreign land. The birthright,
I conceive, had reference first to the priestly office,
which, under the patriarchal dispensation, the first-
born seems to have exercised ; but principally to the
promise of that seed, in whom all the families of the
earth should be blessed—a promise which, no doubt,
the children of Isaac could not understand in its full
meaning; but he who had faith in the God of
Abraham and of Isaac knew that it contained deep
treasures of good things to come. And it was because Esau was wanting in this faith that he did not
value the promise, and was willing lightly to part
with it. For the whole tenor of the history gives us
to understand that Esau's necessities were by no
means so great as he would himself have us suppose
when he says, "Behold, I am at the point to die, and
what profit shall this birthright do me ?" The case of
Esau, who, for one morsel of meat, sold his birthright, was rather that of one whose heart is so madly
set on the present gratification of some appetite, that
he thinks life not worth possessing without the object
of his desire, and that he *must* have it no matter
what price he pays. In fact Esau, as represented in

the history, while not destitute of amiable qualities, shows traces only of a mere animal nature, wholly engrossed with the pursuits of this passing scene, and unable to aspire to the lofty hopes for which the promises to his father gave warrant. And so he has a kind of value for his birthright. It is a thing belonging to him which he is sorry to lose, and is vexed at being deprived of. But yet he does not in real truth feel the value of it. And when he is forced to choose whether he will give up this, or some coveted present pleasure, he chooses the object he really does care for, and exclaims, " What profit shall this birthright do me ?" And thus we can understand how it was that one, of this sensual animal nature, unable to appreciate spiritual blessings, should have been rejected as unworthy to inherit the promises, and Jacob, with all his faults, preferred in his stead.

But there is no reason for supposing that the Bible gives its approbation to these faults. We meet in the Bible as we do in real life with actions of a mixed kind, deserving commendation in one point of view, and not in another. Such cases may be expected to occur frequently in the Old Testament; for the imperfection of the moral training of God's earlier people consisted in this, that certain truths were strongly grasped, but the pressure of surrounding evils sometimes prevented them from giving due weight to the corresponding counter-truths. And so, to use the words of a recent writer, " Their conduct thus presents a blended texture of good and evil. On the side of good we rank the strong faith in God, the

strong resolve that righteousness should conquer, the
steady determination to root out wickedness.   The
evil was, that righteousness was not always tempered
by mercy, nor faith by truth, nor retaliation by justice.
But so far as any of these acts received the expression of God's approbation, we may rest satisfied that
His blessing lighted simply on the virtue, while His
patient forbearance with His creatures' ignorance for-
gave them the accompanying sin."*

In the present case, Jacob was rewarded for his
faith in God's promises, and for his appreciation of
them, when they seemed to bring no immediate
advantage ; not for the deceit by which he tried to
secure them.   In this he showed not his faith, but
his want of faith.   That superiority to his brother,
which was the object of all his scheming, had been
promised him before his birth.   He could not be content, as his grandfather, Abraham, would have been,
patiently to wait God's time for the accomplishment
of His promises ; but when years went on, and no
sign of their fulfilment appeared, he must help God's
plans out by his own schemes and contrivances. Deceit
did not gain him the promises—they had been his
before.   It gained him only twenty years of exile
from the promised land.   It forced him to fly in
terror from his father's roof, it filled his return with
fears at the lasting wrath of a justly offended brother.
Deceit was made the instrument of his punishment ;
it met him in Laban's house, disappointing him of the
wife, for whom he had served, defrauding him ten

* Hannah's Bampton Lectures, p. 177.

times, as he complained, of the wages for which he had bargained, and it well nigh brought his grey hairs to the grave in sorrow for the pretended death of a living son. The Scripture narrative itself, then, teaches us that God's approbation was not given to the means which Jacob used to gain the promises, but only to this, that he really did value the promises of God, little fruit in this life though they seemed to bring—that he set his affections on them, and earnestly strove to obtain them.

You, brethren, are inheritors of promises more full, more distinct, more glorious, than those that inspired the hopes of Jacob. He scarce knew at what he was grasping. He had but dim and shadowy perceptions of future glory, and prosperity, and deliverance for himself and his race; he knew not in what form, or at what time to be realized. But whatever it was, it was a promise of blessing from God, and he had faith to know, that come in what form it might, that was a thing worth striving and working for. Those things, which Jacob, seeing afar off, could but faintly discern, we who have been brought nigh by the blood of Christ, can clearly see. We know exactly what the promises meant that were held out to him, and we have addressed to ourselves promises of things not less precious. A revelation has been made to us in Him of a love surpassing human experience; a love undaunted by danger, unrepelled by the unworthiness of its object; the love of Him who braved tortures, and shame, and death for the sake of enemies, for the sake of ungrateful rebels to His authority, which wearied not till it had

sought out and brought home its wanderers. The
promise held out to us is to have a perpetual share of
that love, to have Jesus as our friend, our counsellor,
our consoler in this life ; to have His Spirit as our
support against temptation, our guide in perplexity ;
and when the house of our earthly tabernacle is dis-
solved, to have prepared for us a house made of
God, eternal in the heavens ; to know that death is
not our enemy, but only the servant who will bring
us close to Him, to be hailed by Him as conquerors
over the same enemies against which He fought—sin
and the world, and Satan—to partake of the glory
into which He entered, to be crowned by Him with
the victor's wreath, and sit down with Him on the
same conqueror's throne, no further enemy remaining
to give battle, no danger being left to make our happiness insecure.   These are the promises held out to
us. Brethren, do you care for them ? None of you
will say you do not ; you have been taught from
your earliest years to look on these promises as yours.
Such was the case of Esau : from his childhood he
had looked on the birthright as undoubtedly his. No
doubt he would at any time, if he had been asked,
have said, that he cared for his birthright until the
moment of trial came, which proved how little real
value he had for it.   Brethren, is it only in the same
way, that you care for the promises of the Gospel ?
Is it that you have a knowledge that they are things
which you *ought* to care for, and that so you regard
them with a traditionary respect ? or is it, that in
your own hearts you do long for them, and covet the
attainment of them ? Because, brethren, if it is only·

in the former way you care for God's promises, it is
easy to predict what the result will be if temptation
comes, and if you are compelled to choose between
things you really do in your hearts long for, and
things which you have taught yourselves to say you
wish for, or which you have merely a feeling that you
ought to like.   Passion will plead strongly that the
objects which it covets are essential to the happiness
of your life, that you are on the point to die if they
be denied you, while the hopes of the Gospel promises retire into cloudy indistinctness, and you say,
What profit shall this birthright do me ?   Never, perhaps, are you aware of the act you are committing ;
never does it occur to you what you are giving up ;
you merely put these distant hopes from your thoughts,
and resolve to take your fill of present enjoyments,
and trust that while you greedily seize on the things
of earth, the things of heaven will not cease at some
day to be yours.   But all the time you may be committing the very act that Esau committed—for one
morsel of meat to sell your birthright !   Beware
that it be not your case also, afterwards to find no
place of repentance, though you seek it carefully with
tears.

Esau is a remarkable instance how that may be
highly esteemed among men which is despised in
God's sight.   Esau, no doubt, held a high place in
the respect and admiration of the generation in which
he lived. ' The favourite son of a wealthy chieftain,
the bold hunter, the daring captain, the successful
warrior ; frank, manly, and generous in his character, Esau might surely feel that he deserved to be

respected; he might surely feel that he was above contempt ; and yet it is precisely to undying scorn and
contempt that Esau's name is handed down in the
pages of inspiration as the unthinking fool, who for
one morsel of meat sold his birthright.

And not less miserably foolish is the choice of any
man who has allowed himself, in the pursuit of present enjoyments, to forget the promises made to those
who love our Lord.   However successful the earthly
career of such a man, however enviable his qualities,
he is still in the number of those, who when
those that sleep in the dust of the earth shall awake,
shall awake to shame and everlasting contempt.   Let
not Satan then delude you, brethren, into imagining
that any object he can present to your desires is
worthy to shut out from your thoughts hopes infinitely more precious.   If you would secure yourselves
against this folly, learn to make Jesus habitually present to your minds.   For if you look on the Gospel as
merely containing a promise of some unintelligible
kind of happiness to be enjoyed in heaven after death,
such a hope is too vague and too remote to compete
successfully with the objects of our present desires.
It is if you have learned to find pleasure in communion with our Blessed Lord now, and to know the
earnest of His Spirit, as containing a pledge and fore-
taste of future happiness, because itself conveying
happiness of the same kind as that to be enjoyed
hereafter —it is then that you feel yourselves to be not
only inheritors, but possessors of a treasure, which you
will not be lightly tempted to surrender.   Pray then,
brethren, to Him who has promised freely to give

His Spirit to them that ask Him ; that that Spirit may reveal to you the things of Christ, may make you to know His love, which passeth knowledge ; and thus filling your heart with love for God's promises, give you the best security for doing that which He commands.

SERMON X.

OBEDIENCE.

"Obey them that have the rule over you, and submit yourselves; for they watch for your souls, as they that must give account, that they may do it with joy, and not with grief, for that is unprofitable for you."—HEBREWS xiii. 17.

THE most important event in the modern history of the Church of these islands is a revolt against authority. By their declaration that no foreign bishop or potentate has any rightful authority in these realms, our ancestors broke the yoke of obedience to a power which had been the growth of centuries, and had been submitted to by the consent of Western Christendom. At the same time, by an act of private judgment, they cast aside beliefs, for which could be pleaded long prescription, and which were supposed to have the sanction of what was reckoned the highest Church authority. It requires an effort of the imagination for us to understand, in any degree, how very bold and daring that act of rebellion was. Sinful and shocking as it seemed to many a good man at the time, we, however, look back to it as the

N

origin of the greatest blessings to our Church. To
it we owe our free access to the Word of God, our
firmer grasp of some of the most important religious
truths, our abandonment of some demoralizing superstitions, and (what has proved more valuable than
correct views as to any one truth) freedom of thought.
We read with pleasure in the Bible, how the Bereans
are commended for their nobleness, in that they
thought it right to verify for themselves the teaching
of inspired Apostles, by searching whether the Scriptures bore out their assertions. And we, too, do not
regard any human authority as having a right to
debar our access to the fountains of truth, or as having
a right to require our acceptance of unproved assertions. We demand proof, and claim a right to weigh
the proofs offered us, and assure ourselves that they
are satisfactory. We are conscious that the freedom
thus claimed for the exercise of thought on religious
subjects, has largely contributed to our intellectual
progress. One science after another has been eman-
cipated from bondage to theology, while all have
made rapid advances, since it has been understood
that reputation is to be no longer gained by retailing
the dicta of some venerated authority, but by enquiry,
research, and independent thought. The course of
our Church history has then had this effect upon her
members, that the dangers we most dread are those
resulting from the abuse and overstraining of authority; the extreme we think most unsafe, is that of
blind submission, while, by a natural reaction, the
just claims of authority run the risk of being slighted.
For certainly, to Protestant ears such a text as,

" Obey them that have the rule over you," (the rulers spoken of being, as the context proves, spiritual rulers,) is less acceptable than such a text as, " Prove all things, hold fast that which is good."

The tendencies which have been produced by the religious history of the nation, have been confirmed by our political history. There was a time when it was fashionable to descant on the absolute right of the civil ruler to exact under all circumstances the obedience of his subjects; not indeed their active obedience when his commands were manifestly unjust and wicked, but at least their passive obedience; that is to say, their unresisting submission to his dealings with them of whatever kind they might be. These speculations as to the theory of the relations between a ruler and his people, were suddenly overturned by the practical experience of misgovernment. Our civil history, as well as our religious, has witnessed a successful revolt against authority. We have had a revolution as well as a reformation. And we are persuaded that the bulk of our people enjoy more security, greater happiness, greater material prosperity under the constitution under which we live, than they could ever have attained, if they had patiently submitted to the government which they then rejected. Hence from the time of which I speak, the duty of subjects to obey their rulers is a doctrine which we hear much less frequently inculcated; the advantages of self-government, and the blessings of civil and religious liberty, have been much more favourite topics of declamation. The tendencies of which I speak as existing among ourselves, have received still greater development on the other side of the Atlantic. The people of the States which have separated from us can boast of yet one more successful revolt against authority than we; and they with justice look to that revolt as the foundation of their greatness as a nation. Constantly recurring with triumph, as they do, to this period of their history, they have learned from it to pride themselves on asserting their freedom from control, and their resolution to submit to no dictation. And the feelings engendered by their political history they apply to religious matters. There is but small veneration for antiquity or authority. Each citizen chooses his religious guide as he will, follows him as long as he will, and forsakes him when he will. Such men, it may be supposed, are not likely to give a very favourable hearing to the exhortation of the text, to submit themselves obediently to other men whose office it is to rule them, and to watch over their souls.

It might seem now that the facts which I have brought forward involve some presumption against the wisdom of the command given in the text. Two nations of the present day, holding the first rank in civilization and power, find that the course of training which has led to their greatness, has indisposed them to accept this command, and has taught them to prefer to a submissive spirit, a spirit of independence and readiness to resist aggression. And, on the other hand, it has been observed, that the nations which in religious matters have paid the greatest reverence to long established authority, are, in the things of

this life, the most backward, and that they lag
behind in the race of civilization. Now, since
Scripture and experience have taught us that "righteousness exalteth a nation," or, in other words,
that compliance with God's commands, as a general
rule, leads to happiness in this world as well as
in that which is to come, there would be a presumption that a system is not really of Divine origin
if it can be said with truth that it generates in those
who adopt it, habits inconsistent with their temporal
prosperity. It is proper, therefore, to remark that
it would be a misrepresentation to say that the
English people are characterized by unwillingness to
submit to authority. What they have been unwilling
to submit to is the *unlawful* exercise of power. Indeed one cause of this unwillingness is their respect
for law, and their readiness to resent a violation of
law. This respect for law is essential to the true
greatness of any people. Where it has been wanting
the absence of restraint on the ambition of the powerful, and on the violence of party conflict, has soon
proved fatal to the state. This respect for law is as
essential to the stability of one form of government
as of another. The republican institutions of our
American kinsmen have been hitherto made to work
well, because, on the whole, the supremacy of law
was cheerfully maintained by the people, and the rage
of party strife was confined within the limits which
their constitution imposed. Notwithstanding excep-
tional irregularities, the feeling of the majority has
been that what is ordained by law must be submitted
to, even by those whom its working unfavourably

affects. Even the present unhappy civil war* has served to manifest how strong was the general conviction that this obedience to law is a citizen's first duty. For a peaceable separation between the two parties might not have been impossible, if it had not been for the strong feeling on the one side that law had been violated, whence arose a sense of unjust treatment and consequent resentment against antagonists, who, it was complained, had upheld the constitution as long as it gave power to themselves, and desired to overthrow it the moment power passed into the hands of their rivals. Thus, then, those very nations which might be instanced as having made great progress in civilization and prosperity, and as owing that progress to their spirit of fiery independence and unwillingness to submit to control, will be found on examination to be characterized by deep respect for the authority of law. If in any parts of either nation that respect does not prevail, it is in the rudest, least civilized, and least prosperous parts of them. But, indeed, it does not require experience on a large scale to establish a truth which forces itself on our daily observation. Men cannot co-operate together successfully for any purpose, unless they comply with the rules which regulate their joint co-operation. Obedience is the key-stone of every society. In some kinds of societies, such as an army, obedience is almost a necessity of their existence. But compliance with rule is essential to the prosperity of

---

* This expression indicates the date when the Sermon was preached. It is needless to say what illustrations a later struggle would furnish of the strength which a community gains by discipline and habits of obedience to rule.

every kind of society, small.or large. It is as essential to the prosperity of a cricket club as of an empire. It is only then what might be expected, that the same rule should hold in things Divine as in things temporal. If human society is held together by the bonds of laws, and threatens to fall to pieces when those laws are disobeyed, far less can we venture to disregard the laws of Him whom to obey is life, whose service is perfect freedom. He has, indeed, as it were, set us the example of obedience to law; for such is the regularity and uniformity of His operations, that we find it most natural to speak of laws of nature, as if the Author of nature were governed in His actions by eternal laws which He had prescribed to Himself. But still more, when God was manifest in the flesh, did He set us an example of obedience. To do His Heavenly Father's will was the object for which He lived on earth; and not less did He submit Himself to His earthly parent, and to every human authority, to which the circumstances of His sojourn here gave a claim on His obedience. When, therefore, on His departure from the world He formed His people into a society, the very fact that He did not connect each separately with Himself, but formed all into one body, of which He was to be the head, implied that every Christian comes under the obligation to obey the laws of the body of which he has been made a member, and which, like every other society, cannot continue in prosperity if its laws are disregarded.

The duty to obey God's laws is one which none of His creatures can have the presumption to dispute;

but it is common with many to draw in their minds
a sharp line of distinction between God's laws and
man's laws, and to profess their readiness to comply
implicitly with every command which can be proved
to come directly from God; while they regard the
rejection of that which rests only on human authority
as rather a meritorious assertion of independence.
In controversies which have raged respecting different
ecclesiastical institutions, infinite pains have been
taken to find Scripture warrant for particular observances, because it has been felt that if a direct Divine
command were not in this way made out, there would
be left for them, in the minds of many, no authority
at all. Now while it is our duty, no doubt, to comply with God's commands wherever He has given us
any, we must remember that it is one of His commands that we shall obey the lawful authority of man.
A law to this effect was one of the ten commandments
given on Mount Sinai ; and the Apostle has declared
that there is no power but of God ; that the powers
that be are ordained of God ; that whosoever resisteth
the power resisteth the ordinance of God, and that
they that resist shall receive damnation. The same
Apostle, when treating of the duties special to different states of life, wherever he inculcates submission on any—whether on wives towards their hus-
bands, children towards their parents, servants towards
their masters—always teaches them to regard the
service which they offer as paid to the Lord, who has
instituted these earthly relations: " With good will
doing service as to the Lord and not to men, knowing that whatsoever good thing any man doeth the

same shall he receive of the Lord, whether he be bond or free." "Obedience for God's sake to a man, clothed with the same circumstances and the same infirmities with ourselves, is a greater instance of humility than to obey God immediately, whose power is infinite, and whose very presence would force obedience from us; just as it is both greater faith and greater charity to relieve a poor saint, for Jesus' sake, than to give anything to Christ Himself if he should appear in the robes of glory and demand it from us." "When saw we thee an hungered or athirst, and did not minister unto thee?" was the cry of those who had hardened their hearts when the saints, in whose person Jesus had besought them, had pined in their presence. "When didst thou command us, and we refuse to obey?" may be in like manner the excuse of those who have stiffened their neck, when commanded by those in whose person Christ Himself commanded them. There would be, after all, little charity and little obedience in giving or obeying at Christ's personal demand, which scarcely any would venture to reject. But true faith is exhibited in recognizing Christ in the calls of daily duty; in knowing that when we see a brother in need, and shut up our compassion from him, we refuse to hear our Lord's represeneative; that when we refuse to obey the lawful authority which He has placed over us, we refuse to obey Him; in knowing that every duty of the place in life which He has assigned us is work given us to do for Him. Our rule of life, then, is God's law, wherever He has expressly made known to us His will; but where God's law is silent, our

rule is man's law, which, when established by rightful authority, has the full weight of Divine sanction.
What has been said as to the sanction impressed
by God Himself on the laws of man applies to the
laws of secular governments, of which primarily it
was said "the powers that be are ordained of
God." But specially it applies to the laws of the
Church, which is a society which our Saviour Himself has founded and endowed with special power.
If there had been no express revelation of our Lord's
will on this matter, we might have inferred from the
mere fact that our Lord instituted this society, that it
was entitled to demand from its members that obedience which is necessary to the prosperous existence
of every society. But this inference has been drawn
for us in several passages of Scripture. When our
Lord sent forth His disciples at the first, He gave
them all the claims on the obedience of those to
whom they were sent which were due to Him, whose
ambassadors they were. "He that heareth you heareth me, and he that despiseth you despiseth me, and
he that despiseth me, despiseth Him that sent me."
And at His last Supper our Lord repeated the same
words, "Verily, verily, I say unto you, He that
receiveth whomsoever I send receiveth me, and he
that receiveth me, receiveth Him that sent me."
To which may be added the well-known promise,
"Whatsoever ye shall bind on earth shall be bound
in heaven, and whatsoever ye shall loose on earth
shall be loosed in heaven." The tenor of these promises plainly forbids us to limit the obligations of
Christians to obedience to the commands which our

Lord may have given in person during His stay on earth. We are here taught to yield like obedience to the commands of the society which He formed and invested with such high authority.

The question, however, arises, Was the power which our Lord then gave, confined to the Apostles on whom it was, in the first instance, bestowed, or is it to be acknowledged as still remaining in force at the present day? Here we make a distinction; with regard to doctrines to be believed as necessary to salvation, we hold, that the Apostles delivered to their converts all that was necessary to be believed; that they kept back nothing that was profitable to them, and shunned not to declare unto them the whole counsel of God. We hold, that the way of salvation is the same now as it was then. We believe that, through the grace of the Lord Jesus Christ, we shall be saved *even as they*. If, then, we would know what *we* must believe in order to be saved, it is sufficient if we know what the Church in the Apostles' days believed; and we acknowledge in the Church of later times no power of making new articles of faith, or of developing old doctrines into forms quite unlike their original. And again, since we have no trustworthy record of what the Apostles taught but the Bible, we hold that in the Scriptures alone all necessary articles of faith may be found; and that no Church or teacher has a right to require any man to receive as an essential truth any doctrine that is not taught in the Bible, or else drawn by fair inference from it.

But the case is different when we are speaking, not of essential doctrines, but of ceremonies or other

188 SERMON X.

similar ordinances. Without some regulations on such matters, a Church could not exist as a society; and we have seen that her Founder gave her full power to frame such as she might require. These may be changed from time to time as expedience may suggest; but as long as they are ordained by lawful authority, are binding on individual members. The private members of the Church would not be justified in demanding a Scripture authority for each of her regulations, before they would yield obedience to it, because we have no right to expect to find a complete code of such regulations in the Bible; and in point of fact we know that none such is to be found there. Nor again, can they refuse obedience, because the observances enjoined are not the most edifying, or the most expedient that could be chosen. When the laws of any society are being framed, it is of course right that the framers of them should strive to make laws as wise and as convenient as possible; and if it should in practice be found that the working of some laws is inconvenient, it is right that individuals should use their influence to have them altered; but still as long as they *are* laws, private members of the society cannot, without a breach of the duty which they owe to it, refuse to obey them. "Although the keeping or omitting a ceremony in itself considered is but a small thing, yet the wilful and contemptuous trangression, and breaking of a common order and discipline is no small offence before God. 'Let all things be done among you,' saith St. Paul, 'in a seemly and due order.' The appointment of which order pertaineth

not to private men ; therefore no man ought to take
in hand, nor presume to appoint or alter any public
or common order in Christ's Church, except he be
lawfully called and authorized thereto." Only one
thing can justify our refusing to obey the commands
of the Church, or of any other lawful authority ; it
is if man's law should be in opposition to God's
law ; then our course is clear, we must obey God
rather than man. We have in the Articles of our
Church the double limitation very clearly expressed,
which God's revealed law places on the authority of
the Church. With regard to rites and ceremonies,
the only limitation is that it ought not to ordain anything *contrary* to God's Word written ; while, with
regard to doctrines, it is, that *besides* the same, it
ought not to enforce anything to be believed for
necessity of salvation ; or, in other words, that it
ought not to enforce anything not contained in the
same. Thus, at the time of the Reformation, the
multitude of ceremonies had grown to a burdensome
excess, and many of these ceremonies were far from
edifying ; yet this alone would not have justified a
separation from the Church. It was not on these
grounds we broke off communion with Rome ; it was
because she herself had made communion impossible,
because (to mention no other reason) we could not
join in her public worship without offering the worship due to God alone, to that which we believe not
to be God.

I may seem to have been stating principles so
generally acknowledged as to be hardly worth dwelling on ; but it would be easy to give instances to

show that they are very often lost sight of. For example, a great many Protestants would think that they had done a good thing if they had convinced a Roman Catholic that one kind of food was as acceptable in God's sight as another—one day as another ; and that, therefore, it was irrational to comply with his Church's ordinance of abstaining from flesh on one day of the week. Nay, some would even be pleased if they had prevailed on him to disobey in practice, though his conscience might be far from satisfied. Or, again, they might be shocked at finding him learning in his catechism the commandments of God and the commandments of the Church, and would urge on him to observe the former alone. The case is much the same as this : Suppose you have the opportunity of instructing the child of one whom you believe to be a bad man, ought you to teach that child never to obey his parent ? It might happen, of course, that the parent might be so depraved that the child ought absolutely to be removed from under his control ; but still this is not always possible : and it happens often, for example, to directors of ragged schools to give instruction to children whose parents, it is to be feared, will teach them to lie and steal. What I suppose any one would say would be the right course to pursue with such a child, is to teach him to reverence God's law ; to instruct him that there are some things which he must not do, even if a parent commands ; but that in all indifferent matters he ought dutifully to obey his parent, so that it might be plain that where obedience was refused, it was not from disrespect, but from reverence to a higher law. And in dealing with a Roman Catholic, the point to assail is not disciplinary regulations, which it fairly comes within the province of a Church to make ; but if you can show him that his Church requires of him that which it would be sinful of him to comply with, then you give him a reason for withdrawing from her communion and refusing her commands.

It is implied in what has been here said, that in the case of no man or society of men, is an individual justified in obeying man's authority so implicitly as to take no heed whether man's law be not in opposition to God's. Yet an opposite doctrine has been taught by those who have most highly exalted the virtue of obedience, I mean by those who have written about monastic obedience. These writers, in describing the qualities of perfect obedience, before insisting that a meritorious obedience shall be prompt and zealous, and so forth, make it the first requisite that it shall be blind obedience. The individual is required by one act to abandon all exercise of his own conscience ; and having thus put out the eyes of his soul, to resign himself blindfold thenceforward to the guidance of another. Each member of a well-known order is to be as passive an instrument in his superior's hands as a staff in the hands of an old man. Legends are told how this unreasoning obedience has been justified by miracle ; how the monk who, at his superior's command, daily watered the sapless staff thrust into the ground found it grow into a tree ; how he who ran across the lake to execute his superior's commands, found the waters bear up his steps. For

such a theory of obedience as this we find no authority in Scripture. The command to obey those who
have the rule over us is not complied with by voluntarily undertaking obedience to those who have not
the rule over us by any appointment of God's, and
whose commands cannot always be satisfied without
withdrawing obedience from some who have a just
claim on our obedience. But even if the power
blindly submitted to were not thus radically desti-
titute of authority, the kind of obedience offered
could not be justified. Those very words so often
quoted, " We ought to obey God rather than men,"
were used to men possessed of no usurped power, but
to the highest authority of the Jewish Church and
nation. And this alone is sufficient to show that the
obedience we are to offer to even the best grounded
authority is not to be blind, mechanical, and irrational, but enlightened, and liable to be withdrawn
should we at any time discover that the guides whom
we are following are leading us astray from the ways
of God.

Yet the practice of even such obedience as this
has its attractions. The theory was framed by men
who well understood human nature; and there has
been no want of men to adopt it in its most slavish
extent. Many of us are apt to take for granted that
the happiest thing is to be self-governed, and to be
subject to no control; but if we look to the opinions
of the bulk of mankind, including both sexes, we
shall find that the vast majority are of the opposite
opinion. They show that they feel that the happiest
thing is to be well governed; to be able to lean on

some intellect which they can respect; to be able to look up to some authority, of the wisdom of whose decisions they can have no doubt, and which shall relieve them from the anxiety of doubt and the terrible weight of responsibility. We recognize in this the natural sanction which God has attached to His law of obedience; and if this pleasure, with which by His ordinance obedience is accompanied, has led men to the excess of obeying where they ought not, it is only in analogy with what takes place in other cases. Our Creator, in His goodness and benevolence, has attached pleasure as a natural sanction to those laws which are necessary for our preservation; and His goodness in so doing is not impeached, because men often, for the sake of this pleasure, indulge their appetites in an excessive and injurious degree.

I have now endeavoured to state some of the limitations with which the command in the text is to be understood. Let me, in conclusion, recommend the command itself to your prayerful consideration and self-examination; that wherever God in His providence has in any way made you subject to authority, you may endeavour, as in His sight, cheerfully to comply with all its lawful demands; with good-will doing service as to the Lord, and not to men.

o

SERMON XI.

THE YOUNG RULER.

"And behold, one came and said unto Him, Good Master, what good thing shall I do, that I may have eternal life? And He said unto him, Why callest thou me good? there is none good but one, that is God; but if thou wilt enter into life, keep the commandments. He saith unto Him, Which? Jesus said, Thou shalt do no murder, thou shalt not commit adultery, thou shalt not steal, thou shalt not bear false witness, honour thy father and thy mother; and, thou shalt love thy neighbour as thyself. The young man saith unto Him, All these have I kept from my youth up; what lack I yet? Jesus saith unto him, If thou wilt be perfect, go and sell that thou hast, and give to the poor, and thou shalt have treasure in heaven, and come and follow me. But when the young man heard that saying, he went away sorrowful; for he had great possessions."—MATTHEW xix. 16-22.

WHEN we read in St. Matthew's Gospel, that our Lord, walking by the Sea of Galilee, saw first Peter and Andrew, then James and John, engaged with their nets, that He commanded them to follow Him, and that they straightway forsook all and followed Him, our first impression is, that those whom He personally called by His voice, were enforced to obey the calling in some way different from His manner of dealing with those whom He now calls by His

Spirit. In St. Matthew's brief account we are not told of any previous knowledge of our Lord possessed by these disciples, and it seems like a miracle, that they should give up every thing on the summons of a stranger. But from St. John's fuller account of this early part of our Lord's history, we learn that the disciples had heard Him described by John the Baptist as the Lamb of God which taketh away the sin of the world; and had received his testimony that the descent of the Holy Spirit had marked Him out as him who was to baptize with the Holy Ghost. On John's testimony they had joined themselves to Jesus, had accompanied Him in His journey from the Jordan to Cana of Galilee, had seen His first miracle; and it was not until after all this gracious training that He gave them His command to follow Him, and become fishers of men. In the case of others, the command to follow our Lord was not obeyed without a struggle. One asked permission first to bury his father; another, first to bid farewell to those of his own house. In the history read as my text, the invitation was actually refused. Thus the things written aforetime are written for our learning, inasmuch as the dispensation, the history of which is recorded, does not wholly differ in kind from that under which we live. Then, as now, the constraining love of Christ drew some after it without a struggle; some after hesitation; some decided to embrace this present world, though casting regretful eyes on the higher path which they abandoned; others seemed unable to lift their eyes at all above the things of earth.

When we compare the accounts given by the Evangelists of any history which they all relate, we almost always find reason to see what a mistake there is in the popular notion which regards Mark's Gospel as a mere abridgment of Matthew's or Luke's. It will almost always be found on examination that Mark throws in some vivid touches peculiar to himself, which clearly show that we have the testimony of an eye-witness (most probably, according to early tradition, of St. Peter) to things which he himself beheld. In this story, for example, St. Matthew says, " Behold one came and said to our Lord ; " St. Luke says, " A certain ruler asked our Lord ;" but Mark says, " When He was gone forth into the way, there came one running, and kneeled to Him, and asked Him." St. Mark brings vividly before our eyes the picture of our Lord going along, followed by His disciples, and this young ruler coming running up, and kneeling down before our Lord, earnestly imploring His answer to his question. St. Mark again alone tells the look of love that Jesus cast upon him— " Jesus beholding him, loved him." This is one of several occasions in which St. Mark records the very look and feelings of Jesus. A little further on in this same story, we are told, Jesus looked round about and saith to His disciples, " How hardly shall they that have riches enter into the kingdom of God." Once more in this history St. Mark tells with peculiar vividness the astonishment of the disciples at our Lord's words. He had said that the disciples were astonished at His words. Then Jesus repeats, " It is easier for a camel to enter into the eye of a needle, than for a rich man to enter into the kingdom of God," and St. Mark repeats, "They were astonished out of measure, saying, Who then can be saved?"

In the history before us, we have the testimony of Origen that according to his copies there was a difference between the story as told by Matthew, and by Mark and Luke; a difference still to be found in our most ancient manuscripts, but which has disappeared in the great mass of modern manuscripts, and consequently in the authorized version. It is a common thing for differences between the Gospels to disappear in the process of transcription; for the copyist, writing from memory, without carefully looking at the page before him, was often in danger of substituting for the words of the Evangelist he was copying the familiar language of another. In the present case, whereas, according to our authorized version, all the Evangelists agree in making the question to be—"Good Master, what shall I do that I may obtain eternal life?" and our Lord's answer—"Why callest thou me good? there is none good but one, that is God," according to the old manuscripts and the report of Origen, Matthew, differing from the rest, gives the question—"Master, What good thing shall I do that I may obtain eternal life?" and the answer—"Why askest thou me about a good thing, there is none good but one." We might suppose this form to be a designed alteration made by some copyist who stumbled at the apparent impeachment of the doctrine of our Lord's Divinity contained in the common form. Yet as there is no reason why a designed alteration should be made in St. Matthew's

Gospel and not in the rest, or why the later transcribers should not be as jealous for their Lord's Divinity as the earlier, the best critics, bearing in mind the tendency of copyists of which I spoke, accept the reading attested by Origen as the genuine one. I think the recovery of this somewhat fuller account of what our Lord said throws light on the difficulty which many of us have felt, why should our Lord seemingly go out of His way to disclaim a title which was His right? "Good Master," said the young ruler. Well, no doubt, he did not know all the reasons why Jesus deserved that appellation; but still He was a good Master, and we should have thought that our Lord might have accepted the title, and gone on to answer his question, how he should have eternal life. But we see the question was—"Good Master, what good thing shall I do?" In other words, he excessively admired Jesus as a man of great virtue and goodness, and having, as the rest of the story proves, confidence in his own fulfilment of the law, he wants to know by what work of surpassing goodness he may merit eternal life. Thus, the very first thing our Lord sees necessary to do is to correct his whole notion of goodness. "Take heed what thou doest when thou ascribest goodness to me, or when thou speakest of goodness in thyself. There is but One good, by walking through whose grace in the ways of holiness eternal life may be obtained."

I see nothing to forbid us to think it possible that this young ruler may have been like the son in the parable who, when ordered to work in his father's vineyard at first refused, but afterwards repented and

went. Certainly the words spoken to him by our
Lord on this occasion were calculated, when pondered
on, to teach him what he was himself and what
was the Master who spoke to him. Was he good?
He thought so when he came to Jesus; he relied
that all the commandments he had kept from his
youth up. Could he think so still, when he went
away sorrowful, his conscience pointing one way, his
will leading him another; clearly seeing his duty to
follow Christ, yet unable to part with the possessions
that he showed he loved better than Christ. Thus
in his case God's Spirit did its work to convince of
sin.

But was Jesus good? Who convicted Him of sin?
as He Himself was able to challenge His enemies to
say. Nay, the more He was known, the more thorough intimacy any gained with His spotless purity,
the deeper the conviction that He was good, as no
other man was. Then comes the question, there is
none good but God: Jesus is good: Who is Jesus?
Certain it is that those who hold our Lord to be only
man, do not deny that He was a good man; good
with a kind of goodness of which there is no other
example. And the question is, whether this acknowledgment does not force them to go a step further.
Christ refuses to be recognized as a good master; to
be singled out from men on account of His pre-emi-
nence in piety and virtue. Is it not that He is good
because He is one with Him from whom all goodness
cometh, and His people good only by being one with
Him. Thus, and not by any good act of theirs, can
they inherit eternal life.

Let us proceed to our Lord's answer to the ruler's question. We can see the frame of mind in which he asked it. He had all the pleasures riches can bestow on earth, but he wished for something more, and was anxious to inherit eternal life. He felt that he was coming to One who could tell him of it. " Lord, to whom shall we go ?" said Peter on another occasion, " Thou hast the words of eternal life." But all this time the young ruler had his own answer partially prepared. That *some* good thing which he should do would secure to him eternal life he fully believed ; all he wanted to know was what it should be. He was very far, indeed, from being able to utter such words as St. Paul afterwards spoke, " I know that in me (that is, in my flesh) dwelleth no good thing." It was necessary that he should be taught this lesson. Now the Great Physician did not deal with all in the same way ; He had different treatment for the desponding and the self-righteous, the timid and the proud, the scorned publican and the Pharisee strong in his own good opinion and in that of his neighbours. Here He uses the law, as the schoolmaster, to bring this young man to Himself, and gradually to convince him that he could not obtain eternal life in the manner he had proposed to himself. Probably, if we had endeavoured to teach such a one the same lesson, we should have told him that he was a great sinner by defect, if not by act ; that if he had kept the commandments in the letter, he had not acted up to their spirit ; that his heart was wrapped up in his wealth ; and that until he had given up his love of riches he could not enter into God's kingdom. Yet probably, too, he would have denied our charges, and gone away angry, not sorrowful.

Our Lord, by the test which could not be evaded, namely, by His command, "Sell that thou hast," forced him to make a choice between the things of earth and of heaven. And then it became evident with which his heart lay. He went away sorrowful, grieving to abandon Jesus, yet unable to resolve to part with his riches. Henceforward he disappears from the Gospel history; yet I think we are not forbidden to hope that the Saviour who loved him may have again repeated to him His command, "Follow me." The sorrow which he felt was, no doubt, real; and it may have been so lasting as to make him reconsider the wisdom of his choice. And the times were coming when his nation was to pass through bitter trials, and when the wealth of many who trusted in riches was suddenly taken from them. In the ordinary course of nature this young man would have lived on to see this time of great calamity for the Jewish people, and it may well have been that he who would not, of his own accord, give up all for Christ, may afterwards have suffered the loss of all things, and yet have found that it was love that sent the trial, and that the Lord was making good His promise to him of treasure in heaven. I scarcely think it is too bold to guess that something like this may have been the after history of one whom we are told that Jesus loved, and of whom the history shows that though, it may be, self-righteous, he was no hypocrite, but one who spoke earnestly, and really strove to keep, as he believed he had kept, God's commandments. And if it were so, it cannot be supposed that his refusal recorded in the Gospels was not sufficiently punished. If afterwards he came to know Jesus, not as a good Master, a holy and virtuous man, but as very God manifest in the flesh, the Lord of life walking incarnate among men, what could ever afterwards in this life repay him for the loss he had inflicted on himself? He might have been His chosen companion, His loved friend, might have dwelt and companied with Him, heard all the wisdom of His teaching, seen to the full His example, might have given Him his sympathy in His sufferings; and he had refused. So sad would be such a thought for any man to carry with him during all his life on earth, that I the more like to think he was not for ever separated from our Lord.

In speaking of this history, it may be proper to say something as to a singular use of it made by Roman Catholic controversialists. They find here, with great ingenuity, an argument in favour of their theory of works of supererogation, an essential part of which is that men may do more to please God than they are bound to do. It is maintained that God has given men certain commands which they *must* obey in order to obtain eternal life, and that in addition He has given them certain counsels of per-fection, which they need not follow if they do not please; but by following which they will obtain a higher perfection, and so merit a higher reward. Here it is said, " Do not kill, do not commit adul-tery," are commands. " If thou wilt be perfect, sell all that thou hast and give to the poor," is a counsel which need not be followed by any one who does not aim at high perfection. But if this were the true explanation of the story, the ruler need not have gone away exceeding sorrowful. He might be cheerful enough if he had done all that was necessary to obtain eternal life, and if he were doing nothing but declining a counsel to aim at some very exalted pitch of saintliness. No, it is quite plain that what our Lord gave him was not a counsel which he might reject if he pleased, but a command. He had asked, "What must I do to inherit eternal life; what lack I yet?" It was in answer to this question that he got the answer, "If thou wilt be perfect, if thou wilt supply what is lacking, sell that thou hast." This was a command to him, to refuse obedience to which was to refuse to follow Jesus on the way that leads to eternal life. The Lord saw his heart, and knew what sign to require as showing that what filled His place in his heart had been dethroned. He would not have done more than his duty had he obeyed the command. In disobeying it he lacked, that is, he failed to fulfil a plain duty, and so was unfit for the kingdom of God. But though I think the attempt an unfortunate one, which has been made to find counsels of perfection in this passage, yet I freely acknowledge that we all make a distinction between duties which a man cannot omit without sin, and things which we highly praise him for doing, yet do not blame him for omitting; and the distinction is felt to be a real one, even if it might be difficult exactly to draw the line. Imagine that you saw an infant on a railway track where it would be certain to

be crushed by an advancing train; that you had
ample time safely to rescue it, and there was no one
else to do it; then, if you passed on and left the
child to its fate, you would be counted as a murderer
in the sight of God and man. But if the train were
so near that interference would involve the imminent
risk of your own life, you would not be blamed for
refusing to venture; and a rescue effected under these
circumstances would count not as as a simple act of
duty, but as one of, it might be, great heroism.
So that if we like to word it so, the act of interference would be in the one case a command, in the
other a counsel of perfection. All this suggests
questions which cannot be followed out without inter-
rupting the course of comment on a Scripture narrative on which I have engaged to-day; but next Sunday I hope to have an opportunity of discussing them
more fully.

After the ruler had departed, Jesus startled His
disciples by saying to them, " How hardly shall they
that have riches "—or, as He presently explains it,
they that trust in riches—" enter into the kingdom
of God :" that it was harder for a camel to enter the
eye of a needle, than for such a rich man to enter
the kingdom of God. The disciples exclaim, " Who
then can be saved ?" for they had not learned to
raise their thoughts above the hopes of a temporal
deliverer distributing rewards among his faithful
followers. This temper of theirs is seen more plainly
in the question put by Peter in the name of the rest
—" Lord, we have left all and followed thee ; what
shall we have therefore ?" We have not held back

like this young man, but have given up everything
for thy sake. What they had given up was not contemptible. James and John, we are told, were rich
enough to have hired servants helping them in their
fishing. Matthew made a great feast in his house
on the occasion of joining our Lord. At any rate,
they felt they had a right that that promise of treasure
in heaven which the young ruler had slighted, should
be repeated, and confirmed to them. In the spirit
in which St. Peter put this question, there was some
self-complacency, perhaps a proud comparison of
himself with others, which deserved blame. On the
other hand, what he claimed was only what our Lord
had promised to give. And we see Christ does not
deny or retract His promise. To those who had made
sacrifices for His sake, He promises a hundred-fold
what they had given up—father, mother, brethren,
sisters, houses, lands, with persecutions, and in the
world to come life everlasting. Yet there is a warning : not they who think that they have the best right
to claim this promise shall be the first to receive it.
There are first which shall be last, and last which
shall be first. And the parable immediately following,
which Matthew alone records—that of the Labourers
in the Vineyard—is intended to bring out this point.
Whatever promises the Lord has made He will undoubtedly fulfil. Yet they who make no bargain
with Him beforehand shall receive from His grace
and bounty not less than those who would claim
their reward as their stipulated due. It may be that
those Apostles who bore the burden and heat of the
day; who confessed Christ when He was yet, in the

eyes of the world, a man like others; who bore the
storms of persecution, and gave up all for Him—it
may be that their reward shall be no greater than
that of others, whose circumstances never called for
any sacrifice for Him, but who in the eyes of Him
who sees the heart were ready to make those sacrifices
had He demanded them. I think if you look at this
parable in connection with its context, you will see
that this is its true explanation. It is a mistake, I
think, to suppose that those who are called at the
eleventh hour can represent those who are not converted till old age. Who is there that has not
followed Christ in youth, who if asked why he stands
all the day idle, could honestly make the excuse,
" Because no man hath hired us ;" who could say,
like these men, that they had obeyed the first summons they had received, and that if they were not
working in the vineyard, it was because they had not
been called before ? No; I think the parable, when
compared with the context, is intended to teach a
different lesson. It is intended to teach the Christian
doctrine of rewards. Rewards we can never deserve
by works of ours. But Christ has promised them to
His disciples, and He has said that even a cup of
cold water given in His name shall by no means lose
its reward. But He would have us understand that
those rewards are by no means proportioned to the
amount of visible work and sacrifice which men can
see to have been made for His sake. And He gives
no encouragement to a spirit such as Peter's was
then—working for Him truly, really making sacrifices
for Him, yet thinking more of the promised reward

than of Him for whom the work is done. Another, seemingly doing much less, but working wholly from love, and not thinking of bargaining for reward, may receive a larger portion.

How faithfully Christ fulfils His promises we can see by looking at the history of those who then received a promise from Him of a return for what they had given up for Him. Not merely in the world to come, life everlasting, but in this life a hundred-fold more than they had abandoned, houses and lands, father, mother, and sisters, with persecutions. One of the first and most cruel sacrifices a Christian was then called on to make was that he must break the dearest family ties. To become a Christian was to lose the good opinion of all whom he loved. Any of you who have looked into the early Christian apologies know what was the belief common among the heathen, as to what took place at the Christian meetings. Stories were told of banquets on infants' flesh, followed by scenes of loathsome debauchery. A man who became a Christian lost the good opinion of his friends as completely as you would do by turning Mormon. He was supposed to have given in his adherence to a degrading superstition, solely in order that he might be able with less restraint to indulge in sensual excesses. In most cases, then, he who thought of embracing Christianity must count that his kinsmen after the flesh would cast him off, hate him, persecute him. And yet he must not hesitate. If he loved father, or mother, or brethren more than Christ he was not worthy of Him. He must give up earthly love, and rely for compensation on the friendship and

love of One unseen. But no sooner had he consented
to do this than he found the earthly love which he
had forsaken given back to him. Instead of the
brethren after the flesh, who had cast him off, he had
a number of Christian brethren, who loved him with
more than a kinsman's love. For even the heathen
took notice how the Christians loved one another.
They would share with him all they had, sympathize
with him in his sufferings, stand by him at the tribunal of the heathen magistrate. Instead of the
earthly father or mother whom he had lost, he had a
friend or counsellor in every aged Christian or Christian matron. If a Christian were forced to leave his
city, he found when he fled to another that he did not
come among strangers, but that he had there a host
of friends, whose resources and active help were all
at his disposal. I believe there is every reason to
think, that notwithstanding their losses from time to
time for conscience' sake, the Christians, as a whole,
were a thriving community, the energetic help which
each gave to the other, more than making up for
what the persecutions of the heathen took from them;
so that if any, counting the cost, had resolved to give
up all for Christ, and had said to himself, Henceforth
I must be alone in the world; my Saviour's love
must be to me now instead of everything else; never
more shall I know the delights of earthly affection:
he found that when he had obeyed the call, what he
had given up was restored a hundred-fold. Probably
he could say, that until he became a Christian he had
never known what brotherly love was, and that in the
cold and selfish system in which he had been brought

up, human affection had never been able to take such
growth as under that system of which brotherly kind-
ness was the rule. And what if, as often would happen, the father or mother, or brethren that were given
back were no strangers, but the very father or mother,
or brethren whom he had lost? How often would it
happen that his meekness under reproach, his patience
under persecution, would touch the hearts of the
kinsmen who had cast him off, and would force
them to see that there must be some reality in a religion which could bear such fruits. And then when
they had searched and found the same Saviour as he,
and had cast themselves into his arms, asking forgiveness for all the injuries that in the times of their
ignorance they had done him, how he would feel
that Christ had faithfully kept His promise, and that
the father or brother in Christ was a hundred-fold
more a father or brother than when merely united
to him by the bonds of earthly relationship.

So, looking back on it now, we can see that our
Lord's promise was kept, even that which seemed
hardest to fulfil ; namely, to compensate in this life
those who in times of severe persecution were giving
up all for Him. It was an Apostle who regarded not
the loss of all things, but counted them as dung,
that he might win Christ, who yet was also able to
report that godliness is profitable for all things, having promise of the life that now is, as well as of that
which is to come.

If we look back now on the choice about which that
young ruler was hesitating ; and if we think not of the
treasure in heaven, but merely ask which course

P

promised him most happiness in this life, I think we
can have no doubt as to the answer. Whether would he
be the happier with his treasure in this world, where
" rust and moth doth corrupt," and where " thieves
break through and steal ;" and at a time when, as
we now know, riches were exposed to more than their
usual uncertainties, and when it is doubtful how long
he could retain those great possessions on which his
heart was set ; *or* if he had exchanged these for a
treasure which could not be taken from him, and cast
in his lot with Him who could compensate him for
the loss of all besides ? 'And we may well trust that
when He says to us, " Follow me," we too shall find
our happiness in obeying His call. It is not for us
to calculate if we give up this or that for Christ,
what shall we have therefore.   But if we follow Him
in faith, we may be assured that even though He lead
us through fire and through water, He will bring us
out into a wealthy place.

   In truth, it seems unreal now to speak of making
sacrifices for Christ.   We can understand what is
meant by men in the Apostles' days taking up their
cross and following Christ.   But now nothing can be
easier than, in the world's opinion, to establish a
claim to the future enjoyment of eternal bliss.   The
good, easy man who quietly drifts down the course of
this world's business and pleasures, (if he have obeyed
the impulses of his own amiable heart in abstaining
from all the more hateful vices, and if he have not
outraged society by any profane contempt of the
national religion,) may, in the world's opinion, full
surely count on a happy immortality.   His obedience

has cost him no sacrifice. He has made no toilsome exertions to run his Christian course, yet he is judged worthy of the prize of successful exertion, and without a contest puts on the crown of victory. I pray you, brethren, each to try yourselves by a more severe standard than that which in charity we apply to others. Still does Christ call on us to deny ourselves for His sake; a call to which the season on which we have entered directs our special attention. He may not call on us for one great act of sacrifice as He did the young man, with the command, " Sell that thou hast ;" but His Apostle, in his direction to the Corinthians, does not tell them to sell all, but weekly to lay by them in store, as God has prospered them ; thus prescribing, as the rule for Christians, an habitual, self-denying forethought. The precept given to this young man was an application of the general principle, " If thy hand offend thee, cut it off and cast it from thee"—a principle to be applied by each of us to our besetting sins. Is it indolence or love of amusement which is making us frivolous and unfit for holy thoughts, then we must cut off what in the case of others would be innocent as that which cannot be harmlessly enjoyed by us. And, in like manner, whatever else our temptations may be. With one it may be to avarice, over-carefulness for the things of this life, fretting anxiety for the future ; with another it may be to waste and extravagance ; with another to impurity ; with another to harsh judgment and evil speaking ; with another to tyranny and selfish disregard of others. Each besetting sin must be given up, whatever it may be, if we would faithfully follow Jesus. He has called us to follow Him, and we must cast off every weight that would keep us back from doing so. That is the broad principle which we must each adapt to his own case. Ask for Christ's Spirit to guide you, and show you the way in which you ought to follow Him; and ask the same Spirit to make you willing to break through every hindrance that would keep you back from following Him, and then you will find that the path along which He leads you will have the same termination for you as for Him, and that if you be partakers of His sufferings, you shall be also sharers of His glory.

SERMON XII.

COUNSELS OF PERFECTION.

"And Jesus answering said, A certain man went down from Jerusalem to Jericho, and fell among thieves, which stripped him of his raiment, and wounded him, and departed, leaving him half dead. And by chance there came down a certain priest that way, and when he saw him, he passed by on the other side. And likewise a Levite, when he was at the place, came and looked on him, and passed by on the other side."—LUKE x. 30-32.

On last Sunday I illustrated the difference between commands and counsels of perfection, by supposing the case of a child in danger of being crushed by an advancing railway train; then, according to the amount of risk involved in an attempt at rescue, and the probability of making the attempt with success, interference might either be a thing which could not be omitted without barbarous inhumanity, or the omission might be excusable, or the attempt at rescue might be highly heroic, or it might be culpable rashness. In reading this parable of the good Samaritan, most persons think of the act of the priest and Levite as one of the first kind, the omission from sheer inhumanity of a simple act of duty; and in so judging

of the case, they lose some of the practical lessons
which the parable teaches ; for of inhumanity such as
this they feel they never could be guilty. I think
nothing forbids us to think of that priest and Levite
as conscientious men, who fully acknowledged the
duty that lay on them to love their neighbour as
themselves, and were not at all aware that they were
overlooking any obligation which that duty imposed
on them. If they had been called on to give any
help to another man, which it seemed to them that
it was their business to give, for all that appears in
the story, they would have given it. In the case
actually represented, I suppose they would have ac-
quitted themselves of all blame, by reflecting that
this man was not their neighbour ; or, in other
words, that the case was one in which it was not
their business to interfere. What was the case ?
They were hurrying along a dangerous road, one well
known to be infested with robbers. They see cast by
the side of the road, what would seem to be the
naked corpse of some victim of a previous robbery
and assassination. We are told that this man had
been stripped and wounded and left half dead ; and
it is likely that his body presented to a hasty passer-
by little signs of life. It does not seem very unnatural then, nor perhaps unpardonable, if travellers
coming after him on the same road, thought less of
him than of themselves. They might exclaim,
" Here has been another assassination ; see where
these robbers have been at work again ; let us lose
no time in hastening past this dangerous part of the
road, and getting into a place of safety." If the

thought occurred to them, perhaps this man is not already dead, perhaps he may stand in need of succour, they might quiet their conscience with the thought that, in all probability, it was now too late to give effectual help to one so far gone ; or that to be of any real use to him would require an amount of trouble and time which it was quite impossible they could give, and that in any case it was no business of theirs. And so they passed on. We have read in tales of shipwreck something of the torture of disappointed hope. We have read of the joy spread among the survivors of some disaster, when, after having for days endured hunger and heat and thirst, they see from their little raft an approaching sail, and imagine their signals have been observed, and feel sure that relief is at hand ; and then of the agony when their hope changes into despair, as the ship proceeds on its course without seeming to have perceived them, and as they watch its receding sails, until at last, as far as their eye can range along their horizon, they find themselves in hopeless solitude. And we may fancy that something of the same kind was the disappointment of this wounded traveller, each time that the tramp of the approaching beasts gave him hope that succour was nigh, as the noise passed on and died away, and left him abandoned. Our Lord represents him from whom succour eventually came as a Samaritan ; one with whom the Jews held no dealings ; one, therefore, who had a better right than others to say that the wounded traveller was no neighbour of his, and that it was not his business to help one whom his own countrymen neglected. But you see this man showed that he alone understood the meaning of the command to love his neighbour as himself, who made that *his* business, which did not seem to concern him more than others; who regarded not the difference between Jew and Samaritan; who regarded not the trouble, nor cost, nor delay, nor danger to himself, but only saw that there was a fellow-creature hanging between life and death, and resolved, at whatever sacrifice to himself, to remain to help him.

I have no doubt that if the priest and the Levite could have seen the sufferer relieved by one on whom he had claims far less strong than on themselves, their duty would have struck them in quite a new light, and they would have owned with shame that he whom they had neglected to help *was* their neighbour. Has it never happened to any of you to ask yourselves whether it was your duty to do something not quite agreeable to you; and when you had come to the indolent or self-indulgent decision that it was a thing you were not obliged to do, to be shamed at seeing the work that you were refusing to do performed by some one of whom you must own that it was less his business than yours? It might be a case exactly parallel to that described in the text, where you happened to be brought into the close neighbourhood of bodily suffering, and you held back from offering your aid because you feared that the sacrifices the effort would impose on yourself were more than you would like to undertake, and because it seemed that the matter did not closely enough concern you; or it might be a case of bereavement, where an afflicted family needed comfort and sympathy, or perhaps other active help; or it might be merely some common little acts of neighbourly courtesy which were needed, and from which you held back because they would be troublesome, and because it did not seem that you were actually obliged to offer them; or it might be that wrong words were spoken, or wrong things done in your presence, against which it was a Christian duty that a protest should be made, but where you decided that it was not incumbent on you to speak. In all such cases if, while we are hesitating, and (what comes practically to the same thing as refusing,) by our delays, neglecting to act, we hear the right word spoken, or see the right thing done by some one else not more bound to do it than ourselves, how quickly a new view of our duty flashes on us. There are many little obligations which no one has a right to compel us to fulfil; little duties of which we must ourselves be the judge, and very self-indulgent judges we often are. In such cases it is often the sight of the unselfishness of others, and the very different spirit in which they judge what they are bound to do, which teaches us to distrust the judgment we had given in our own case, and makes us submit it to further deliberation.

After the experience of a few instances of the kind of which I have been speaking, where things which had once seemed to us not duties incumbent on us, as our consciences become more enlightened, are felt to be what cannot be neglected without sin, we perceive, I think, how hard it is to draw any definite line separating duties and counsels of perfection. Compare

our modern philanthropy with that of past times,
and how many things are there which we regard as
plain duties to be performed for the benefit of their
poor neighbours by those to whom God has given
wealth, which in former days were not dreamed of,
and which one who should then have fulfilled, would
be regarded as going much out of his way. There
was a time when the rich and noble scarce looked on
themselves as beings of the same race as the low-
born poor. In battle the fate of the knightly anta-
gonist was marked with sympathy and respect, but
scarce any heed was taken how many of the rascal
scum were swept away. At home who thought it his
business to mind in what hovels they dwelt, what
food they ate, to what seeds of disease they were exposed ? If the poor were not patient and submissive
in their misery, they were sternly repressed by law.
For sixty years the law of England punished an able-
bodied beggar with whipping at the cart's tail for the
first offence, with mutilation for the second, with
death for the third. Down to almost living memory
offences against property were visited with merciless
severity. I need not repeat the well-known story of
the starving wife of an impressed sailor, put to death
because she had taken up and immediately laid down
again a piece of goods on a shop counter. In reading
of some of the severities of law in former days, I am
less startled by the coarse jesting with which some of
the unfeeling carried out their work than by the
kindly tone of humane judges. They seem to have
felt towards the condemned as we might towards men
whose limbs had been entangled by some powerful

machinery; pitying their fate, yet never dreaming that in the course of nature things could be otherwise. Everyone has heard what prisons were before Howard's time—seminaries of crime and disease, for the horrors of which no one felt himself responsible, and no one thought it his business to reform. Amiable, good, pious men made their fortunes by the slave trade, and never suspected that their money came from a polluted source. It was after his conversion John Newton acted as supercargo of a slaver, and knew not that his employment was work unfit for a Christian man. How slowly it dawned on the minds of the English nation that we owe duties to the souls of the Africans whom we carried from their own lands, or of the natives of the countries which we have colonized. In our own time almost has it been acknowledged that exertion should be made for the religious enlightenment of heathen who were not by God's providence made our spiritual charge. The Society for the Propagation of the Gospel, whose special field is the colonies of Great Britain, dates only from the time of William the Third; the Church Missionary Society, which undertakes completely foreign missions, was founded in our own century.

When I thus point to duties which we acknowledge, and which our fathers overlooked, it is not in order to make you think with complacency how much we are better than our fathers. Very probably our descendants may be able to point with equal wonder to the blindness of this generation to duties which will then appear obvious. My object has been rather to show the difficulty of drawing a definite line between commands and counsels of perfection., A man may seem in his time to be following out a counsel of perfection, who is in truth only quick-sighted to perceive a duty which his generation is neglecting. Not one word would I say in diminution of the praise and honour to which such a man is entitled; but if a theological theory is built on the assumption that he has done something with regard to which God has given no command, to that I must take exception. Who could more be said to have followed out a counsel of perfection than Howard, when he made that his business which was not his more than another's, and devoted to the relief of the sufferings of prisoners his labour, his fortune, his health, his life. Yet if it be said that it was no duty to make exertions for the relief of such misery as that which he encountered, we have only to ask ourselves should we not each think it a personal reproach if we knew of the present existence of evils such as he exposed, and if we stirred no hand to remove them? The exertion would cost us less than it did him, because thousands of ardent helpers would now join in the work at which he laboured single-handed. And similarly it may be said of others, whom we know as having undertaken extraordinary toils for the good of men's souls or bodies, that it is not so much that they have gone beyond God's commands, as that they have understood better than others what is meant by these two great commands, " Thou shalt love the Lord thy God with all thy mind, and all thy heart, and all thy soul, and, Thou shalt love thy neighbour as thyself." I am sure these men themselves would be the first to own that when they had done all, they were still unprofitable servants—they had done no more than was their duty to do. We claim no merit to ourselves because we recognize and act on duties which men wiser and better than ourselves in former days, as Sir Thomas More, Sir Matthew Hale, did not perceive. Now that God has opened our eyes to see more plainly the answer to that question—" Who is my neighbour ? " we feel, that however neglect might be pardonable in others with less light, we cannot without sin act otherwise. Surely, if we in any degree comprehend the depth and width of these two great commandments which I have quoted, we must own that there is no act of love towards God or towards man that is not included in the command ; and any attempt to measure the extent of that command forces from us the exclamation, " Who then can be saved ? " Nay, by merit of ours none can. Yet we know that we have to deal with a merciful and gracious Judge, who by His blood has purchased pardon for our sins of omission as well as of commission, for our neglects as well as for our trespasses—for those secret sins into which we fall from the bluntness of moral apprehension, as well as those presumptuous sins which we commit in defiance of greater light. And they who have done more than others—who have taken upon themselves the duties which their brethren were neglecting as well as their own—shall doubtless find that nothing which they have done for Christ's sake has been forgotten by Him. We shrink from the word merit, as used by men towards God with reference to works,

the best of which, no doubt, are tainted with imperfection ; but it is quite scriptural to speak of rewards,
inasmuch as Christ has promised them to the most
trifling service performed for His sake, and has said
that even a cup of cold water given in His name
shall not lose its reward. We may fully believe,
therefore, that those whose pre-eminent self-denying
labours in the cause of Christ have been honoured by
the love and praise of saints on earth, have also not
been unmarked in heaven. Nay, how could it be
otherwise ? Is not the love of Christ a thing which
inevitably brings its reward with it ? Must it not be
that in proportion as a man has given his heart and
soul in love to God, so is he capable of knowing the
love of Christ which passeth knowledge, and of being
filled with all the fulness of God ; so is he capable
of feeling and appreciating those pleasures which
God bestows on them that love Him ? We may well
believe, then, that in the day when " they that be
wise shall shine as the brightness of the firmament,
and they that turn many to righteousness as the stars
for ever and ever," it will be found also that one star
shall differ from another star in glory.

I was led last Sunday incidentally to speak of
counsels of perfection, because the mention of them
was suggested by a passage, of which a well-known
controversial use has been made. And I, perhaps, gave
you reason to expect that I would to-day discuss the
question controversially, and shew that Scripture
does not really warrant the consequences that have
been drawn from it. Yet it seems to me now that it
would be unprofitable to spend time in any detailed

refutation of a system so artificial, that were I to try to drag it out of the schools, and present it before you here, it would drop to pieces in the handling. The whole object of maintaining that some men may do something over and above what God commands, is in order to establish also, that the efficacy of their super-erogatory works can be transferred from the doers to others. Yet, if we admit to the full, that some have been enlightened by God's Spirit to see duties to which their contemporaries have been blind ; that God has given them the will to take on themselves work to which they were not more bound than others ; for the sake of the fulfilment of it to deny themselves com-forts, which they might lawfully have enjoyed ; and if we admit, too, that God not only found means by His love to compensate them richly in this life for what they had given up for Him, but that He is also their everlasting portion ; still how is all this con-sistent with the notion of transfer ? If they whom God has more abundantly filled with His love, are, perhaps, from some special act of God's, but certainly from the constitution which He has imprinted on the nature of things, capable of enjoying in greater fulness those good things which He has prepared for those that love Him, are we to turn about and say this is not so, such men enjoy no greater happiness ; suffi-cient for them be such merit as is enough to gain admission to heaven—let anything, over and above, be transferred to others? But an assertion so contra-dictory as this to all the arguments on which it has been founded is made by no one : the merits, as they are called, of the saints, are confessed to be in their nature untransferable. But it is said that it is God's ordinance that every Christian man should, by a certain amount of pain and suffering, in some degree make up to God's honour, the affront it has suffered by his sins, and that every good work has a double efficacy; by its merit deserving eternal reward, by whatever pain and labour it has cost making satisfaction for sin. And it is said, that though merits cannot be transferred, satisfactions may; that a saint may keep all the merit of his good works, and receive an eternal reward in proportion to them, and at the same time transfer the satisfactions of these works over and above what were necessary for himself to the score of some other person paying in purgatory the satisfactions which he had failed during his earthly life to pay. The highly artificial character of this theory seems to make it as needless as it is unsuitable to discuss it here. It certainly has not the smallest connection with the difficulty which has come under our consideration. That difficulty may be stated thus. Is it the duty of every man to give up all the comforts of home, and go out as a missionary, or in some other way endure as much toil and privation, and suffering, for the Gospel's sake, as St. Paul did? Do we sin who neglect to make any such sacrifices? If we do not, did not St. Paul, and such as he, do something over and above his duty, for which he may justly claim a higher reward than others? Well, suppose we granted that he did, what justification would this give to a theory which proposes that he should be paid twice over, not only receive the reward of his labours himself, but also transfer the benefit of

them to others.   It is to be judged that this method
of applying the good works of saints to relieve the
sufferings of sinners in purgatory, is nothing but a
fictitious remedy for a fictitious disease.

But, in truth, the subject which has come before
us to-day is one which it is more important to discuss
practically than controversially.   It was surely not in
order to cast odium on the ruling classes of His time
that our Lord represented in the parable the priest
and the Levite as passing by on the other side.   By
making a Samaritan the repairer of their neglect, he
shewed that his object was not to array one class of
Jews against another, but rather to force all Jews,
even those most in esteem for piety and virtue, to ask
themselves did they fully understand the extent of
that command, "Thou shalt love thy neighbour as
thyself;" and did they in their practice carry it out as
it ought to be done?   I have tried to shew that the
neglect of duty, for which the names of the priest
and Levite in this parable have become a by-word,
did not necessarily imply any extraordinary hardness
of heart, and that their case rather illustrates that
slowness to recognize obligations not strongly enforced
by law or by public opinion, of which our own consciences must frequently condemn us.   I have reminded you of instances of neglect in past days which
shock us now, but which scandalised nobody then.
For, both to the eye of the body and of the mind, it
constantly happens that there are things which are
easily overlooked, which are even hard to see, but which
when they have been pointed out to us, and we are
once able clearly to distinguish them, ever after appear

Q

to us so plain that it seems amazing any could cast a glance without taking notice of them. Surely, it would be absurd to flatter ourselves that we are so clear-sighted now that none of our duties escape our observation, and that the men of this generation need not fear that their descendants should ever wonder at *their* strange blindness.

Certainly the men of this world would much prefer that those who pay attention to neglected duties, should profess to follow not duties but counsels of perfection. If such persons would only own that they are treading on paths where they do not ask others to follow them, they would find favour enough with the world, which likes to have saints as objects of admiration, not imitation. But if they profess that the things they undertake are obligations binding on every Christian man, they cast a reproach on others, and at once provoke opposition. It is not inappropriate to refer to the objections which have been urged against Christian missions. Many of them do, in fact, resolve themselves into this, that the precept to love our neighbour as ourself, cannot possibly apply to men who live so far away, and who have habits and manners so different from ours, and even (for no topic of ridicule has been more effective) who call their hamlets by such uncouth names as those by which the people of Africa absurdly designate their villages. Then it is urged that, if we take an interest in the welfare of a people so far away, our neighbours at home must suffer. I believe exactly the reverse is the truth, and that those whose sympathies are quick enough to be touched by distant claims, will also be affected in the most lively way, and be the most ready to respond to calls nearer home. At all events, the parable we have been considering has taught us, when a call for help is made us, not to delay till we have satisfied ourselves, Is the sufferer our neighbour? Is it our business in particular to help? Is there no one else on whom he has stronger claims than he has on us? True Christian sympathy and love will often make that our business which before had seemed to be anybody's business. True Christian love will discover opportunities of usefulness and means of promoting God's glory, which one, who has not His cause at heart, will overlook.

Brethren, if you wish to be sharp-sighted in such matters, the method is willingly to obey any call to do God's work which presents itself. For every time you decide that you need not do something which your conscience tells you that you ought to do, you make it less likely that the thought should occur to you again. But on the contrary, ready obedience to what you feel to be God's commands will make you quick to hear His voice speaking to you again. And the Holy Spirit, who alone can give you the will to work for Him, will also open your eyes to know the wondrous things of God's law, to understand the value of the privileges He bestows on you, to recognize the opportunities He presents to you of promoting His glory. And if, as I said, nothing shames us more out of our indolence and selfishness than the example of others, who, without hesitation, fulfil the duties from which we are inclined to shrink; so there is no means which the Holy Spirit is wont to employ more successfully in subduing our selfish love of ease than the example of Him who pleased not Himself, whose whole earthly life was one of self-sacrifice, terminated by that crowning sacrifice, in which He freely gave His own life for us, that we might live through Him. May God make us to live the life of Christ on earth, and so make us conformed to His example here, that we may be with Him hereafter in His glory.

SERMON XIII.

CERTAINTY.

"That thou mightest know the certainty of those things wherein thou hast been instructed."– LUKE i. 4.

IN the words I have read you will have recognized part of the well-known preface of St. Luke's Gospel, in which the Evangelist declares his object in writing to be, that his disciple might not be dependent for his knowledge of the great facts of the Saviour's life on the accounts, oral or written, of men not entitled to speak with authority, but might have a trustworthy record of the testimony delivered by those who had been from the beginning eye-witnesses and ministers of the Word.

In St. Luke's history of the preaching of the Apostles.he gives especial prominence to their office as witnesses of Christ. He describes the capacity to bear this witness as the qualification required for election to the Apostolate. More than once in the specimens of the Apostles' preaching which he has preserved, they attest that they had seen the Saviour many days after His resurrection; that they had eaten and drunk with Him after He had risen from the dead. You will remember also the language in which another Apostle claims to have personal knowledge of the things of which he writes. " That which we have heard, which we have seen with our eyes, which we have looked upon, and our hands have handled of the Word of life; that which we have seen and heard declare we unto you."

The facts thus delivered by men whose sincerity it was impossible to doubt, and who professed to speak from personal knowledge, were received by the first generation of converts with the undoubting confidence with which first-class human testimony is accepted. Convinced by these facts that Jesus was the bearer of a Divine revelation, they accepted with equal confidence His assurance of a future resurrection, of which His own resurrection had been the earnest. And so the most striking and attractive feature of the new religion was, that it offered a certain knowledge of the true solution of great problems, concerning which men elsewhere were hopelessly perplexed. I speak of those great questions, the most important which man can put : Is there a Supreme Being who cares for man, and in whose wisdom and goodness man may confide ? Is there an after-life and a retribution ? Is there forgiveness of sins with God ? At the time when Christianity was published the old traditional answers which heathenism gave to these questions had been worn out. The poets' tales of subterranean realms, of Styx and its frogs, of Charon and the single boat in which so many thousands of souls must daily cross, were discredited by boys as

soon as they came to be old enough to be chargeable
for admission to the public baths. Educated men
regarded it as an insult to their understanding if they
were deemed capable of believing these portentous fic-
tions of poets and of painters. But philosophy, which
swept away the religion of the vulgar, had nothing
wherewith to replace it. It either frankly declared
that men had nothing to hope for beyond the grave,
and had no reason to count on protection or sympathy
from any deity here; or if it ventured to speak in
more hopeful accents, did so with such tremulous
uncertainty that it won no confidence. At such a
time one of the things by which an inquiring heathen
was most struck in Christianity was the tone of assured conviction in which its professors spoke. Their
confidence might be well or ill-founded, but it was
an undoubted fact that, while all else was perplexity,
there were thousands who declared that their feet
had found sure standing-ground in the drifting waters
of religious opinion, and who called to all around to
plant their feet on the firm rock on which they stood.
A lively picture of the attraction which such an invitation offered is presented in a work probably written
about the end of the second century, which, though
a fiction, is clearly one drawn from real life in the
representation it gives of the agonies of doubt and
disappointment suffered by a sincere inquirer for
truth before he at length found refuge in the sure
haven of the soul. "From my youth," says the
writer, "I was exercised with doubts which had
found an entrance into my soul, I know not how—
Will my being end with death? Will the boundless-

ness of time in the end consign all things to oblivion
and silence; so that not only we shall cease to be,
but there shall be no remembrance that we have ever
been? When was the world created, and what was
there before the world? If it has always existed,
will it continue to last for ever? If it had a beginning, will it likewise have an end? And after the
end of the world, what then? The silence of the
grave, or something else of which we can form no
notion? Haunted by such thoughts as these, which
came I know not whence, I was sorely troubled in
spirit; I grew pale, and wasted away. When I strove
to drive them from me, they returned again and
again with increased violence, so that I suffered
greatly. I knew not that in these very thoughts I
enjoyed a friendly companion guiding me to eternal
life, not allowing me to rest till I had found it. But
while thus perplexed, I ran to the schools of the philosophers, hoping to find a foundation on which I
could rest in safety; but nought could I see but the
building up and tearing down of theories, nought but
endless disputes and contradictions. Sometimes, for
example, the demonstration prevailed of the soul's
immortality, then again of its mortality. When the
one prevailed, I was happy; when the other, I went
away sorrowful. But neither doctrine had the power
of truth over my heart. I was tossed to and fro by
contending arguments, and forced to the conclusion
that opinions were accounted true, not from their
accordance with the truth of fact, but from the ability of those who maintained them. I grew dizzier
than ever. I could neither lay hold on any of those

things which were spoken as firmly established, nor
yet was I able to lay aside the desire of inquiry ; but
ever when I would shake it off it recurred with greater
force." It were tedious to pursue the story; but you can
easily conceive the contrast which the enquirer found
between the doubtful utterances and uncertain gro-
pings of a blind philosophy, and the steadfast belief
of the Christian teachers who claimed to walk in the
light of God's truth.

They had many opportunities of showing that
their conviction was not an assumed confidence.
All the power of the rulers of the world was exerted to wrest their faith from them. Nay, they
might keep their faith if they would but dissemble
it. Some trifling compliance, and they were free ;
to cast a few grains of incense into the fire, to
swear by the fortune of Cæsar ; but rather than do
aught inconsistent with their Christian name, they
preferred the dark stifling dungeon, the rack, the
wild beasts, the hot iron chair. The genuine records
of their martyrdoms are not scanty ; and one feature
is common to them all, that to the sufferers the unseen world is a greater reality than the things of
sense. To use the words of one of those early
documents, " they were eager to put off this light, in
order that, at the Lord's command, they might pass
to the brightness of the eternal dwellings of salvation;
for they preferred the true to the false, the heavenly
to the earthly, the eternal to the perishable. By the
suffering of one hour, they gained a joy which never
should decay." In their struggles, too, they felt that
they were contending against an unseen enemy, and

that they had unseen support. A favourite thought
with them was, that it was not so much that they
were enduring man's cruelty, as that they were
champions chosen by Christ to combat for Him under
His eye against Satan in person. They triumphed
in declaring that they were trampling under foot the
head of the dragon, whose malice had stirred up the
wrath of man against them. And they owned the
present support of Him for whom they fought. As
the spectators of some of their martyrdoms write,
"They made it evident to all, that in the midst of
those sufferings they were absent from the body, or
rather that the Lord stood by them and walked in
the midst of them." Repeatedly those histories exhibit how an overpowering idea can confer absolute
unconsciousness of bodily suffering. A delicate woman, when torn by a savage beast, showed indeed
her sense of what was passing, by re-arranging her
torn raiment, by knotting up her fallen hair, lest the
sign of mourning, dishevelled hair, should disfigure
the joy of her espousals; yet, when released, asked
when she was to be cast to the beast, and, until
shown on her person the marks of the conflict, could
not be persuaded that she had already undergone the
trial.

It is needless to inquire what answer would have
been given by sufferers, who showed so plainly that
to them the things of faith were greater realities than
the things of sense, if asked were they *certain* of the
truths for which they were content to give their lives?

The age of persecution passed away, and with
prosperity an age of speculation succeeded. The first

controversy related to the question, what they were
to think of the Master whom all who bore His name
agreed in worshipping. Did they pay this honour
to a creature, or to one who had existed from eternity? The Emperor, to whom the dispute appeared
unpractical, bitterly disappointed to find disunion
where he had hoped for peace, strove to silence the
controversy. But his efforts being vain, he conceived,
as he tells us, by a divine inspiration, the idea of
invoking, in order to decide the question, representatives of the whole Christian world. Thus in an
age of despotism and political inactivity, was brought
together the greatest representative assembly which
the world had yet seen.* Spectators were reminded
of the day of Pentecost by the assemblage of men
from every nation under heaven. There came scholars from Alexandria, and from the more civilized
cities of the empire; there were Copts from the desert,
hermits from the East. Outside the limits of the
empire, Persia had its representative. There was a
Scythian from the extreme North; a Spanish bishop
took a leading part in the proceedings. Among these
representatives of universal Christendom, were many
venerated for the testimony they had borne in the
then recent persecutions. A thrill went through the
assembly, as one bishop lifted up to bless them a
right hand seared by the fire. Others could show in
their bodies other marks of the Lord Jesus, marks
of stripes, an eye thrust out, a crippled leg. When
it turned out that in an assembly with such claims on

* See Stanley's "Eastern Church;" De Broglie's "*L'Église et
L'Empire Romaine.*"

the veneration of the Christian world, Arius could not muster a score of followers, and that the vast majority regarded his doctrines as offensive and blasphemous, it could not be but that in the mind of the great masses of Christians, the question was completely set at rest by the concentrated testimony of the leaders of Christian thought in every part of the empire, as to what the religion taught which they had received from their fathers. And, although the waves of controversy did not at once subside, yet, during every year that passed of the subsequent peaceful times of the Church, the authority of the men of the heroic age, which had triumphed over the last persecution, waxed greater and greater, and the decisions of the Nicene Council, ratified by subsequent acceptance, were held to be as binding as Scripture. Christians had no hesitation in ascribing to them the attribute of certainty.

After the settlement of the Arian disputes, new controversies arose in the Church on points more subtle and perplexing; and the same expedient as before — namely, the assembling of councils — was resorted to for a solution of them. But the success of this expedient was less each time that it was repeated. After each decision of a council there was a longer and longer period of struggle whether the decree should be recognized as authoritative, and more and more numerous dissentients, who ultimately withdrew, refusing to be bound by it. Take, for instance, that which is counted as the fourth of these councils, to the conclusions arrived at by which our own Church assents; and it may be said that among all the councils there was not one which had greater *prima facie* claims on the respectful submission of the Christian world. The number of bishops was at least twice as great as that which had assembled at Nicea; the decree was drawn up by one of the ablest and most energetic of the Roman Popes, the only one of them who took an effective part in determining any of the early controversies; and it was supported by all the authority of the Emperor. Yet it wholly failed to give peace to the Church. After the decision of the council, the heresy which it condemned developed itself with fresh vigour. It spread itself over the whole East, enthroned its adherents in some of the chief patriarchal sees, found support in Constantinople itself, and its prevalence was for centuries a source of perpetual weakness and of actual danger to the Empire. The West, however, was not touched by these storms, and Pope Gregory the Great only gave utterance to universal western opinion when he described the four councils as the four-square stone on which the structure of faith rises—whose decisions he received with entire devotion, with most complete approbation.

Still, however, fresh controversies arose, necessitating fresh decisions, and resulting in new separations. Actually, you are aware, the state of the Christian world is, that there is one body claiming indeed to represent the original stock, but which does not include within it half the professed disciples of Christ. In that body, by the double process of silencing of dissentients, and of expelling those who refuse to be silenced, enough of practical unanimity has been

obtained to allow of decisions being made which are
outwardly acquiesced in by all, and which, no doubt,
are also in the case of most of those who are not too
indifferent to have opinions at all, accepted with
internal assent as certain truth. Outside that body
there are a number of communions differing among
themselves, and in each of which considerable liberty
of diverse opinion is permitted ; but on some points
also holding very strong convictions, not the least
strong being the falsity of the peculiar doctrines
asserted by the Church of Rome. The intensity of
that conviction they had, through what must be pronounced a blunder on the part of their opponents,
an opportunity of testifying ; for of the Protestant
Churches, as well as of the early Christian Church,
it was true that the blood of the martyrs was the
seed. There are few who are not in some degree
affected by the strong and genuine convictions of
others ; and it was no small gain to Protestantism
that so many of its adherents exhibited by the surest
of tests that they had such unhesitating conviction of
the truth of their doctrine, that they dared not to be
false to the light that was in them ; and when offered
the alternative of tortures and death on the one side,
recantation on the other, they spurned life when to
be had only on the terms of saying one thing with
the lips, thinking another in the heart.

What I have said has been intended to prepare the
way for the consideration of the palmary argument, to
which in the present day the whole Roman Catholic
controversy has reduced itself, namely, that in that
Church alone can Christians have certainty of the

truths they are bound to believe. All other lines of argument have now been abandoned. The Roman Catholic advocates have now retired, or have been driven from the field of Scripture and of history. Indeed their own learned men have failed them. We have lately heard outcry in abundance against the pride of human learning presuming to dictate to the Church—an outcry raised, because men whom their Church had hitherto justly accounted its most distinguished ornaments, were not content to take positiveness of assertion as equivalent to proof, but ventured to attempt to verify what they were required to believe. But it is hoped now to replace the failure of all other lines of proof by the one argument to which I have referred. This argument would run somewhat thus :—The mark which, as I said in the beginning, distinguished the Christian teachers from the schools of the philosophers, was that the latter could only profess to follow probable opinions more or less doubtful, while the Christians professed to have certain knowledge of the dogmas they proclaimed. Nothing but this intense faith of its adherents could have saved the religion from being uprooted by the desperate assaults which the Roman rulers made upon it. Faith is indeed the life of, every great movement. To doubt, to balance arguments, to criticise, is the intellectual pastime of men of culture and leisure ; but if the result of the process is only negative, if the critics have only been able to destroy, not construct, if they are not capable of feeling and exciting some high enthusiasm, they have no in-fluence on the world's history. But the mass of mankind do not obtain their convictions by the process of balancing arguments—a process for which they have neither inclination nor leisure; they accept what is delivered to them by authority, and which commends itself to their feelings.*

It is urged, that where action is necessary, reasoning keeps us back from action, impressions lead us to it. To most persons argumentation makes the point in hand more doubtful, and considerably less impressive. Life is for action; to act you must assume, and that assumption is faith. It is argued then that Christ did not leave His people to depend for their knowledge of the truth of His doctrines on the slow and doubtful process of argumentation; that, on the contrary, he provided in His Church a means of teaching them with authority what they must believe; and that He bestows on them the supernatural gift of faith, enabling them to hold with perfect certainty what is delivered to them. Certainty, it is alleged, is unattainable by the Protestant method of reasoning and proof. All the arguments employed are in their nature moral, not demonstrative, and the conclusions can only be received as true with more or less probability. A Protestant may hold that it is no doubt true, with a very high degree of probability, that there is a God, and that He has sent His Son into the world; but his system renders him unable to accept these or any other propositions with the unhesitating certainty of faith. The Roman Catholic, on the other hand, receives

* The arguments quoted are taken from Dr. Newman's "Grammar of Assent."

what is delivered to him by the Church with absolute
certainty; there being no higher evidence for anything than the testimony of God Himself. And they
proceed to say that this certainty is indefectible. It
would be pyrrhonism to deny that on some subjects
men can attain to certain knowledge. Now, whatever
we certainly know to be true can never be shown to be
false. If, therefore, we have attained to a certainty
that the Church of Rome is infallible, it matters not
if she goes on to assert doctrines, which we never bargained for when we submitted to her; such as the
Immaculate Conception and the personal Infallibility
of the Popes; doctrines, which may appear to our
unassisted reason absolutely opposed to the truth of
history, and such that it seems that the hampering of
the Church with them must indefinitely postpone the
conversion of the world. Still, having once had a
certitude that the decisions of the Church can
never be wrong, we must hold that certitude fast,
persuaded that no evidence whatever can possibly
overthrow it.

I had designed to-day to examine this whole theory,
and to enquire what certainty of religious truth is attainable by man. I had proposed on next Sunday to
examine a kindred theory held by Protestants, and to
enquire how far it is true, that men can have certain
assurance of present and eternal salvation. I perceive
that time will not permit me fully to carry out my
plan; but it is impossible not to notice the resemblance between the story told of Cromwell, as to how
his disquietude as to his religious state was removed,
by recalling his former certainty, that he had once

R

been in a state of grace, and Dr. Newman's theory, that his past certainty as to Roman Infallibility is sufficient to quiet any distress caused by proof of actual error committed by the Church of Rome. Although I must postpone to the next day a fuller examination of the argument I have stated, I would remark now that in the whole controversy there is no greater source of fallacy than the abuse of the word certainty. We are said to have a certainty when there is undoubting persuasion in our minds, and when the thing of which we are persuaded is actually true. If we were quite infallible these two things would always go together. But as long as we are liable to mistake, it can only mislead us if we give to our own convictions the name of certainties—to other people's convictions differing from ours, some weaker name ; and if we assume, that because truth can never change, therefore, that of which we claim to be certain must never be reexamined, no matter what fresh evidence may offer. On the contrary, no wise man holds any conclusion of his to be absolutely irreversible. There are some things that we may firmly believe with a full persuasion that no new evidence will turn up to contradict them. In this persuasion we may legitimately refuse to attend to opposing evidence that is manifestly not of the first class. For instance, we should not lightly give heed to stories affecting the character of a person in whom we felt confidence. Yet, if we made it a canon, that on no evidence whatever would we believe anything to that person's disadvantage ; or if in any case we maintained that the conclusions we had drawn from our study of one class of facts must never be abandoned, no matter what new facts might come to light, then our belief could no longer be called faith : it would be prejudice.

I do not think that I need regret that I have not now time for a refutation of the Roman Catholic arguments which I laid before you, because it scarcely needs that I should point out how little is gained by disparaging the kind of certainty we can obtain without help from an infallible Church, since, unless we begin by assuming the thing to be proved, we can have no greater certainty that the Church is infallible than that which we can arrive at without her help; and the logical problem is one of the most hopeless character with which some of the ablest Roman Catholic divines have been trying for the last two or three years to grapple, namely, how, from probable premisses, we can draw an absolutely certain conclusion : how we can have greater certainty of anything we receive on the Church's authority, than we have of her title to speak with authority.

It will suffice now to call attention to the practical working of the theory, that the Christian Revelation will have been a failure, unless we can have as high certainty of the right solution of every problem that speculative theologians can raise, as we have of the truths that Jesus suffered under Pontius Pilate, and rose again from the dead. It is in order to satisfy the supposed necessity for such certainty, that in our own time there has been created—what Christendom existed so many centuries without finding out its need of—a living tribunal competent to give an infallibly correct answer to every question that may be propounded to it. We may judge of the need of such a tribunal, by referring to the last occasion on which it exercised its function. A dispute was raised some five centuries ago, between two powerful parties in the Roman Catholic Church, as to whether or not the mother of our Lord had been conceived without original sin. There was no practical difference between the parties as to the honour which was to be paid her. All were united in offering her a worship which we believe cannot rightly be given to any creature. All, too, were willing to own that she had been born without original sin. But the point at issue was how long before birth she had been cleansed from it, whether at the very instant of her conception, or as some said, a few moments, or possibly two or three hours afterwards. Thus the problem was to fix the time within a few hours, when a supernatural privilege was conferred some nineteen centuries ago, no practical consequence whatever being to follow, no matter which way the question might be determined. We can understand the craving for certainty which the so-called Clement describes himself to have felt in the passage I already read to you, as his mind brooded over some of the most important questions that affect man's future destiny. But it is difficult to conceive how a craving for certainty as to the right answer to the problem I have just stated, could break the rest or spoil the appetite of a single human being. It must be owned, however, that the point was hotly disputed; that men called each other heretics, and asserted that the eternal salvation of others was imperilled by wrong opinions on it. But all this time the Infallible tribunal abstained from interfering. And now that it has broken its centuries of silence, in order to pronounce a decision on an extinct controversy, nothing can be more depressing than the indifference with which the decision has been received by the lay members of that communion. Can we rightly give the name of Faith to the disposition which leads a man to acquiesce without inquiry, while dogmas are added to his creed; may we not fairly conclude that the same man would be likely to acquiesce with equal ease if dogmas were taken from it?

Brethren, I have occupied you to-day with a subject of controversial Theology, but it suggests a practical question, which I would wish you each to put to himself. You very intelligently reject the superstitious additions which those of another communion have made to their creed; but what is the nature of your faith in the truths you hold in common with them? Your faith may be indolent assent to traditional doctrine, it may even rise as high as passionate attachment to the correct enunciation of a theological formula; but if it has not become the spring of your practical principles of action, if it does not work by love and overcome the world, then your belief in our Lord's death and resurrection is, in God's eyes, of no more value than the belief which others hold of the reality of the apparition of La Sallette, or of the miracle of the melting of the blood of Januarius.

SERMON XIV.

CERTAINTY.

" Be ready always to give an answer to every man that asketh
you a reason of the hope that is in you with meekness and fear."—
I PETER iii. 15.

THE Christian religion makes a double appeal—to
the intellect and to the heart. It has shown itself
capable of exciting passionate devotion in those who
receive it ; yet the power to excite enthusiasm is
common to it with many a false religion. Enthusiasm (both name and thing) is far more ancient
than Christianity. We need not doubt the reality of
the passionate religious emotion which impelled the
Bacchanals to their mountain orgies, or which dic-
tated still wilder modes of Eastern worship, such as
those of which we get a glimpse in Scripture, where
the prophets of Baal are described as cutting themselves with knives and lancets till the blood gushed
out upon them. But powerful as heathen enthusiasm
has been, it seems almost a degradation to Christian
enthusiasm to mention one in comparison with the
other. The one has been but a temporary possession,
impelling the votary to acts on which, when restored

to his right mind, he looks back with surprise or sorrow or shame ; the other is a permanent indwelling of the Divinity, moulding the character of the whole life. And while the heathen religious emotion seems to us irrational, and to our different habits of thought almost unaccountable, the Christian was ever guided, controlled, and justified by reason. I spoke last Sunday of the power which intense religious conviction bestowed on those who were called to suffer for their faith ; how to them the unseen was far more real than the things of sense; 'how they showed themselves indifferent to, and almost unconscious of, bodily torture, so as to move the wonder of heathen spectators at the inconsistence of men who, professing their faith in the resurrection of the body, declared that they thought their bodies so precious that God must needs exempt them from the corruption which appeared to be their natural lot ; yet acted as if nothing were in their eyes more contemptible than their own bodies. But it is striking to notice what an amount of calm good sense, as a general rule, controlled the enthusiasm which was content to brave martyrdom. When we consider that the sufferers for Christ were all through their trial accompanied by the hearty and admiring sympathy of their fellow-believers; that they were certain, in case they survived the conflict, of holding a permanent position of honour and influence in the Church—if they died, of having their memory so venerated that, as we know happened in the end, the martyrs came to be worshipped as a kind of minor divinities ; and when we consider that they were fully convinced that death would be to

them an exchange of earthly fluctuations and troubles
for abiding happiness, with which their light affliction that endureth but for a moment was not worthy
to be compared, we need not wonder if martyrdom
seemed to them a thing more to be coveted than to
be dreaded. There were, consequently, cases from
time to time of persons who voluntarily sought for
martyrdom, or threw themselves in the way of it;
yet, unless there were some worthy cause exceptionally
to justify such an act, it was not stamped with the
seal of Church approbation. Nay, to draw back from
persecution when sought out for it—that is to say,
to flee or conceal oneself from the enemies who sought
his life — though objected to by the fanatical, was
commended by the prevalent voice of the community
as an act of Christian prudence, and justified by our
Lord's own command, " When they persecute you in
one city, flee into another." Such flight or concealment was actually practised by leading men, who
afterwards proved, by the constancy of their death,
that want of courage was not the cause why they had
not faced the combat sooner. So, again, if there were
an external resemblance between the rapt ecstasy of
Christian prophets and that of heathen seers, there
was the fundamental difference that Christian inspiration was consistent with complete self-control—that
the spirits of the prophets were subject to the prophets.
This difference was much insisted on as exposing the
falsity of the pretence to inspiration made by certain
fanatical sects, whose prophets were the organs of
frenzied utterances which they had no power to control. And generally the Christians claimed, not to

have caught up their belief in some unaccountable way by sympathetic contagion, but they declared themselves to be ready, as the words of the text direct, to justify it by proof. Several of the apologies are still extant which were offered, in order to defend by argument the doctrines which they held so firmly.

It is plain from what has been said, what a very imperfect view of our religion is taken by those who practically regard it as appealing but to a single part of our nature. There are some who look only to the effects of religion in securing virtuous conduct, and who hold that provided a man's life be in the right, he may allow graceless zealots to dispute about doctrine as they please. Others again care only for the excitement of religious emotion. It matters not to them that the feelings raised end in nothing, that they die away without having wrought any permanent change of character; nor do they care to justify by argument the reasonableness of the emotions they value. They regard a preacher's time as equally wasted, whether he speak of moral duties, in which case they set him down as a mere legalist, or whether he attempt to maintain by argument either the fundamental doctrines of the Gospel, or his deductions from them. Anything of mental effort they dislike, and they count all words out of place in the pulpit which are spoken to the head, not the heart. Lastly, others convinced that mere excitement of feeling, if there be not a basis of fact to justify that excitement, is as unpractical as the emotion felt by the spectators of a tragedy, or the readers of a novel, and as irrational as the frenzied passion of the Mænads, have so devoted themselves to proving the truth of Christianity, that they seem to have forgotten that there was any use to be made of it after it had been proved. They have disparaged the value of the faith of the unlearned, unless it had been commended to their reason by some instruction in evidences ; or they have occupied themselves in controversy and in the refutation of heresy. And there are, doubtless, many to whom the study of the theory of Christianity merely as an intellectual problem has interest ; yet if they occupy themselves exclusively in such studies, and offer their results to others as their spiritual nutriment, their own hearts are forced to confess that their disciples are not without reason when they express their dissatisfaction, and declare that those are dry husks with which their souls cannot be fed.

In short, then, Christianity is mutilated, if it is regarded exclusively from its intellectual, or its emotional, or its practical aspect. It can never be unimportant what a man's belief is, for his conduct is always liable to be more or less influenced by it ; yet conclusions may be admitted by the reason as true, and still may lie dead in the mind for years, never coming into contact with the practical springs of action. It needs that emotion should quicken into life those germs of action, before their fruit can appear. Christian faith, then, does in its idea include an intelligent reception of the great facts which the religion has revealed ; but this alone is nothing, unless emotion lay hold on these facts, deriving from its sense of their reality a strength, which the most highly raised efforts of the imagination never could have given it, and thus gaining power to conquer the engrossing influence of sense, and to guide the whole course of life.

On last Sunday I considered a theory which virtually amounted to discarding from the notion of Christian faith all the rational part, and retaining merely the emotional, and it is to be hoped the practical part. It is observed that a state of doubt is incompatible with the excitement of strong feeling. If you have received a benefit from an unknown source, you will not be quite indifferent to one who you think may possibly have bestowed it on you; but until you have received some positive assurance on this point, you are not likely to entertain any lively emotion of gratitude towards him. It was urged, then, that the proofs and evidences, on which it has been attempted to establish a foundation for Christian belief, are in their nature probable, not demonstrative arguments, and are therefore incapable of yielding that certainty which is essential to true faith. And as scarcely any of the beliefs by which mankind are influenced have been argued out by themselves, but almost all have been taken up on the authority of others, so it is contended that the mode by which God has provided that Christian belief should be generated is not argument, but the authoritative teaching of a Church always inspired to give absolutely correct instruction, and to which they who submit themselves receive in the supernatural gift of faith undoubted assurance that they are in the right way.

And thus it is hoped to meet the obvious difficulty to which I referred on last Sunday—namely, if our

reason cannot give us certainty in our investigation
of religious truth, what certainty can we have of our
belief that Christ has founded a Church infallibly
guarded from error ? what certainty that we have
found the Church so guarded if there be one ? what
certainty of anything we receive on the authority of
the Church whose teaching we have accepted ?　It is
replied, that it is not by logical proof we discover the
Church.　Faith must make a venture ; it must begin
by assuming the truth of the Church's claims.　After
you have submitted you find you have done well ;
and experiencing in the bosom of the Church rest,
peace, certainty, you know that she who has bestowed
those gifts on you must be Divine.　Assuredly, it
cannot be denied that an alleged revelation may
powerfully commend itself by internal evidence.　He
who has received such a revelation on its external
proofs may find an additional reason for trusting it
in the consistence of its doctrines with each other,
their reasonableness, their holiness, their adaptation
to the wants of his nature.　Such arguments as these
go to make up great part of the grounds of the conviction we all feel that the Bible is the Word of God.
But this rational conviction can be felt by no disciple
of a Church which claims to be infallible ; for her
first principle is that her teaching shall be subject to
no criticism.　A disciple of the Church of Rome is
bound to crush down every doubt as sinful : he must
reject as heretical every attempt to test the teaching
of his Church by reason, or Scripture, or antiquity ;
consequently her teaching can never receive any subsequent verification.　The certainty of her disciples

can never rise higher than it was at the first moment they submitted to her. A guide who points out to those whom he conducts the land-marks on each step of the way, may give them much additional assurance that they are on the right road, to confirm the confidence which first induced them to put themselves under his guidance. Such was the method adopted by the ancient Church, and such is the method adopted by our own, which teaches nothing to be believed as necessary to salvation for which she does not offer Scripture proof. But a guide who insists on blindfolding his passengers can do nothing to add to the confidence they first felt in him. It certainly is no proof of his competence, that those whom he conducts feel great comfort and satisfaction in being relieved from the anxiety and perplexity of having to choose a way for themselves.

It remains to notice the assertion, that after submitting to the Church we receive a supernatural assurance of her claims, faith being a supernatural gift with which we cannot tamper without impiety. This is an assertion which it is difficult to discuss, because anyone who declares that he knows something by means of Divine revelation made directly to himself, declares what it is as difficult for anyone else to refute as it is for him to establish it to the satisfaction of others. We do not deny the work of the Spirit of God in producing the faith of the believer; but we deny that that work violates any of the laws of our nature. We say that it is performed in strict conformity with these laws, by supplying evidence which ought to convince, and by removing the moral hindrances which might impede the fair consideration of that evidence, as when He opened the heart of Lydia to attend to the things spoken by Paul. If a Church shows by its conduct that it dare not submit to examination the evidence which it offers, and if it declares that the conviction resulting from that evidence is altogether of supernatural origin, it does its best to justify the infidel scoff that its doctrines are such that, by its own confession, it requires a miracle to make a man believe in them. It remains also to explain how it is that others who also claim to have been taught by God's Spirit, are led to quite opposite conclusions. Certainly, to us who stand outside it requires no miracle to account for the feelings of rest and peace experienced by those who submit to the guidance of an infallible Church. There is nothing miraculous in the fact, that men who cease to inquire, and who take their opinions on trust from others, are not troubled with the doubts and anxieties which attend the task of weighing evidence, and forming a judgment for ourselves.

But we may fairly ask—Is the release from such anxiety a blessing or a curse? In the case of secular knowledge do we think the independent enquirer to be pitied, because, in his investigations, he may have to encounter perplexity, disappointment, failure, and may even fall into error. Do we think *him* happier who without mental effort gets by heart second-hand knowledge, which gives him as little interest as it has cost him trouble. The independent enquirer may be often baffled, only partially successful; but whatever knowledge he has attained has yielded him infinitely more pleasure than the most accurate information that has been taken on trust from others. Our Heavenly Father has dealt with us in respect to the supply of knowledge for the mind as He has with respect to the supply of food for our bodies. In neither case has it been His will that the way of acquirement should be too easy. The food necessary to sustain life cannot be gained without toil. From time to time some actually perish for want of it. But the struggle has drawn forth man's energies, and braced his powers. In those climates where the struggle has been hardest, the greatest advances in civilization have been made ; and the condition of mankind in those tropical lands where the bounty of nature is greatest, enables us easily to judge into what a state of drowsy inactivity the race would have sunk had the poets' dreams been realized of a golden age, when the leaves dropped honey, and the rivers ran wine. Thus we can understand how it has been that the knowledge which distinguishes the civilized man from the barbarian, essential as it now seems to the comfort and security of our daily life, was not at once bestowed as the common property of mankind, but has been attained with painful effort by slow and successive steps, stimulating and rewarding the research of many generations of successful enquirers.

If, then, with respect to all else the rule holds good, that life gives nothing without toil, is it likely that religious knowledge is the only thing which can be got by indolent effortless reception, that he who seeks for theological truth need bestow no labour of thought, but has an oracle provided, ready to give an infallible

solution of every problem which may be propounded
to it. How paralysing the effect of such an institution must be there needs no other example than that
which I used last Sunday, the dispute about the doctrine of the Immaculate Conception. When the point
at issue is explained, it is now seen to be quite unpractical, and one which in our judgment does not justify
the zeal which was roused by it. But at least we
must allow, that at the time when men called each
other heretics for differing on this subject, and when
they threatened eternal damnation to their opponents,
they did feel a lively interest in the question debated,
and all the faculties of their minds were strained to
obtain the true answer to it. All this interest continued so long as there was no practical belief in the
Church of a tribunal empowered infallibly to decide
the question ; for that there was no such practical
belief is proved by the fact, that the Church authorities never dared to pronounce a decision, because
they knew that the party which might be defeated
would not recognize the decision as infallible, and
would make a schism rather than submit to it. In
our own time the claim of infallibility has come to
be practically recognized, and wherever this has been
done, the result has been utter stagnation of religious
thought, the laity receiving with profound indifference
the sentence which was to decide whether their faith
was to embrace a dogma more or less.

It may be objected that my argument would be successful if man was a purely intellectual being; then,
indeed, the search for truth might be made the
business of this life, and the possession of truth

might be regarded as a subordinate matter. But in religion the case is otherwise. There it is necessary, not that we should seek for truth, but that we should have it, that we should embrace it with the full assurance of faith, and that this faith should become our practical spring of action. I admit that this may be truly said with respect to certain great fundamental doctrines; but this admission does nothing to establish what is really contended for, namely, the necessity of a means for obtaining an infallibly correct solution of every theological question that may be debated. For analogy shows that even if such knowledge be very important, yet in God's dealings with us, its importance may constitute it the fitting reward to stimulate our research. Of the great and fundamental truths to which I have referred, we have no cause to complain of want of certainty. It is quite untrue to say that certainty cannot be the result of argument, unless the argument amount to a mathematical demonstration. On the contrary, the convictions which practically regulate our lives are all the result of arguments, which theoretically would be classed as probable. But the assurance produced by such arguments rises exactly in proportion as they are tested by examination, and as the proof of them is found to be convincing by other men. We count that we have absolute certainty that we live on an island, and that there is such a city as Rome, just because we know that men are perpetually acting on the faith, that the maps that make these assertions are correct, and because we have never known any one complain of being deceived

S

by them. The method of teaching by authority is God's appointed means for the instruction of mankind ; but the confidence with which we can trust such teaching is altogether proportionate to its willingness to submit to correction. The teaching of our Church, or of the primitive Church, may be as safely trusted as the uncontradicted statements of the newspaper press in a free country, where we know that anything erroneous that may be published is likely to be met by an immediate counter-statement : the teaching of a Church which claims infallibility is as little worthy of confidence as what is published in the newspapers of a despotic country, where nobody is permitted to deny whatever it may be the will of the government to have believed. The device, therefore, of having an organ, whose utterances shall be subject to no question, so far from giving certainty, actually takes it away.

It is childish to disparage the assurance we have as to the facts of religion, because the evidence which establishes them belongs to the class which is technically called probable. " Probability is the very guide of life;" and we need not murmur if the facts of religion are established by the same kind of proof as that on which we act in our most important earthly concerns. You complain that probable arguments will not make it certain to you that there is a God who created you, a Redeemer who died for you, a Holy Spirit who sanctifies you. You might as well complain that you cannot be certain that the couple who reared you are your father and mother—the playfellows, with whom you have been brought up, your brothers and sisters. The evidence on which men believe such facts is not demonstrative, and instances can be produced of people who have been deceived by trusting to it.

In conclusion, I would fully concede that we may have reasons for the hope that is in us, which we cannot always easily produce for the satisfaction of other men. We are perpetually forming judgments on the characters of those with whom we mix in daily life. One person we dislike and distrust; in the uprightness and integrity of another we have implicit confidence; on the truth of another's love to ourselves, we would stake all we have in the world. We should find it hard to gather into a formal argument all the looks or gestures, chance expressions, or other little circumstances which had resulted in forming one definite impression. And yet, each little incident that may have passed from our own memory was a perfectly legitimate source of inference, and we have no reason to distrust the conclusions we have drawn from them. In like manner, the belief of the unlearned may be completely rational, and founded on very real arguments, however difficult they might find it to marshal them in order. In their study of the Bible, the aggregate impression produced by a number of minute touches, is one of full confidence in the artless truth of the relaters, miraculous although be the facts to which they bear witness. Does not the character of Paul reveal itself in his writings in the same way as does the character of those with whom we hold oral converse. And if the result of our study of his writings is to produce in us the conviction, that he is one whose word we may safely trust, is not such a conviction as entirely reasonable as a similar

judgment formed of men, in whose characters our intercourse with them leads us to put reliance ? There
are statements of the Bible, too, which admit of experimental verification ; its doctrines concerning sin,
and concerning the need of a Saviour ; its doctrine concerning a God willing to answer prayer, and with whom
His creatures can have personal intercourse in every
time of need. I do not say that the testimony of our
hearts and consciences to such doctrines would dispense with external proof of the Divine authority of
the book that contained them ; but yet, when such
proof has been furnished, they who are unable to
examine it for themselves, in addition to the confidence
arising from the knowledge, that their religion fears
no light and shrinks from no examination, have
accessible to them evidence attested by their own
experience, and not by the report of others. And the
love of God being shed abroad in their hearts by the
Holy Ghost given unto them, they know that their
hope is one which maketh not ashamed.

SERMON XV.

ST. PATRICK'S DAY.

"And when Hadad heard in Egypt that David slept with his fathers, and that Joab, the captain of the host, was dead, Hadad said to Pharaoh, Let me depart that I may go to mine own country. Then Pharaoh said unto him, But what hast thou lacked with me that behold thou seekest to go to thine own country? And he answered, Nothing : howbeit, let me go in anywise."—1 KINGS xi. 21, 22.

THE verses preceding the text tell how this Hadad, escaping in his childhood the massacre which aimed at the extermination of his people, found in Egypt shelter, house and land, a royal alliance, reception for his own children among the members of the king's acknowledged family. Yet all this luxury could not weigh against the name of country, or bring him to own Egypt as his home. And no sooner does a chance seem to offer of successfully asserting his country's independence, than he abandons his Egyptian ease for a life of privation and adventure. Something like this had occurred before when Moses, refusing to be called the son of Pharaoh's daughter, preferred to cast in his lot with the fortunes of his

own oppressed race. But something more than mere
patriotism inspired the resolution of Moses. He,
we are assured, was so gifted to put faith in a promised Redeemer, that the reproach which he esteemed
greater riches than the treasures of Egypt might
fitly be called the reproach of Christ. In the present
case it does not appear that any religious motive
actuated Hadad; and it is doubtful whether his
patriotic struggles met with any success. According
to the Septuagint, he did ultimately establish himself
as a king in Edom. According to Josephus, the
power of Solomon was too strong for him there, and
he was compelled to content himself with harassing
the adversary of his race in conjunction with Syrian
allies, but without thereby gaining the liberty of his
own people.

If we wish to speak of patriotism, we are almost
compelled, if we desire a Scripture illustration, to
turn to the Old Testament. One affecting example,
indeed, there is in the New: the tears shed by the
Saviour over the doomed city which refused to hear
His call; but yet this is a virtue to which He nowhere exhorts His followers, and about which His
Apostles, in their Epistles, are equally silent. Are
we to consider this as a defect in Christian morality?
It seems as if the Christian teachers were unable to
appreciate moral beauty of a kind, the excellence of
which it might have been expected that they would
have been most ready to acknowledge. The virtue
most strongly commended in the New Testament is
that of self-sacrifice. The most impressive thing in
the Gospel is its exhibition in the highest degree of

the love which prompts a man to give his life for his friends. But patriotism had already elicited examples of this kind of self-sacrifice which men had ever repaid with their highest honours. History or legend fondly commemorated the deeds of Codrus, Leonidas, the Decii, many another hero who had not feared to die for his country ; nor was the humblest soldier insensible to the same motives ; and with but little hope of fame for their reward, whole legions had often advanced to posts whence they knew that none of them should return. Admiration of such deeds was felt as keenly by the Jews as by Greeks or Romans, or any other people ; and not to speak of elder national heroes, the acts of the Maccabees and their followers were, at the time that the Apostles taught, living in the memory and the praises of their countrymen. It may not be amiss, then, to inquire why the New Testament is silent on this subject, and contains no exhortations to the practice of a virtue which heathens admired, and the beauty of which none can dispute.

I shall not inquire whether, as some have asserted, all sin can be reduced to selfishness ; for it will not be denied that the selfish spirit is utterly opposed to the Christian, and that out of it naturally spring most of the faults and vices which our conscience condemns. And it must be admitted that selfishness is natural to fallen man ; and that not to speak of voluntary sacrifice of our own rights, even due regard to the rights of others is a thing which must be taught by education and training, and by experience, that we are sure eventually to suffer ourselves if we disregard what others may claim from us. Yet there are implanted in our nature principles antagonistic to selfishness, the most striking being the domestic affections. Even in the lower creatures we know how parental affection will triumph over the instinct of self-preservation, and how the most timid of animals become courageous in defence of their young. In the case of every animal, instinct impels the mother to grudge no sacrifice of ease or sleep necessary for the care of her little ones during their period of helplessness ; and in the human species reason prolongs parental care beyond the time of infancy, and calling forth feelings of gratitude and duty in return, establishes the family relations whence much of our best and purest happiness is derived. Undoubtedly, as a general rule, to undertake the duties of wedded life is an important step in a man's moral training; and he who takes upon him to provide for others whom he learns to hold dearer to him than himself, is thereby lifted out of selfishness and placed in a higher moral condition than his whose conduct had no end but to provide for himself the greatest amount of pleasure. Yet with many family love is but an enlarged selfishness. With many the duty of providing for those of his own house is but an excuse for rapacity, of which, without some such apology, he would be ashamed. So mischievous has at times appeared the selfishness of family love, that some legislators, practical or speculative, have regarded it as a thing to be warred against, and have devised plans for training the young, so that they might regard themselves rather as children of the State than as members of a private family.

It is a remarkable example of God's power to bring good out of evil, that it is war which has elicited some of man's noblest qualities. In the security of our daily life we scarcely can conceive a state of things when war was the rule, peace the exception ; when neighbouring states thought it natural to inflict injuries on each other, unless they had made some compact to the contrary ; when no comity tempered the rights of war, and each citizen knew that the overthrow of his state would involve possibly the loss of his life, certainly the loss of his personal liberty, and that of his family. All that he owed to the parents who had shielded his early years from harm, was little in comparison with what he owed to the city, whose laws had given him his moral and political education, and to the fellow-citizens, from whose daily protection he received the enjoyment of every other blessing, wife, children, personal freedom. On each man's consciousness of this obligation, and on his willingness loyally to return it, the safety of the State depended. And thus was generated a state of feeling, in self-sacrificing grandeur rising as much above mere family affection, as that does above the selfishness of the celibate. Each then felt that his life was an offering, which it would be most glorious to pay if demanded as his club-contribution for the common safety. Not merely his own life, but the lives of those most dear to him, must not be grudged if needed by the State, but for whose protection he never could have enjoyed their love ; and thus, a mother, whose son had gone forth to battle in her country's defence, would feel it less painful to see

him returning on his shield than without it. Yet,
noble as these patriotic feelings are, they too, may, in
their narrowness, be chargeable with being but a still
enlarged selfishness. The two precepts seemed to
have gone together—" Thou shalt love thy neighbour
and hate thine enemy." Often has the patriot thought
it laudable to aggrandise his own state at any cost to
other nations. That they had rights which justice
required him to respect he did not dream. Scarcely
would he own that they had virtues which demanded
his esteem; but representing them to his mind as
cruel, insolent, perfidious, he little recked what injuries he did them. Greece, which has exhibited some
of the noblest examples of patriotism, has exhibited
also some of its abuses. Great part of its history is
an account of miseries inflicted on each other by
inhabitants of cities, of what we should count the
same country, and whose geographical proximity
marked them out as natural friends. Nothing would
seem to us more unnatural than if the relations between Dublin and Bray were the same as those between
Thebes and Platæa, or if all the principal cities of our
own island were mutually hostile communities constantly seeking each others' ruin. We can hardly
sympathize with the jealousy with which these
Grecian cities guarded their autonomy, and resisted
all attempts at amalgamation. And the evils arising
from their mutual animosities would have been far
greater if it had not been for that fortunate calamity,
the common danger of all the Grecian cities from
barbaric invasion, which early roused the Hellenic
feeling, so that they could never after quite forget

their common brotherhood. It was this feeling which saved Athens when she lay prostrate at her enemies' feet, at the end of the Peloponnesian war; it was this which made it easy for Greeks of different cities to unite in presence of the barbarian, and made, for example, the exploits of the Ten Thousand, matter of pride to every Grecian heart. And there is something resembling this in the feeling of common brotherhood, that in greater or less degree exists between European Christian nations, which mitigates the asperities of war, and continually tends to exempt non-combatants from its severities. We ourselves now are ready to own the injustice of many of the beliefs held by our fathers during the great war, concerning Frenchmen and their Corsican master. We begin to feel that the conduct of State to State, as well as of individual to individual, ought to be governed by the Christian rule, of not doing to others what we would not that they should do to us; and that patriotism itself may be selfishness in disguise, if in zeal for its own country's greatness it transgress the bounds of justice. Thus, then, patriotism marks but a stage in the progress of the expansion of men's sentiments, not the final result. It is much to teach a man that he must live not for himself alone, but for his family, yet if he rests in this, his moral growth is stunted. Still more, to teach him to live, not for his family alone, but for his city: more again, to teach him to live, not for his city alone, but for his country—for all those who speak the same tongue, or who own a common origin or a common worship. Yet, in each of these cases, that which is a real

moral advance, when it is a step in lifting a man out
of self, may become mischievous when it is the means
of confining or suppressing sympathies which are
striving to diffuse themselves more widely. It is one
thing for a man to prefer his city's welfare to his
own ; another to prefer the welfare of a province to
that of an empire.

And now we can answer the question why the Gospels are silent as to the virtue of patriotism. This
was, of all others, the duty which the Jews of our
Saviour's time least needed to be taught. The time
had been when the patriotic feeling of the Jew had
in more than one terrible crisis preserved the existence of his nation, and so preserved also the treasure
of religious truth deposited in their keeping ; but
now, soured by the contrast between their actual state
and their former glory, and their hope of future
glory, their national pride had degenerated into an
intolerant hatred of strangers, presenting externally
as narrow and unamiable a form as patriotism had
ever assumed. There was no need to stimulate feelings already in excess ; and the time had come to
teach them the lesson that they were citizens of a
better country ; to teach them to recognize as fellow-
citizens and as brethren men whom they had hitherto
hated as aliens in language and in blood. In that
city all the distinctions which had heretofore caused
jealousy and disunion were to be abolished. There
was to be neither Greek nor Jew, circumcision or
uncircumcision, barbarian, Scythian, bond nor free,
but Christ was to be all and in all.

Thus far I have only touched on matters undis-

puted among Christians, but I come now to what is
at the present day a subject of lively controversy.
In what sense are we to understand the verse I have
just cited? Is the catholicity which it proclaims
absolutely opposed to Nationalism? If at the time
of the Persian invasion an orator had proclaimed
that there was now to be neither Athenian, Spartan,
Arcadian, Argive, but each was to be Grecian, he
might mean one of two things — either the abolition
of the autonomy of the separate cities, or he might
mean only that all were to be animated by a sense of
common brotherhood and common interests, in which
their previous jealousies should be forgotten. In
which of these two senses are we to understand the
corresponding declaration of the Apostle? The
Church of England, you know, holds that the abolition of national distinctions in Christianity gives to
men of every land equal privileges in the Redeemer's
kingdom; that it proclaims brotherhood between men
in every country who acknowledge the same Master;
but that it does not destroy the autonomy of independent Christian communities by constituting some
central authority to which all are bound to submit;
in particular, that the Bishop of Rome hath no juris-
diction in this realm of England. In the unreformed
Church also a great stand was made in defence of
the principle that national privileges and the reten-
tion of national peculiarities are quite consistent with
the catholicity of the faith. I allude in particular to
the four celebrated propositions of the Gallican clergy
in 1682. Now, however, the theory once called ultra-
montane seems to be completely in the ascendant in

the Church of Rome, and nationalism is denounced as a deadly heresy. Implicit submission to the decrees of the Sec of Rome is declared to be the great duty of Christians ; and even local variation from Roman usage in things indifferent—the use, for instance, of a liturgy different from the Roman—once freely permitted, is now as much as possible discouraged.

In order to judge whether this were truly the meaning of the Gospel declarations, let us go back to the principles we have already laid down. The New Testament is silent as to the virtue of patriotism ; but passages may be cited from it apparently hostile to the domestic affections. " If any man hate not father and mother, wife, brethren, and sisters, let him not come after me." " I am not come to give peace on earth, but rather division." " The father shall be divided against the son, and the son against the father ; the mother against the daughter, and the daughter against the mother. A man's foes shall be they of his own household." " Ye shall be betrayed both by parents, and brethren, and kinsfolk, and some of you shall they cause to be put to death."

We have no difficulty in understanding the meaning of these texts. The time was one when undue regard for family ties would have stood in the way of the fulfilment of a higher duty ; but it is quite certain, from other passages, that Christianity, instead of being hostile to the domestic affections, enjoined their highest cultivation. " Let every one of you in particular so love his wife even as himself, and let the wife see that she reverence her husband." Still

less, then, does the silence of the New Testament
concerning patriotism afford a proof that that virtue
is not to be cultivated under the Gospel. The writings
of that Apostle who was hated by his own countrymen as anti-national, and as an enemy of his country's
privileges, contain perhaps the strongest expression
of national feeling which is anywhere to be found.
" I could wish that myself were accursed from Christ
for my brethren, my kinsmen according to the flesh."

In short, then, the sum is, that in each of the
stages of our moral training which I have already
sketched, the discovery of a higher duty, though it
may sometimes limit the claims of duties previously
acknowledged, leaves these claims in full force where
the higher duty does not interfere. It may be the
duty of a man to sacrifice his own ease, in some extreme cases his own life, for the welfare of his family;
yet on the whole, it is for the interest of the family
that their head should act in the way that rational
self-love would direct him to act. Patriotism may
sometimes demand that family affection shall not interpose to prevent a member of the family from
making a sacrifice which his country's good requires.
Yet, on the whole, it is for the interest of the country
that the sanctity of family ties shall be upheld. Even
when different provinces unite to form one kingdom,
although, as we unhappily know, there may be an
attachment to the part which implies disloyalty to
the whole, this is not necessarily so. It is not dis-
advantageous to the community that different portions of it should strive in honourable emulation with
each other, one cultivating with pride memories

and associations not common to it with the rest. There is no disloyalty to Great Britain in the attach- ment which a Scotchman feels to his native land, nay even when it leads him to recal former successful struggles with England; nor is there disloyalty in our allowing this day to remind us that we are Irish- men, bound to feel peculiar love and concern for the welfare of our own island; just as the peculiar con- cern we each feel for the welfare of our own family is perfectly consistent with our duty to our country. And so again, the members of the different nations which constitute the Church universal are not dis- loyal to the whole, because of the attachment and pride with which they regard each his own national Church: just as a soldier feels pride in the exploits of his own regiment, and in the names inscribed upon its colours; and such a feeling is not incon- sistent with his duty to the army of which his own regiment is a part, but rather the honourable emula- tion between regiment and regiment increases the efficiency of the whole. Our national Church feeling would be wrong if it led us to narrow our sympathies to our own land; if it made us forget the ties of brotherhood, which bind us with Christians of other nations. Still more would it be wrong if it led us to aggrandize our own Church at the expense of theirs, or to make it tyrannise over them; as if, for ex- ample, we proclaimed the Church of England to be the mother and mistress of all other Churches, and if we claimed for it the right to give them laws and demand their obedience. As we cannot find that Christ gave to any one bishop the right to constitute

himself bishop of bishops, so we desire to show our
unity by acts of mutual love and co-operation against
the common enemy—the vice and ungodliness of the
world—without either making for ourselves, or submitting to in others, a usurpation of authority, to
which our Lord has given no sanction.

It so happens that we can recall with more pride
the religious than the political history of our island.
There was a time when from this land sounded forth
the Word of the Lord; so that her faith was spoken
of through the whole world, and she deserved the title
of Isle of Saints. Enjoying, from her remoteness of
position, exemption for a time from the foreign invasions which left no security elsewhere, her ecclesiastical
schools flourished, and this land became the seat of
learning and education. From her went forth the
missionaries who evangelized first the highlands of
Scotland and the north of England, then the nearer
German tribes, then the more remote, and even so
far as Switzerland, which names an Irishman as its
Apostle. And at the Council of Constance the right
of England, which was there represented by an Irish
prelate, to vote as a separate nation was sustained on
the ground of her inheritance of the ancient prerogatives of Ireland.

It may, perhaps, be expected that I should say
something as to our right to look back on these successful labours as part of the history of our own
Church. We may test the identity of our Church
with that which existed in this island in former
times, either by comparing our doctrine with that
which was anciently held, or by tracing down the

T

history of the Church, showing that it is the same
body which has continuously existed, bishop replacing
bishop, in regular succession, from St. Patrick's time
to Primate Beresford's.　As to the results of the former method, all parties are coming now to a tolerable
agreement.　The result is not very different when
we compare our doctrine with the remains of St.
Patrick, or any other Irish saint, from what we get
when we compare it with any other writings of equal
antiquity.　In all cases we find that almost everything we most object to in modern Romanism seems
to be unknown to the ancient writers ; and this is a
matter of such notoriety, that the dispute now is not
so much about the fact as about the principle whether
changes, or as they are euphemistically called, deve-
lopments of doctrine, are necessarily improvements,
and whether on points concerning which the early
Church could find that nothing certain had been
revealed, the modern Church has the power of attain-
ing infallibly certain truth, and imposing it on its
members to be believed for necessity of salvation.

It would not be reasonable to discuss such a principle as this at the end of a sermon ; but the very
starting this theory of development is significant
evidence even to those unacquainted with ancient
authors what their testimony is.　On one point, I
may mention, the evidence of early Irish writers is
stronger in our favour than that of English writers
of the same date, I mean the supremacy of the Roman
See.　In any country that had been evangelized from
Rome there would naturally be paid as much deference to the Roman See as is paid by the bishops of

our own Church in India to the See of Canterbury; and examples of such deference are sometimes taken as proving more than they really do. But the early missions to and from Ireland having been made without reference to Rome, as the diversity of usages proves, there was naturally in the Irish Church a tone of independence of Rome, which we need not expect to find in Rome's daughter Churches.

With respect to the regular succession of our bishops, it is only recent controversies* that make it necessary that anything should be said. This is not the place, nor would there be time, for entering into any complicated historical discussion; and I am glad that it is not necessary to do so, and that the main facts of our case admit of being simply stated. It is for the interest of those who desire to obscure the truth to muddy the waters. Most men are too indolent to be willing to examine closely any difficult discussion, and therefore if you show them any conclusion that they like to adopt, and give them something like a chain of reasoning in its favour, you may safely calculate that if you only make the argument a little hard to follow, they will adopt the conclusion without examining the reasoning. Our Church has many political enemies, who are only too glad to believe anything to her disadvantage, and any Irish

---

* At the time of the agitation against the Irish Church Establishment, very vigorous efforts were made to show that there had been a failure in the succession from St. Patrick of the bishops of our Church. Although I have scarcely heard anything of such attempts since the passing of the Irish Church Bill, yet in the possibility of their being hereafter revived, I think it better not to suppress what I said on the subject at the time.

clergyman who will give them the sanction of his
name for so believing, can acquire on the cheapest
terms a reputation from them for candour, impartiality, and even for learning. I will, however, state
the conclusions to which I think a person of real
impartiality must come ; and I think I am competent
to pronounce judgment in this matter, because, for
reasons which I shall presently give, I do not myself
regard the question at issue as one of vital importance
on the one side or the other. The history, then, of
what took place at the accession of Queen Elizabeth,
which has hitherto been generally accepted, is as
follows :—In England none of the bishops who were
found in possession would take part in consecrating
the bishops of the Reformed Church, and accordingly
Archbishop Parker was consecrated, not by any of the
Marian prelates, but by bishops who had been in
office before Mary's accession, but were dispossessed
or disowned by her. In Ireland, on the contrary,
only two bishops refused to conform, and were deprived by Elizabeth ; and the consecrations, therefore,
of new prelates took place without the smallest difficulty. One of the Irish bishops appointed by Mary,
Archbishop Curwen, took so active a part in the
proceedings of the Reformed Church, that with respect to him at least no one has ventured to make a
question. About fifty years after the event, a ridicu-
lous attempt was made by some Roman Catholics to
dispute the validity of the English consecrations,
and a fable was invented, that for want of bishops to
consecrate them, the candidate bishops met at the
Nag's-head tavern, and after supper went through

some mummery of consecrating each other. This fable is now quite exploded, but at one time it was necessary seriously to argue against it. And one of the arguments relied on was, that there was no necessity for the reformed to have recourse to any irregular process of obtaining consecration. "Why should a rich man steal?" says Fuller. The letters patent for the consecration of Parker were directed to seven Protestant bishops, and "if there had been any need," says Archbishop Bramhall, in 1653, "they might have had as many more out of Ireland. For Ireland never wanted store of ordainers, nor ever yet did any man object want of a competent number of consecrators to an Irish Protestant bishop. No man did ever question the ordination of the first Irish Protestant bishops, to this day. They who concurred freely in the consecration of Protestant bishops at home, would not have denied their concurrence in England if they had been commanded."

This testimony is proof enough of what is otherwise certain, that for a hundred years after the event, no one dreamt of disputing that the bishops whom Elizabeth's accession found in Ireland, concurred in the consecration of their Protestant successors. From time to time, however, historical paradoxes find supporters. Nero is found to have been much maligned; Richard the Third to have been well made and handsome; Henry the Eighth a conscientious man, compelled to behead his queens by a sense of painful duty. For all these paradoxes I think much more can be said than for that started some little time ago by the Roman Catholic Doctor Moran, that the Irish prelates whom Queen Elizabeth's accession found here, refused to conform to the Reformation, or to take part in the consecration of the Protestant bishops; that Queen Elizabeth was so weak, or so mild and merciful, that she contented herself with the deprivation of two of their body, leaving the rest in quiet possession of their sees; that meanwhile the Protestant bishops got consecrated nobody knows how, perhaps by Archbishop Curwen, singly, which might be granted, since he having been consecrated in England, it is supposed could not transmit the Irish succession. I could almost wish that some evidence could be found in proof of this wild imagination. For if so, it would appear that Queen Elizabeth's reformations were made with such universal assent, and in such complete absence of unfriendly witnesses, that the most flagrant irregularities could be committed in the consecration of the Protestant bishops, yet no one on that account raise the slightest objection to their validity, no one make the smallest mention of these irregularities, and no suspicion of them arise for three hundred years, that is to say, until the present day. One would imagine that an hypothesis so incredible would not have been put forward unless some new evidence had been discovered disproving the received opinion. Now the whole of the new evidence brought forward by Dr. Moran amounts to this, that it appears from Vatican manuscripts, that certain of the bishops who were supposed to have concurred in the Protestant consecrations, were, notwithstanding, till their death recognized at Rome as bishops, the proof of this being, that successors are said to have been appointed to vacancies made by their deaths, showing that they had not been previously deprived. I have no suspicion that Dr. Moran misquotes the manuscripts from which he cites, but it is inconvenient that he should bring forward witnesses, whom we have no power of cross-examining. It is quite possible that the result of a cross-examination would be to turn this witness against us, to a witness in our favour. For example, suppose that in that document the names of deceased bishops were ordinarily inserted with " bonæ memoriæ," or some other note of praise, the absence of such a note in the case of the majority of the bishops cited by Dr. Moran, would show, that though never actually deprived by the Pope, they had committed acts which had incurred the displeasure of Rome. But if we were even to apply to the entire the note, " bonæ memoriæ," which is said to be affixed to five out of thirteen, the assertion that a prelate performed certain official acts commanded by Queen Elizabeth is not contradicted, or even made improbable by the assertion, that he died in good odour with the Pope. In unsettled times, men of not very high principles comply with the demands of the dominant power, and yet strive to retain the favour of the party which may be in power again. How many noblemen attended Parliament, or performed other official acts under William III., and yet contrived to keep in good odour at St. Germains. Some of the Irish Prelates in question were not men of very high principle, and so alienated the property of their sees, that *we* should not affix to them the note, " bonæ memoriæ." Such

men were very unlikely to make themselves martyrs in opposition to royal authority. There was
no disposition on Elizabeth's part to drive matters to
extremity, her wish was rather to make the Church
comprehensive; nor would those who acknowledged
her supremacy and complied with her commands,
find any difficulty in retaining their sees, even though
they held in their hearts many points of Romish doctrine. But we are concerned with the official acts of
these men, and not with their private opinions; nor
do I think is there the smallest pretence for disturb-
ing the received opinion, that the prelates of
Elizabeth's appointment, from whom our present
bishops derive their succession, were duly and regu-
larly consecrated by men who held the same office
under Queen Mary.

Many persons, and in my opinion Mr. Froude
among the number, have contradicted our assertions
from sheer ignorance of what it is that we do assert.
And when it is explained to them, they will, perhaps,
think that the point for which we contend is one of
no great importance. Well, I have said already, that
in my opinion the point is not one of vital importance. Those who do not hold the doctrine of Apostolic succession, will naturally regard any question
of succession of bishops as of no importance at all.
They will attach much more importance to the fact,
which constitutes the chief strength of Romanism in
this country, and which we unfortunately cannot
deny, namely, that the Reformation, which was
pushed successfully as far as the English language
and English influence extended, however successful

with the clergy and other educated classes, did not reach the native Irish-speaking population, who, therefore, knew no reason when emissaries came from Rome, why they should not accept teachers who had at least the merit of being Anti-English.

But this is not even a question of succession from the Apostles ; it is a question of succession from St. Patrick and other early Irish bishops. When we have proved our case against the Romanists, they are in no worse position in Ireland than they confessedly are in England. However long the Roman Catholic hierarchy in England may last, it can never connect itself with the early Church that existed there previous to the Reformation ; it must be content to trace its origin, not to the mission of St. Augustine, but to the mission of Cardinal Wiseman ; and whatever justification there is for the Bishop of Rome's intruding bishops into occupied sees in England, the same applies to Ireland. If he can dispense with establishing any connection with St. Augustine, he can dispense equally with St. Patrick. On the other hand, if Roman Catholics could succeed in proving all they have tried to prove against us, our position would not be in the least affected. It is needless to discuss a supposition which savours so completely of the nineteenth century, as that the new Elizabethan bishops were not consecrated by any body. The very invention of the Nag's Head fable shows that to men of former times it was absolutely inconceivable, that a man could take on himself the work of a bishop without going through, at least, some ceremony of consecration. And in this case

there was not the slightest temptation to such irre-
gularity, since it is confessed that Archbishop Curwen
was at hand, able and willing to perform the consecration. Even then, on the improbable supposition
that he did this work single-handed, he is still
left as a link, to connect us with the ancient Irish
Church. And this·is sufficient; for, though he was
consecrated in England, the connection between the
Irish and English Churches was one of old standing,
and some of Curwen's English consecrators themselves traced their ecclesiastical descent to Ireland.
One thing is certain, either the succession from St.
Patrick has perished, or we have it; our adversaries
certainly have not. For they are compelled to fill
up the gap that separates them from the Pre-Refor-
mation bishops with the names of men ordained by
Italian not by Irish prelates, whose relation to Ireland was, in many cases, purely titular, and who had
no more real connection with the history of Ireland,
than a divine just named had with the history of
Melipotamus.

But though, as I have said, the question I have
been considering is not one of vital importance, it
does not follow that we are not right in defending
our position when it is attacked. An officer of the
52nd would not forfeit his commission if it could be
proved that his regiment had taken no part in the
repulse of the Guard at Waterloo, and so far the
question might be said to be one of no real importance to him ; yet the question is one in which he
would most properly feel a lively interest, and we
should consider him as deficient in true military

spirit if he had no concern for the historical reputation of his regiment. In any case, those who deny our assertions respecting our Church have no right to raise the question whether these assertions are important. That would be to fling a stone and run away; first to contradict us, then, when they find that what they have disputed is likely to be proved to be perfectly true, to turn off and say—After all, what does it much matter?

What I believe to be the result of the discussion is, that it is a certain historical fact, that both in England and Ireland the succession of bishops, from the earliest evangelizers of these countries, is preserved in the Established Church, and nowhere else. This is a point of no importance in our favour if it can be proved that by God's law any foreign bishop has a right to rule over us, and that we sin in asserting the independence of our National Church. But if no such right can be established, then foreign interference with us was an act of schismatical intrusion. It is not, however, in a spirit of unreasoning dread of foreign interference, or out of any mistaken pride or love of isolation that we assert the claims of our ancient Irish Church. It is because attacks on the independence of our Church have been combined with attacks on its purity; and the teaching of doctrines unknown to St. Patrick and the Church of his time has been a principal cause why our country has lagged behind in enlightenment and civilization. For these reasons we think it no ill-spent time to vindicate our right to recall memories which ought to be dear to all Irishmen; and in the name of these memories invoke our fellow-countrymen to shake off a foreign yoke, and cast away the superstitions which their foreign instructors have taught them.

Let us ask of God, my brethren, to bestow on our land the blessings of unity and peace ; that its citizens may be bound together, not only by their common regard for the country in which they dwell, but because they own each other as fellow-citizens of a better country, Zion, the city of the living God, the heavenly Jerusalem, for whose welfare all work and pray, and to which may He vouchsafe to bring us, there with Him eternally to dwell.

SERMON XVI.

PRESENT SALVATION.

" He that believeth on the Son hath everlasting life."—JOHN iii. 36.

OF all the heresies that have disfigured the Christian Church there is scarcely one that has commenced by the assertion of simple falsehood. In most cases the heart of the leader of the movement has been stirred by the rediscovery of some truth which had been lost sight of in the current theology. And in rescuing this truth from disregard, and in proclaiming it to the world, he has done good work. But the evil has been, that commonly this truth becomes in his eyes so large that it eclipses every other, that the favourite texts which assert it come to be his whole Bible, that other truths, which seem to him to be antagonistic to it, are thrown into the background, or even denied, so that in the end, the system which he teaches is a worse mutilation of the Gospel than that, the imperfections of which had first moved his indignation.

The danger of this exclusive contemplation of a
single truth is exemplified in the case of the doctrine
of present salvation, which constitutes the sum and
substance of the teaching of a certain class of preachers of the present day. This doctrine does contain
a great and precious truth, distinctly taught in the
text, and in other passages of Scripture; yet, as we
shall presently see, when it is separated from the
rest of the Gospel, this very truth itself loses its
essential character, and becomes identical in its effects
with the falsehood to which it is opposed. But as I
say, there are those to whom the whole of the Divine
Revelation seems to be compressed into this one text,
" He that believeth *hath* everlasting life." Their
test question, by which they try the state of those
whom they meet, is, "Are you saved?" If the
person interrogated reply, "I hope to be saved," he
has failed to pronounce the Shibboleth correctly, and
is discerned to be one of the unconverted. And our
Church is condemned, because in so many places its
formularies fail to comply with the rules of this new
theology. The Prayer-Book puts into our mouths
the petitions, "O God, make speed to save us,"
"O Lord, save Thy people," "Show Thy mercy upon
us, and grant us Thy salvation"—petitions, it is said,
inconsistent with the Scriptural truth, that we already
have the salvation which we ask God to grant us.
The Prayer-Book teaches us to ask for forgiveness of
sins, whereas it is said we ought to believe that our
sins have already been forgiven. It contains the
prayer, "O Lamb of God, that takest away the sins
of the world, grant us Thy peace," whereas, it is

said, St. Paul teaches us, that being justified by faith, we *have* peace with God, through our Lord Jesus Christ. I may remark in passing, that this very text, which is one of the main pillars of the system of doctrine which I am considering, is now given by the principal critical editors, in the form, " Let us have peace," according to which reading the text changes sides, and makes St. Paul guilty of the same error that is reprehended in our Church, namely, ex-horting his converts to a peace which they had already. I mention this various reading, not that I myself prefer the altered reading, but as the immense pre-ponderance of ancient witnesses, whether manuscripts or early citations, is in favour of it, the example shows how very precarious is the deduction of a doctrine from a single text, and how true is the remark, that a doctrine, which is supposed to rest on a single text, will, on examination, be found to be supported by no text at all.

In the present case, it is easy to show that Scrip-ture does not bear out the inference which has been drawn from the use of the present tense in the text, namely, that it is improper to speak of salvation as a future thing—a doctrine, indeed, which amounts to this, that Christians have no better salvation to look forward to than that which they enjoy already. We can point out that the petitions in our Liturgy, which have been objected to, " O God, make speed to save us," " O Lord, grant us Thy salvation," are themselves couched in the words of Scripture. To this it is replied, that the words of an Old Testament writer do not express the privileges that

are enjoyed under the Christian dispensation. I will
not delay to examine the correctness of a theory,
according to which the Christian Church has been
wrong from its first foundation to the present day, in
supposing that, whether in its public worship, or in
the private devotions of generation after generation
of its most saintly members, it could find in the
Psalms of David adequate expression for its deepest
feelings ; for there are abundant examples from the
New Testament, of the use of the future tense in
connection with salvation. In St. Peter's address to
the Council at Jerusalem, given in Acts xv., he says,
" We believe, that through the grace of the Lord Jesus
Christ, we *shall* be saved, even as they." St. Paul,
in his description of the Christian's armour, 1 Thess.
v. 8, makes the helmet not present salvation, but the
hope of salvation. Hope essentially has reference
to the future ; for as the same Apostle elsewhere
says, " We are saved by hope ; but hope that is seen
is not hope ; for what a man seeth, why doth he yet
hope for ?" It is needless to refer to the number
of passages which speak of hope as a Christian grace.
That most to my purpose is that in Rom. v., where
in proving that the Christian hope maketh not
ashamed, the apostle argues, " While we were yet
sinners, Christ died for us. Much more, then, being
now justified by His blood, we *shall* be saved from
wrath through Him. For if, when we were yet
sinners, we were reconciled to God by the death of
His Son, much more, being reconciled, we *shall* be
saved by His life." In like manner, Paul repeatedly
breaks the rule which has been deduced from his

writings, that because Christians *have* peace with God it is improper they should ask for peace. He prays for the Romans, (Rom. xv. 13,) "The God of hope fill you with all joy and *peace* in believing, that ye may abound in hope." He prays for the Thessalonians, (2 Thess. iii. 16,) "The Lord of peace himself *give* you peace alway by all means." I need not take further pains to show on how superficial an examination of Scripture the teaching of our Church has been objected to, and how inferences have been rashly drawn from one or two texts, without observing whether those inferences were consistent with what is elsewhere taught in the Bible.

If we are to do justice to the entire teaching of Scripture, we must give equal prominence to both parts of the truth : to the truth that salvation is not some unknown blessing to be enjoyed in the future, but a thing to be grasped in the present, and to the truth that that which we can now enjoy is but the earnest or first-fruits of a more perfect future. The Bible speaks of the very admission into the Christian Church as an act of salvation. In the account of the miracle of the day of Pentecost, "being saved" and "being added to the Church," are spoken of interchangeably. St. Peter exhorted his hearers to be saved from that untoward generation. (Acts ii. 40.) And then it is said, they that gladly received his word were baptized, and there were added on that day about three thousand souls. And subsequently, the Lord added daily, not, as our version has it, those that were afterwards to be saved, but τοὺς σωζομένους, those that were then being saved. And in remarkable

U

conformity with this, St. Peter, in his Epistle, speaks of baptism as saving us; (1 Pet. iii. 21;) but yet it would be unscriptural if baptism were represented as anything more than the first step in the Christian life; and in the 2nd Epistle of Peter, (ii. 21,) it is said of those who do not lead their lives according to the beginning then made: "If, after they have escaped the pollutions of the world through the knowledge of our Lord and Saviour Jesus Christ, they are again entangled therein, and overcome, the latter end is worse with them than the beginning; for it had been better for them not to have known the way of righteousness, than, after they have known it, to turn from the holy commandment delivered unto them."

I wish to speak at somewhat more length on this great Christian doctrine of a salvation begun in the present and perfected in the future; for if we understand all that is meant by it, we shall have the best safeguards against the abuses of which this doctrine has been the subject. It cannot be too often repeated that the great characteristic of our Saviour's teaching is His perfect fusion of religion and morality into one homogenous whole. In heathen systems, religion and morality were things apart. Men, who had often seen their best-laid plans shattered by powers against which they were helpless to struggle, listened eagerly when they were told that it was possible to control the unseen forces of the universe. The history of what is called by the opprobrious name of priestcraft, is the history of devices by which certain men gained wealth and power through successful inculcation of the belief that they specially understood the art of conciliating the favour of the divinities, and so, of gaining the good things of this life for those who employed their services. And in popular heathenism, in order to conciliate the favour of the divinities, morality was not essentially necessary. The gods, conceived as of very imperfect morality themselves, were regarded as willing to make favourites of the men who paid them due sacrifices and other marks of honour, and in consideration of merit of this kind to look with a lenient eye on their failures of duty towards their fellow-men.

The mere revelation of a future life had not, of itself, the power to bring morality and religion into closer union. It but threw open a wider field in which those tendencies of human nature, which had exhibited themselves in heathenism, might have room to operate. There is nothing essentially holy in the craving after future happiness. The same spirit which prompts a man to push himself forward,.and gain for himself as large a share as he can of the good things of this life, will, if he believe in another, prompt him also to push himself forward, and gain for him-self as large a share as he can of the good things of that. There is identity between the spirit of worldli-ness and the spirit of what Coleridge called other-worldliness. As men's knowledge of natural laws increased, they learned how to govern forces which once had terrified them ; and as far as this life was concerned, they felt less strongly their need of divine assistance to gain for them good things, which they now understood how to win for themselves. But over that unseen world they were obliged to own that they had no power, and therefore were still ready to welcome the aid of those who undertook to secure their happiness there.

And it must be owned, there have been professedly Christian teachers who, like the heathen priests of old, have degraded the majesty of heaven by likening the Eternal King to some of those weak earthly sovereigns who, by acts of homage and professions of personal attachment, can be induced to advance unworthy favourites. In various ways, the doctrine has been taught that God cares more for men thinking rightly about Himself, or about their paying Himself due honour, than He does about their conduct to each other. In one of the earliest heretical writings that have come down to us, (the Pseudo-Clementines,) wrong belief about God is made the worst of sins. We are told that adultery is a terrible sin, insomuch that it deserves the second degree of punishment, for the first degree of punishment is due to those that are in error, even though they live chastely. A similar doctrine has been maintained amongst ourselves. Not long since, it was elaborately argued in the columns of one of the religious newspapers, that a life of unrepentant malignity, falsehood, and impurity, if coupled with accurate orthodoxy, would be a less outrage upon God than a life of unrecanted heresy, coupled with a course of purity, charity, justice, truth, and prayer.* Outrageous as this proposition is, it is but the following out to its

*See Letters in *The Guardian*, Sept. 4, and following weeks.

legitimate conclusion the teaching of Roman Catholic Divines, as to the infinite superiority of what are called the theological virtues to any other—a doctrine defended by Dr. Newman, and from which he draws the conclusion that one who has been a bad Catholic may have a hope in his death to which the most virtuous of Protestants are necessarily strangers.* And it is notorious how this doctrine has been carried into practice; how, for example, there have been in Roman Catholic countries, robbers and assassins most constant and scrupulous in their acts of piety and devotion.

But this Antinomian teaching is not confined to Roman Catholics. By Protestants also it has been maintained that provided a man be a true believer, his sins, however great they may be, do not diminish God's love and favour towards him. In our own time, the teaching has been reproduced by Protestants almost in identical words, by which Tetzel caused so much scandal at the time of the Reformation, when, as it is said, he undertook to assure his penitents of pardon, not only for their past, but for all future sins.

It is scarcely necessary to remind you how anything approaching to Antinomianism is condemned by our blessed Lord. Human teachers have often yielded to the temptation of condoning their disciples' faults in consideration of their personal attachment and their zeal in their cause. Not so He. Those who were bound to Him by the closest ties of

---

* *Anglican Difficulties.* Lecture IX.

earthly relationship were not on that account to
occupy higher places in His Kingdom. His mother
and His brethren were those who heard the word of
God and kept it. They who kept it not, albeit they
had been on terms of intimacy with Him, and had
eaten and drunk in His presence, were warned that
they should one day hear from His voice the sentence,
"I know you not: depart from me, ye workers of
iniquity." . . "Why call ye me, Lord, Lord," He
cried, "and do not the things that I say?" And his
Apostles learned from Him to pronounce worthless
and unreal all that called itself religion, but which
neglected duty towards man, while professing to
observe duty towards God. "If a man say, I love
God," says one Apostle, "and hateth his brother, he
is a liar: for he that loveth not his brother whom
he hath seen, how can he love God whom he hath
not seen?" (1 John iv. 20.) "If any man among
you seem to be religious," says another Apostle,
"and bridleth not his tongue, but deceiveth his own
heart, this man's religion is vain." (James i. 26.)
And future happiness is represented, not as coming'
by an arbitrary decree on certain favourites of heaven,
but as following in strict conformity with the laws
which God has ordained. "Be not deceived," says
St. Paul; (Gal. vi. 7;) "God is not mocked: for
whatsoever a man soweth, that shall he also reap.
For he that soweth to his flesh, shall of the flesh
reap corruption; but he that soweth to the Spirit,
shall of the Spirit reap life everlasting." And it is
well to observe that it is in connection with the fulfilment of our duty towards our fellow-men that this

warning is given, for he goes on to say :—" Let us not be weary in well doing : for in due season we shall reap, if we faint not. As we have therefore opportunity, let us do good unto all men, especially unto them who are of the household of faith."

From this doctrine, that what a man soweth he must reap, that future happiness or misery is the natural fruit, according to God's appointed order, of the character that is formed in us here, the doctrine of present salvation necessarily follows. Nothing would be more agreeable to the corrupt nature of men, than if some plan could be devised by which they might be Christ's hereafter without being Christ's here, by which they might be enabled to live in this world as they pleased, and yet not fail to secure eternal happiness. But what the New Testament teaches is, you cannot be saved hereafter unless you have been saved here. " Now is the accepted time ; now is the day of salvation." Only embrace that salvation, only join yourself to Christ now, only strive to be like Him through the aid of that Holy Spirit whom He has promised to give you, and you will not have to wait for a future life in order to taste the happiness which is the portion of His people. Even in this world of care and sorrow and tears, Christ can bestow a peace which the world cannot give, a joy which the world cannot take away, in the assurance of His love, from which nothing earthly can separate us.

This doctrine, that it is possible—nay, necessary— to begin on earth the life of heaven, is a very different thing from that into which the doctrine of present

salvation has been distorted. Mankind are impatient
of doubt, and eager for certainty. Millions of Christians have accepted, without inquiry, the claims of
a so-called infallible Church to give them absolute
assurance of the true solution of all doctrinal controversies, merely because they otherwise would be
obliged to own that there was a possibility of their
going wrong on points on which they deemed that
error would be fatal. Much more would men, believers in a future state, be eager for certain assurance
as to their future portion in it. Our Lord more
than once warned His disciples that there was a
possibility of self-delusion in this matter, self-delusion continuing to the last. He represents those
whom He would denounce as workers of iniquity as
confidently calling on Him to open to them. (Matt.
vii. 22.) He represents those placed at the left hand
of the Judge as confident that they had never failed
in duty towards their Master. (Matt. xxv. 44.) Notwithstanding, men commonly seem practically to
hold that self-delusion is a thing impossible, and
that the opinion men form as to their own condition
in the sight of God must necessarily be correct. I
recently heard, in the North of England, that a
common formula in which a dying man is there
addressed by his surrounding friends is, " Lad, art
going to heaven? Do say yes." If he can gasp
out a " yes," their minds are at ease. He *is* going
to heaven. And I suppose there is scarcely one of
ourselves who would not be distressed if a dying
friend expressed doubts as to his acceptance with
Christ, or whose mind would not be relieved if these

doubts were removed. If a man can thus judge with certainty of his own state before God, it seems only reasonable that he should not wait to the end of life in order to obtain an assurance so important to his peace. And, accordingly, it is taught that if a man can only find courage to pronounce himself saved, he *is* saved. No matter into what sins he may afterwards fall, his acceptance with God remains unshaken, for he has once for all passed from death into life. Such teaching as this is precisely opposite in its tendency to the doctrine of present salvation as taught in the New Testament. The tendency of New Testament teaching is to draw into closest union the present life and the future, the latter being the natural continuation of the former, the character moulded in the training of this life abiding with us permanently. On the contrary, the doctrine against which I contend puts an arbitrary break between our future portion and our present life; nor can I conceive teaching more heathen and less Christian than that sin can take place without injury in the case of those who have once been made favourites of Heaven.

Take the case of an absolute unbeliever, who, from prudential regard to his happiness in this life, regulates his conduct according to strictest rules of morality, but who altogether denies that there is a possibility of punishment in another world. If a man is safe for thinking himself safe, this man is in no danger. But you are alarmed at his state; you labour to convince him that he is in a position of awful danger: and if you succeed, the next thing

is to assure him that if he will only believe that he
is in no danger, he *is* in none, and that, in regulating
his conduct, he may dismiss from his mind any
apprehension that it will affect his condition in the
future state. May he not fairly say, "You are but
bringing me back to the point I was at before you
preached to me." And the truth is, that if the
Gospel be, what some would reduce it to, a mere
contrivance for quieting men's fears of hell, it would
have been simpler if such fears had never been
excited.

But it will be asked, "Do you teach, then, that the
Christian must remain always in doubt, whether or
not his sins have been forgiven, always in trembling
apprehension whether he may not be eternally parted
from his Saviour?" No, I do not. The cure for such
apprehensions is faith; but by faith I mean, as the
New Testament teaches, faith in Christ, not as some
modern teachers would have it, faith in ourselves.
"Believe on the Lord Jesus Christ, and thou shalt
be saved," was the answer of Paul to the Philippian
jailer; and if it be asked, what is it we are to believe,
Paul tells us in his Epistle to the Romans, " If thou
shalt confess with the mouth the Lord Jesus, and
shalt believe in thine heart that God hath raised
Him from the dead, thou shalt be saved." Nay,
it is said there are some who confess with their
mouth the Lord Jesus, and yet to whom His Resurrection does not in the end prove a source of salvation. And the thing that you must believe, in order
to be saved, is that you yourself are one of those
whose state of mind in accepting the Gospel message

is such that it will prove to you a savour of life. Nothing is more unscriptural than any teaching which makes your hope depend on your looking into yourself, instead of looking unto Christ. Men's temperaments vary. Make the test of their state before God the confidence they can feel in the reality of their own faith, and the heart of the timid righteous one may be made sad, and the hands of the confident wicked one may be strengthened. Bid them look to Christ ; and though there is no comfort there for those who willingly continue in sin, there is abundant comfort for those who desire to escape from its bondage. If you believe in Christ, you believe in a God who so loved you that He spared not His own Son, but freely gave Him up for us all. You believe in a Redeemer who gave Himself for us, that He might redeem us from all iniquity, and sanctify us unto Himself a peculiar people, zealous of good works. You believe in a Holy Ghost, ever ready to aid in the conflict we must wage. Can you believe all this, and doubt that God desires our happiness, desires our holiness, (for these two things are one,) more than we can wish it ourselves? Can you believe this, and doubt with whom the victory must be ?

Nay, you may say, "I doubt not God; I doubt myself. I doubt not His love to me. But I doubt whether my love for Him will continue as I feel it now, whether I may not fall away as others have done." Such doubts can only arise from our refusing to admit those rules of practical probability which are the very guide of our present life. Do such doubts ever disturb the security of earthly love? Does it ever occur to any man who really loves, to say, I know that the object of my love is abundantly worthy of love, even far greater than I can bestow. I know that my love is returned to a degree immeasurably beyond what I deserve, and I know that it will continue to be so returned; but since other men have been inconstant, I doubt the permanence of my own feelings. Perhaps my own love will not continue as I feel it now, and perhaps I may prove inconstant, as they have done. If a man asked your advice, who was disquieted by such doubts as these, and if contempt would permit you to advise him, would you not say, Think no more about your own feelings; think of the object of your love; cherish such love as you now feel, and strive habitually to show it forth in act, and have no care beyond.

We may say something of the same kind as to doubts whether God has forgiven our sins. Questions have been raised, as to the moment when God forgives the sins of those whom He admits to His kingdom; whether from all eternity, or at the moment of their conversion, or for each sin, at the moment it is repented of with due contrition, or at the judgment day. The doubting sinner may easily entangle himself in a theological labyrinth, if he insist on determining the relation to time of the acts of an Infinite Being. Is it not enough for him to know this, that whatever his past sins may have been, he may trust in Christ's atoning work, that they are not an impediment to his now experiencing the love of God, and obtaining from Him strength to live the rest of his time in the flesh, no longer to the lusts of men, but to the will of God? The blessed doctrine of the forgiveness of sins delivers the soul from cruel and profitless remorse, and enables it to turn away from the dead past, and make the future its own. If, on the one hand, I must condemn as ungenerous and odious the doctrine, that we are to feel no shame or sorrow for sin because God has forgiven it, just as if it were possible that pardon granted for our offences towards one whom we loved could make us cease to regret these offences; on the other hand, I cannot agree with those who recommend it as an exercise profitable for deepening the spiritual life, to strive artificially to heighten our sorrow for past sin, by reviving the memory of it, meditating on it, and confessing it to others. I do not think that we shall do well in tearing open those sores which we have committed to the healing of the great Physician, gazing on them ourselves, and asking others to gaze on them. Does a sculptor, who aspires at perfection, collect his early works, and spend his time in gazing on them, and mourning their imperfections? Does he not rather, when once he has recognized their faults, cast them aside, and obtaining the very best model he can, fix his eyes on *it*, and strive to make his work like that? And so, when once you have owned that the time past of your life may suffice you to have wrought ungodliness, instead of fixing your eyes on that past, I would have you fix them on Christ, and obtain from Him grace to become such as He was; assured of this, that you cannot be so

ready to ask that grace as He to give it. In the
closeness of your life with Him, you will find present
salvation.

I, too, brethren, would ask each of you the question—Are you saved ? But saved from what ? Are
you saved from sin ? Are you saved from anger,
bitterness, uncharitableness, untruthfulness ? Are
you saved from sloth and frivolousness ? Are you
saved from impurity, from unclean thoughts, and
words, and deeds ? Are you saved from selfishness
in all its manifestations ? Ask those questions to
yourselves, ask them of any one who tells you he is
saved. If you have learned to mortify these works
of your earthly members, bless God for it ; and be
confident that He who has begun a good work in you,
will perform it unto the day of Jesus Christ. But if
you dream that you can be saved from the punishment of sin, without being saved from sin itself,
Christ has commissioned me to preach no such
Gospel to you. It is not true that you can ; and if
it were true, a miserable Gospel it would be.

SERMON XVII.

THE WORK OF A DISESTABLISHED CHURCH.*

"Jesus Christ, the same yesterday, and to-day, and for ever."—
HEBREWS xiii, 8.

WE live in a world of constant change. All living
creatures run the round of birth, growth, development, maturity, decay, death; and then are succeeded by others which run round the same circle.
"Man cometh up and is cut down like a flower; he
fleeth as it were a shadow, and never continueth in
one stay." For a while one day may pass like
another, and we see little mark of change; yet,
from time to time, the most quiet lives are startled
by events which break their monotony. We have, as
it were, been gliding down the current of a quiet
sluggish stream, and suddenly we find ourselves in
troubled waters. We have to pass through a season
of anxiety, distress, perplexity; and when it is over
we may have some loss to mourn, and have to

* Preached in St. Andrew's Church on January 1, 1871, the day
on which the Irish Church Act came into operation.

continue our journey under changed circumstances. We are most struck by change, when we are forced to compare the present state of things with that which existed at some interval of time. If we return to a place where we lived some years ago, we are struck by finding, not to speak of outward and visible changes in the aspect of the place, that of the friends we had known there, some are dead, some departed, the survivors greatly altered, and a new generation sprung up who know us not. And occasions like the present—the first day of a New Year, naturally lead us to carry our minds back, and compare the present with the past. Even if we go no further back in our comparison than the first day of last year, it cannot be but that many of you have changes to report. Changes there are certain to be in every one of us, visible to God's eye if not to ours. His eye can see in some, new graces developed by the working of His Holy Spirit, good habits strengthened by exercise, power to resist temptation gained by frequent victory over it; in others, alas! His eye may see the fences broken down which early education had raised, while they who have not sought His guidance, stray further and further from the way of peace. Every one of us, too, more particularly if he be young, has gained something in knowledge and experience. But changes there must have been in the outward circumstances of many. In this congregation there must be some in whose family circle death has, during the last year, made a breach ; and it is certain that those who count their's entire, know not in what state the beginning of another year will find it.

In public affairs the events of the last year have preached an eloquent sermon on the uncertainty and change in human concerns. Two of the chief of the temporal sovereigns of Europe have been forced to descend from their position. One of them, the Pope, governed but a small extent of territory; nor do we yet know for certain whether his dethronement will be permanent. Yet, on account of the use he has made of his temporal possessions to support his spiritual pretensions, and on account of the passionate outcries made by his adherents, as to the injury which the interests of their religion are likely to suffer, that change which took place last summer almost without a struggle is a very memorable one. The interests of their religion have, during the last year, received a far more fatal blow in what they regard as a great triumph. They have assembled what they call a general Council for the first time these three hundred years; and there, in order to do more honour to their ruler, have made a decree so outrageously at variance with Scripture, tradition, and history, that all the men of real learning in their body, who protested in vain against this new dogma, are now at their wits' end what course to take. They have proclaimed all their lives that they are bound to accept the decrees of a general Council as infallibly true; and here is a Council which has made a decree which they know to be false, and which they cannot defend in controversy without abandoning the ground of history altogether.

The other sovereign who has been dethroned, was one whom Europe had been in the habit of watching, in order to know whether it was to have peace or war.

x

I remember, and so do many of you, how one New
Year's day a few years ago, Europe was startled by a
speech from him, which announced the breaking out
of that Italian war, which was the prelude of many
coming changes ; and so on succeeding New Years'
days his words were anxiously marked. This New
Year's day there is no one here whose utterances
have not almost as much power to influence coming
events. A new empire, and it would seem a new
Emperor, have seized the foremost place in Europe ;
and that great city, which was long the home of
luxury, whither lovers of pleasure repaired from many
a distant land, is now cut off from intercourse with
its own provinces.

But we need not go abroad to look for instances of
change. To-day, for the first time I may say since
Christianity was planted among us, this country, as
a State, makes no profession of religion. From
henceforth we, the members of what used to be the
State Church, cease to enjoy any privilege over our
fellow-citizens. We have even lost our property,
which had been secured to us firmly by long possession, and by statutes most solemnly sanctioned. On
the other hand, every one of us is now given powers
in the direction and management of Church affairs
which we never exercised before.

I have tried to describe to you what a world of
change we live in. Contrasted with this incessant
fluctuation, the Scriptures present to us Him who is
above all change. "I am the Lord, I change not,"
was the character in which He revealed Himself by
His prophets. " Thou, Lord, in the beginning hast
laid the foundation of the earth, and the heavens are

the work of thine hands. They shall perish, but
thou shalt endure. They all shall wax old as doth
a garment, and as a vesture shalt thou change them,
and they shall be changed; but thou art the same,
and thy years shall not fail." Among the proofs
that our Blessed Lord is God as well as man, this
holds a foremost place, that in the New Testament
the attributes of God are ascribed to Him, in particular, that attribute of unchangeableness, which
belongs to no creature, and that He is described,
as I read in the text, as "Jesus Christ, the same
yesterday, and to-day, and for ever."

Our faith that the great Head of the Church is
unchangeable need not in the least be shaken by the
fact that He permits His Church, like everything else
human, to be affected by change. As men change,
He sees that the instrumentality must be changed by
which His work in them can be done. As years go
on, men's habits of thought change; new forms of
error become attractive; the truth must be presented
in a new form, and be defended by new arguments.
If I were to take the best sermons of the ablest and
most successful preachers who lived a century or two
ago, not to speak of those of still earlier time, and
were to preach them to you now, you would feel them
to be out of date; the whole form and style would
be different from what you are accustomed to; you
would find things dwelt on at length in which you
would take no interest, and other things omitted
more suitable for your immediate wants. There is,
in fact, a collection of old sermons published by
authority for the use of the clergy—I mean the Homilies. They were drawn up at the time of the

Reformation, because many of the clergy of the unreformed Church had not been in the habit of preaching, and required help in the exercise of this ordinance. They were written by some of the ablest and soundest divines three hundred years ago, and they contain some very clear and beautiful statements of Gospel doctrine. Yet no clergyman now thinks of using them for the purpose for which they were intended, and if he were by any cause prevented from preparing a sermon, he does not think of reading one of the homilies for his congregation. I mention this as an illustration how the instrumentality well adapted for doing God's work in one generation is often ill suited to another. And this is why God sees that the ministers whom He employs in His work must be constantly changed, because with age their character hardens and stiffens, and they are incapable of accommodating themselves to the changed wants of the new generation. So He takes them away when they have done their work, often to our eyes before they have done their work, and while they are still capable of great usefulness, and replaces them by others not better in themselves, but better suited for the work He has for them. It is always a matter of great grief to the Church when men tried and approved are taken from her, and when she has to exchange men of known faithfulness and zeal, hallowed by years of usefulness, and beloved for their work in the Lord, for others of whose qualifications she has had no experience, and who are unable to exercise the same influence. At such times we are bound to remember that we are not dependent for our intercourse with God on a succession of many priests, who are not suffered to continue by reason of death, but on one great High Priest, who continuing ever, hath an unchangeable priesthood, which passes not by succession from one to another. If His earthly ministers have done work of which we feel the benefit, the work is not theirs but His, and whatever else be taken from us He remains. Perhaps for this reason He changes from time to time the human agents whom He employs, in order that we may look above them to Him, that our faith should not stand in the wisdom of men, but in the power of God.

And in God's providence not only individuals but institutions are thus taken away and replaced by others. But assuredly the breaking up of the old order is a time of perplexity and anguish of spirit. Men feel sorely the death of the old, but they see not the birth of the new; nor can they perceive how it can possibly make up for the loss of what is taken away. Take, for example, the breaking up of the old Roman empire by the invasions of swarms of northern barbarians. Nothing could seem more unmixed calamity than this, which was the ruin not only of civilization but of Christianity. The Gospel had painfully won its way from the lowest place in Roman society to the highest. It had begun by being the religion of the slaves and of the poor. At Rome it had been a foreign superstition ; sometimes receiving contemptuous toleration, sometimes attempted to be outrooted by bitter persecution ; and yet, notwithstanding all, ever growing and spreading, until at length it seated itself on the imperial throne, and made itself master of the civilized world. And now all the work had to be done over again. The civili-

zation which Christianity had conquered was overthrown ; and the mastery of the world was again in
the hands of heathens, fiercer and seemingly less
open to the influences of the Gospel than before.
What wonder that men's hearts should have sunk
within them ; and yet it proved that all this dismal
anarchy attending the break-up of a worn-out organization was the birth of a new system, containing
elements of healthy, vigorous life, and that Christianity gained immensely both in purity and in
expansive energy as it passed from the effete Roman
empire to the German tribes who constituted our
modern Europe.

. Take, again, the Reformation. To us the work it
effected seems unmixed good ; but it did not seem
so to many pious and excellent men at the time. To
them it seemed the introduction of lawless questioning of everything established by authority. There
were many who brought scandal on the Reformers by
the extravagance of their doctrines, in which they
assailed fundamental principles not only of Christianity, but even of ordinary morality. By these
extravagances the minds of many were revolted
against all innovation ; and it seemed better to them
to bear patiently some things which they owned to be
abuses, rather than run the risk, in the removal of
them, to destroy the Church which they were trying
to amend.

Take, again, the French Revolution. That was
attended with so much bloodshed, so much violence,
so pitiless overturning of all old structures, however
great their claims to reverence, such bitter hostility
against Christianity itself, that the vast majority of

thoughtful men in these islands looked on it with
horror as an unmixed calamity. Yet, notwithstanding all this great temporary evil, now that it has
passed away, a work remains which most of us will
acknowledge to be good. Few of us would wish to
restore that system of class privileges involving much
cruel oppression of the poor by the rich and noble,
which that revolution swept away. But whether we
like it or not, we can see that it was the appointed
means in God's Providence for reconstituting European society on a new basis; for the Europe of the
past is not the Europe of the present and the future.
And we may well believe that it is not without cause
that God has seen fit that Europe should suffer all
the miseries of the present war; and that when it is
over, it will be acknowledged that the new state of
things is better than the old.

My hope and trust is, that we shall be able to make
the same acknowledgment about that change which
more immediately affects ourselves, and of which I
am expected to speak specially to-day. There is no
difficulty in understanding that a great change in the
political constitution of a society may make a great
change necessary in the constitution of the Church,
which is best qualified to do God's work amongst
them. In former times the State was everything,
and the individual nothing. In temporal matters it
was thought right that the sovereign should decide
what was most for the good of his people, and that
they should quietly submit to his decrees. The rule
was laid down, that people in general had nothing to
do with the laws but to obey them. At such times,
too, they naturally were willing to submit to the

guidance of authority in Church matters also, and thought it very little hardship to have no voice in making ecclesiastical laws. But now, that in political affairs we like to have a voice in making our own laws, and prefer to do things for ourselves, rather than have them done for us by the wisest rulers, it is natural that we should have the same preference in Church matters also ; and so the system of State Churches, which was well adapted for old monarchical Europe, may require to be exchanged for a freer organization in our modern democratical society. I think if the change that has taken place in our Church's constitution had gone no further than this, we should all rejoice at it. It had been a couple of hundred years since the Church in this country had any power of legislation for herself, and now that we have recovered our liberty of action, we have used it not by reviving convocation in its antiquated form, but by adapting our governing body to the exigencies of the present time. I think we have every reason to be satisfied with the manner in which this work was done last year ; and when we consider that a body of men, wholly inexperienced in working together, was called on suddenly to perform the delicate and difficult task of framing a new Church constitution, the amount of ability that was shown, and the temper in which they acted together, making mutual concessions when it was necessary for the sake of agreement, must be pronounced highly creditable to them. But we have had to purchase our freedom at a heavy price. Our recovery of the right to legislate for ourselves has been only gained on condition of the forfeiture of the endowments which were intended to secure the permanent publication of Christ's Gospel in this country. Now, a few years ago it was often discussed whether the voluntary system or a system of endowments was the best for the Church. On the one hand, it was urged that the clergy of an endowed Church, whose income in no way depends on the manner in which they do their work, are under temptation to be indolent, and also to disregard the reasonable wishes of their people. On the other hand, it was said, that in the voluntary system, the clergy are so dependent on their people, as to be under a temptation, instead of faithfully delivering God's message, to tell them only what is agreeable to them ; that for example, when slavery was an institution in the United States, it was defended in the slave states by the clergy of all denominations. It has been urged, and it is a thing that we are justly proud of, that our's has been the Church of the poor, that voluntary Churches are naturally opened where there are congregations rich enough to pay the pastor, and that even, when in the migrations of fashion, a part of the town is given up by the rich to the poor, the voluntary Churches in the district are apt to be closed, or else removed to the more fashionable neighbourhood ; whereas, our Church undertook territorial responsibility, and made it her boast that she brought home the preaching of God's Word impartially to every district, rich or poor. It was urged, and proved by the confession of some of the most brilliant declaimers in defence of the voluntary system, that the remuneration it provided for the clergy was in many cases miserably insufficient ; that while men of great talents were, no doubt, handsomely paid,

men of ordinary ability found it hard to obtain a
mere livelihood; while all alike ran the risk of being
left destitute if, through age or sickness, decay of
mental power, or decay of popularity, their congregations deserted them. And then it was asked,
When there are so many openings as there are at
present for young men of ability, and so much com-
petition for their services, how can we, on the voluntary system, keep up that superiority in learning,
ability, and influence which hitherto has honourably
distinguished the clergy of our Church? How shall
we prevent our ministry falling into the hands of an
inferior class of men if every young man of ability
who thinks of choosing this profession is likely to be
told by his friends that, in a worldly point of view,
his choice is the most imprudent he can make?
These were the arguments which induced the majority of the members of our Church to resist as long
as they were able the attempt to deprive the Church
of her endowments; but now that we have failed, it
is our duty to accept cheerfully the condition God in
His Providence has seen to be best for us, and to try
to gain the full benefit of all the advantages which it
offers, while we do our best to guard against the dangers to which it is exposed. A man who had inherited
a large estate would be quite justified in resisting any
attempt to deprive him of it; but if he failed, it would
be childish were he to sit down and lament, as if God
had sent him unmixed calamity; for it is quite possible that his children, forced to earn their own bread,
might be happier and even richer in the end than if
they had succeeded to an inheritance without any
exertion of their own. My own belief is, that if we

take timely measures we may put our Church on a
firmer basis than ever; and that by a mixture of the
endowment system and the voluntary system, we may
gain all the advantages of both and avoid some of
their evils—have all the energy of one, and much of
the security of the other. What we aim at doing is
the formation of a central fund, sufficient to pay half
the salaries of the future clergy. By a central fund
we can take care that the wants of the poorer districts
are provided for; for by all sharing together we can
make the abundance of one place supply the defi-
ciency of another. We can give permanence and
security to the position of the clergy, while since
there will still be a necessity for a considerable sum
to be raised by annual subscriptions, the necessity of
harmonious working between clergy and people will
be evident to everybody; and our people will be in
no danger of sinking into that state of languid indifference into which are apt to fall the members of a
State Church which demands no exertion from them.
Now the raising of this central fund is possible *if we
begin at once, and not otherwise.* We of this generation have the power, if we please, of taking all the
sweets of disestablishment, and refusing to touch any
of the bitters of disendowment. We may claim as
our own at once all the rights and privileges of legis-
lating for the Church; and as the services of the present clergy are secured to us for their lives, we may
cast on the next generation the task of paying their
successors. So again, if we choose to take a selfish
view, we who live in a great city may think the formation of an endowment fund a matter of very small
importance. It may be expected that the respectable

people who form the congregations of the principal
Dublin churches would never feel any difficulty in
paying their clergy without any help from a central
fund. The prophet Ezekiel long since told how there
were in his time many who gathered to hear the
teaching of the prophet, in the same manner as they
would gather to hear the very lovely song of one that
had a pleasant voice and could play with an instrument ; and so there are many in every large town
who, merely for intellectual gratification, will gather
round the preaching of a man of ability, and will be
willing to pay for the privilege as they would for any
other public exhibition ; but I need not tell you that
money given from no higher motive than this cannot
be set down to the account of Christian charity. If
we give from love to Christ we must not think merely
how to please ourselves, but must strive to consider
how the efficient working of His Church over the
whole country can be best provided for. In this
country we have to contend with a most powerful organization ; for the Church of Rome sacrifices everything, even truth itself, in order to maintain unity of
action ; and it is plain that, humanly speaking, it is
only by union among ourselves that we can contend
with success ; and that if our efforts are selfish and
partial, the end will be the abandonment to the Roman
Catholics of all the districts where our people are
poor and scattered. But now if we make good use
of the interval while we have the services of the present clergy without charge upon us, we can, without
unduly burdening ourselves, secure the permanence
of our Church's organization by the raising of a central fund. It may be said roughly, that by the

operation of compound interest a subscription of £1 a year begun at once will effect as much as one of £2 delayed until the pinch begins to be felt. So that all we have to do is now to raise half the annual sum necessary for the working of our Church. If we are incapable of doing as much as this, what hope have we that the future Church can be sustained ?

I hear the question sometimes asked by different people, If we raise a central Endowment Fund, what guarantee have we that some future Government will not lay hands on it? Others say, What guarantee have we that the reforms will be made in the Church which we think desirable? Others again, What guarantee have we that such sweeping changes will not be made, that the money will be hereafter applied to objects of which we completely disapprove? I think good answers can be given to these questions. For instance, it can be said that funds raised by voluntary subscriptions, will stand in the same position of legal security as any other private property; that Roman Catholics and members of every other religious body have the same interest as ourselves, in maintaining the security of such funds, so that nothing less than a revolution can touch them; it may be said, that we have given so completely popular a constitution to our Church that it cannot fail to be in thorough harmony with the feelings of the Protestant people of this country, while we have provided sufficient securities against rash and ill-considered change. These I count sufficient answers to these questions; but I would rather reply to the spirit which puts them; for when God points out to men a work which it is their duty to do for Him, He never condescends to satisfy them, should they faithlessly insist on first being given some guarantee that their exertions must be sure to be crowned with success. In the management of our own worldly affairs, we do not insist before we act, on having absolute certainty that our schemes will turn out well; we engage in business, though we cannot be sure of success; we lay up money for our families, without any certainty that our investments may not turn out differently from what we calculated on. And in the same spirit we must work for God. We send out missionaries. One may bring in a large congregation of converts; another, equally able and zealous, may not gain a single disciple. God warns us to make this uncertainty of return a reason for trying diligently every form of work for Him. "In the morning sow thy seed, and in the evening withhold not thine hand, for thou knowest not whether shall prosper, either this or that, or whether they both shall be alike good. Cast thy bread upon the waters, for thou shalt find it after many days." And so I think all that it concerns us to know is, that if we do not use this breathing time before we lose the services of our present clergy, it is certain our Church will fail to provide the means of grace to our poor people scattered over the land, and will shrink into the large towns; while, according to the best calculations of human prudence, a timely effort now will put our Church on a basis of permanent efficiency. If we see this, shall we not have faith to do our part, and leave the result to God? His promise to be ever with His Church does not prevent any particular Church from having its candlestick removed from its place. Some of the most famous Churches

of former times have fallen away, as for instance, the
Churches of Asia Minor, to which St. John was
commissioned to send his letters in our Lord's name ;
and so if we be unfaithful, our national Church may
also fail.   But this we may be sure of, that the death
of a Church never comes from without.   It is not
such a blow as that which our enemies have inflicted
on us that can injure us.   Taking away our wealth
or worldly position, does not touch the Church's real
life.   Such losses only prove us; and if we do not
flourish separated from the State, it will only be because, while united to it, our love has grown cold,
so as not to be strong enough to induce us to make
the sacrifices and exertions to preserve the union
among ourselves that is essential to success.   But,
brethren, I am persuaded better things; and I do
trust there is enough of zeal for God's cause among
us, as to make such exertions now, that this Church
of ours may be, for many long years to come, a
witness for God's truth and a blessing to the land.

One word I would add, that while your present
gifts will be acceptable in helping to swell the not
inconsiderable sum which I hope will be raised in
this diocese to-day, still what is most important of all
is that you shall give systematically, and according
to your means.

There are three objects you have to provide for :—
you must first make up the annual expenses of the
working of your own church—heating, lighting, and so
forth, which heretofore were supplied by the Ecclesiastical Commissioners.   Secondly, you must take
timely measures for the supply of clergy for your
own church, whenever our Great High Priest takes to

Himself those ministering servants of His, who are the instruments by which He now does His work among you. And thirdly, I hope you will not be content with providing in this way for yourselves, but that you will also contribute for the needs of the poorer parishes of this city, and of places in other parts of Ireland unable to help themselves. One way in which we may answer these calls is by taking advantage of the weekly collections in Church. In these the sums given by each person have usually been trifling, and the collections have chiefly served as a formal acknowledgment of our duty to give of our substance to the service of Him to whom we owe everything we enjoy. By increasing the amount we are in the habit of giving, we can make these collections answer the new calls on us, without injury to those charitable purposes, for which they have been until now applied. We may also undertake to give a certain sum annually, or at such other intervals as best suit our convenience. And by giving to-day we shall give some earnest of the spirit which may be expected to animate us through the year which we commence with the Lord's own day. Offer to Him of your substance, but above all offer to Him yourselves; and then whatever are the changes and chances of this uncertain life, His everlasting arms will be your support; He who has been His people's help in ages past will be your never-failing strength in time to come.

Porteous and Gibbs, Printers, 18 Wicklow Street, Dublin.

June 1872.

A Catalogue of Theological Books, with a Short Account of their Character and Aim,

Published by

MACMILLAN AND CO.

Bedford Street, Covent Garden, London.

Abbott (Rev. E. A.)—BIBLE LESSONS. By the Rev. E. A. ABBOTT, M.A., Head Master of the City of London School. Second Edition. Crown 8vo. 4s. 6d.

Among the subjects treated in 'this volume are:—"The Times of Christ," "The Life of Christ," "Christ's Miracles," "Christ's Sacrifice," "Love," "Forgiveness," "Faith," and "Prayer." The book is written in the form of dialogues carried on between teacher and pupil, and its main object is to make the scholar think for himself. "Wise, suggestive, and really profound initiation into religious thought."—Guardian. The Bishop of St. David's, in his speech at the Education Conference at Abergwilly, says he thinks "nobody could read them without being the better for them himself, and being also able to see how this difficult duty of imparting a sound religious education may be effected."

I

Ainger (Rev. Alfred).—SERMONS PREACHED IN
THE TEMPLE CHURCH. By the Rev. ALFRED AINGER,
M.A. of Trinity Hall, Cambridge, Reader at the Temple Church.
Extra fcap. 8vo.   6s.

This volume contains twenty-four Sermons preached at various times
during the last few years in the Temple Church, and are charac-
terised by such qualities as are likely to make them acceptable to
cultivated and thoughtful readers.   The following are a few
of the topics treated of:—" Boldness;"   " Murder, Ancient and
Modern ;"   " The Atonement;"   " The Resurrection ;"   " The Fear
of Death ;"   " The Forgiveness of Sins, the Remission of a Debt"
(2 Sermons);   " Anger, Noble and Ignoble ;"   " Culture and
Temptation ;"   " The Religious Aspect of Wit and Humour ;"
" The Life of the Ascended Christ."   " It is," the British Quarterly *says,   " the fresh unconventional talk of a clear independent*
thinker, addressed to a congregation of thinkers . . . .   Thoughtful
men will be greatly charmed by this little volume."

Alexander.—THE LEADING IDEAS of the GOSPELS.
Five Sermons preached before the University of Oxford in 1870—
71. By WILLIAM ALEXANDER, D.D., Brasenose College ; Lord
Bishop of Derry and Raphao ; Select Preacher. Cr. 8vo.   4s. 6d.

Each of these Sermons is on a characteristic text taken successively
from each of the four Gospels, there being two on that from St.
John ; viz.—St. Matt. i. 1 ; *St. Mark* i. 1 ; *St. Luke* i. 3 ; *St. John*
i. 1, 14.   *" Dr. Alexander is eminently fitted for the task he has*
undertaken.   He has a singular felicity of style, which lights up
the discourse and clothes it with great beauty and impressiveness."
—Nonconformist.

Arnold.—A BIBLE READING BOOK FOR SCHOOLS.
THE GREAT PROPHECY OF ISRAEL'S RESTORATION (Isaiah,
Chapters 40—66). Arranged and Edited for Young Learners. By
MATTHEW ARNOLD, D.C.L., formerly Professor of Poetry in the
University of Oxford, and Fellow of Oriel. 18mo. cloth.   1s.

Mr. Arnold has undertaken this really important task, on account of his conviction " of the immense importance in education of what is called letters ; *of the side which engages our feelings and imagination." Mr. Arnold in this little volume, attempts to do for the Bible what has been so abundantly done for Greek and Roman, as well as English authors ; viz.—to take " some whole, of admirable literary beauty in style and treatment, of manageable length, within defined limits ; and present this to the learner in an intelligible shape, adding such explanations and helps as may enable him to grasp it as a connected and complete work." Mr. Arnold thinks it clear that nothing could more exactly suit the purpose than the last twenty-seven chapters of the Book of Isaiah, beginning "Comfort ye" &c. He has endeavoured to present a perfectly correct text, maintaining at the same time the unparalleled balance and rhythm of the Authorized Version. In the copious notes every assistance is given to the complete understanding of the text. There is nothing in the book to hinder the adherent of any school of interpretation or of religious belief from using it. The Preface contains much that is interesting and valuable on the relation of " letters" to education, of the principles that ought to guide the makers of a new version of the Bible, and other important matters. Altogether, it is believed, the volume will be found to form a text-book of the greatest value to schools of all classes.*

Baring-Gould.—LEGENDS OF OLD TESTAMENT

CHARACTERS, from the Talmud and other sources. By the Rev. S. BARING-GOULD, M.A., Author of "Curious Myths of the Middle Ages," "The Origin and Development of Religious Belief," "In Exitu Israel," etc. In two vols. crown 8vo. 16s. Vol. I. Adam to Abraham. Vol. II. Melchizidek to Zechariah.

Mr. Baring-Gould's previous contributions to the History of Mythology, and the formation of a science of comparative religion are admitted to be of the highest importance ; the present work, it is believed, will be found of equal value. He has collected from the Talmud and other sources, Jewish and Mahommedan, a large number of curious and interesting legends concerning the principal characters of the Old Testament, comparing these frequently with similar legends current among many of the peoples, savage and civilised, all over the world. "*These volumes contain much that is strange, and to the ordinary English reader, very novel.*"— Daily News.

Barry, Alfred, D.D.—The ATONEMENT of CHRIST. Six Lectures delivered in Hereford Cathedral during Holy Week, 1871. By ALFRED BARRY, D.D., D.C.L., Canon of Worcester, Principal of King's College, London. Fcap. 8vo. 2s. 6d.

In writing these Sermons, it has been the object of Canon Barry to set forth the deep practical importance of the doctrinal truths of the Atonement. "The one truth," says the Preface, "which, beyond all others, I desire that these may suggest, is the inseparable unity which must exist between Christian doctrine, even in its more mysterious forms, and Christian morality or devotion. They are a slight contribution to the plea of that connection of Religion and Theology, which in our own time is so frequently and, as it seems to me, so unreasonably denied." The Guardian *calls them " striking and eloquent lectures."*

Binney.—SERMONS PREACHED IN THE KING'S WEIGH HOUSE CHAPEL, 1829—69. By THOMAS BINNEY, D.D. New and Cheaper Edition. Extra fcap. 8vo. 4s. 6d.

*In the earnestness and vigour which characterize the sermons in this volume the reader will find a clue to the vast influence exerted by Mr. Binney for forty years over a wide circle, particularly young men. In the concluding sermon, preached after the publication of the first edition, he reviews the period of his ministry as a whole, dwelling especially on its religious aspects. "Full of robust intelligence, of reverent but independent thinking on the most profound and holy themes, and of earnest practical purpose."—*London Quarterly Review.

Burgon.—A TREATISE on the PASTORAL OFFICE. Addressed chiefly to Candidates for Holy Orders, or to those who have recently undertaken the cure of souls. By the Rev. JOHN W. BURGON, M.A., Oxford. 8vo. 12s.

The object of this work is to expound the great ends to be accomplished by the Pastoral office, and to investigate the various means by which these ends may best be gained. Full directions are given as to preaching and sermon-writing, pastoral visitation, village education and catechising, and confirmation. Under the heading of "Pastoral Method" the author shows how each of the occasional offices of the Church may be most properly conducted, as well as how a clergyman's ordinary public ministrations may be performed with the greatest success. The best methods of parochial management are examined, and an effort is made to exhibit the various elements of the true pastoral spirit. "The spirit in which it approaches and solves practical questions is at once full of common sense and at the same time marked by a deep reverential piety and a largeness of charity which are truly admirable."—Spectator.

Butler (G.)—Works by the Rev. GEORGE BUTLER, M.A., Principal of Liverpool College :

FAMILY PRAYERS. Crown 8vo. 5*s.*

The prayers in this volume are all based on passages of Scripture—the morning prayers on Select Psalms, those for the evening on portions of the New Testament.

SERMONS PREACHED in CHELTENHAM COLLEGE CHAPEL. Crown 8vo. 7*s.* 6*d.*

These Sermons, twenty-nine in number, were delivered at intervals from the opening of Cheltenham College Chapel in 1858, to the last Sunday of the year 1861, and contain references to the important events which occurred during that period—the Indian mutiny, the French campaign in Italy, the liberation of Sicily and Naples, the establishment of the kingdom of Italy, the American Civil War, and the deaths of many eminent men. "These sermons are plain, practical, and well adapted to the auditors. . . . . We cordially recommend the volume as a model of pulpit style, and for individual and family reading."—Weekly Review.

Butler (Rev. H. M.)—SERMONS PREACHED in the CHAPEL OF HARROW SCHOOL. By H. MONTAGU BUTLER, Head Master. Crown 8vo. 7*s.* 6*d.*

Whilst these Sermons were prepared to meet the wants of a special class,

Butler (Rev. H. M.)—*continued.*

there is a constant reference in them to the great principles which
underlie all Christian thought and action.   They deal with such
subjects as " Temptation," " Courage," " Duty without regard to
consequences," " Success," " Devout Impulses," and " The Soul's
need of God."   " These sermons are adapted for every household.
There is nothing more striking than the excellent good sense with
which they are imbued."—Spectator.

A SECOND SERIES.   Crown 8vo.   7*s.* 6*d.*

"Excellent specimens of what sermons should be,—plain, direct,
practical, pervaded by the true spirit of the Gospel, and holding up
lofty aims before the minds of the young."—Athenæum.

Butler (Rev. W. Archer).—Works by the Rev. WILLIAM
ARCHER BUTLER, M.A., late Professor of Moral Philosophy in
the University of Dublin :—

SERMONS, DOCTRINAL AND PRACTICAL.   Edited,
with a Memoir of the Author's Life, by THOMAS WOODWARD,
Dean of Down.   With Portrait.   Eighth and Cheaper Edition,
8vo.   8*s.*

This volume contains twenty-six Sermons by one of the most earnest,
thoughtful, and eloquent preachers of his time, treating of almost
every point of evangelical doctrine and Christian practice.   The
following selections from the titles of the sermons will give a fair
idea of the contents of the volume:—" The Mystery of the Holy
Incarnation;" " The Daily Self-Denial of Christ;" " The Power
of the Resurrection;" "Self-Delusion as to our Real State before
God;" " The Faith of Man and the Faithfulness of God;" " The
Wedding-Garment;" "Human Affections Raised, not Destroyed by
the Gospel;" " The Rest of the People of God;" "The Divinity of
our Priest, Prophet, and King;" "Church Education in Ireland"
(two Sermons).   The Introductory Memoir narrates in consider-
able detail and with much interest, the events of Butler's brief life;
and contains a few specimens of his sweet and tender poetry, and

Butler (Rev. W. Archer.)—*continued.*

a few extracts from his thoughtful addresses and essays, including a long and eloquent passage on the Province and Duty of the Preacher.

A SECOND SERIES OF SERMONS. Edited by J. A. JEREMIE, D.D., Dean of Lincoln. Sixth and Cheaper Edition. 8vo. 7s.

In this volume are contained other twenty-six of the late Professor Butler's Sermons, embracing a wide range of Christian topics, as will be seen by the following selection from the titles:—" Christ the Source of all Blessings;" " The Hope of Glory and the Charities of Life;" "The Holy Trinity;" "The Sorrow that Exalts and Sanctifies;" "The Growth of the Divine Life;" "The Folly of Moral Cowardice;" "Strength and Mission of the Church;" "The Blessedness of Submission;" "Eternal Punishment." The North British Review *says, "Few sermons in our language exhibit the same rare combination of excellencies; imagery almost as rich as Taylor's; oratory as vigorous often as South's; judgment as sound as Barrow's; a style as attractive but more copious, original, and forcible than Atterbury's; piety as elevated as Howe's, and a fervour as intense at times as Baxter's. Mr. Butler's are the sermons of a true poet."*

LETTERS ON ROMANISM, in reply to Dr. Newman's Essay on Development. Edited by the Dean of Down. Second Edition, revised by Archdeacon HARDWICK. 8vo. 10s. 6d.

*These Letters contain an exhaustive criticism, written in the author's most vigorous and polished style, of Dr. Newman's famous "Essay on the Development of Christian Doctrine." An attempt is made to shew that the theory is opposed to the received doctrine of the Romish Church; that it is based on purely imaginary grounds, and necessarily carries with it consequences in the highest degree dangerous both to Christianity and to general truth. Whilst the work is mainly polemical in its character, it contains the exposition of many principles of far more than mere temporary interest. "A work which ought to be in the Library of every student of Divinity."—*BP. ST. DAVID'S.

LECTURES ON ANCIENT PHILOSOPHY. *See* SCIENTIFIC CATALOGUE.

Cambridge   Lent   Sermons. — SERMONS   preached
during Lent, 1864, in Great St. Mary's Church, Cambridge.   By
the Bishop of Oxford, Revs. H. P. Liddon, T. L. Claughton,
J. R. Woodford,   Dr. Goulburn,   J. W. Burgon,   T. T.
Carter, Dr. Pusey, Dean Hook, W. J. Butler, Dean Good-
win.   Crown 8vo.   7s. 6d.

> *The names of the preachers of these Sermons are a guarantee that they
> are worth reading.   They were preached on the Wednesdays and
> Fridays during Lent 1864, and treat of the following among other
> subjects:—"God in His Perfections the Measure of the Sinfulness
> of Sin in the Creature," by the Bishop of Oxford; "Adam hiding
> himself from the Presence of the Lord," by the Rev. H. P. Liddon;
> "God the Hope and Joy of the Penitent," by the Rev. T. T. Carter;
> "David in his Sin and his Penitence," by the Rev. Dr. Pusey;
> "God the Consolation of the Afflicted," by the Very Rev. Dean Hook;
> "God the Reward of the Faithful," by the Rev. W. J. Butler.*

Campbell.—Works by John M'Leod Campbell :—
THE NATURE OF THE ATONEMENT AND ITS
RELATION TO REMISSION OF SINS AND ETERNAL
LIFE.   Third Edition, with an Introduction and Notes.   8vo.
10s. 6d.

> *Three chapters of this work are devoted to the teaching of Luther on
> the subject of the Atonement, and to Calvinism, as taught by Dr.
> Owen and President Edwards, and as recently modified.   The
> remainder is occupied with the different aspects of the Atonement as
> conceived by the author himself, the object being partly to meet the
> objections of honest inquirers, but mainly so to reveal the subject in
> its own light as to render self-evident its adaptation to the spiritual
> wants of man.   The book has been found richly suggestive by many
> of the profoundest minds in the Church.   Professor Rolleston, in
> quoting from this book in his address to the Biological Section of
> the British Association (Liverpool, September, 1870), speaks of it
> as "the great work of one of the first of living theologians."
> "Among the first theological treatises of this generation." —
> Guardian.*

Campbell (J. M'Leod.)—*continued.*

CHRIST THE BREAD OF LIFE. An Attempt to give
a profitable direction to the present occupation of Thought with
Romanism. Second Edition, greatly enlarged. Crown 8vo. 4*s.* 6*d.*

*In this volume the Doctrines of the Infallibility of the Church and
Transubstantiation are regarded as addressed to real inward needs
of humanity, and an effort is made to disengage them from the
truths whose place they usurp, and to exhibit these truths as
adequate to meet human cravings. The aim is, first, to offer help
to those who feel the attractions to Romanism too strong to be overcome by direct arguments addressed to sense and reason; and,
second, to quicken interest in the Truth itself. "Deserves the most
attentive study by all who interest themselves in the predominant
religious controversy of the day."*—Spectator.

Cheyne.—Works by T. K. CHEYNE, M.A., Fellow of Balliol
College, Oxford :—

THE BOOK OF ISAIAH CHRONOLOGICALLY AR-
RANGED. An Amended Version, with Historical and Critical
Introductions and Explanatory Notes. Crown 8vo. 7*s.* 6*d.*

*The object of this edition is to restore the probable meaning of Isaiah,
so far as can be expressed in appropriate English. The basis of
the version is the revised translation of* 1611, *but alterations have
been introduced wherever the true sense of the prophecies appeared to
require it. The* Westminster Review *speaks of it as "a piece of
scholarly work, very carefully and considerately done." The*
Academy *calls it "a successful attempt to extend a right understanding of this important Old Testament writing."*

NOTES AND CRITICISMS on the HEBREW TEXT
OF ISAIAH. Crown 8vo. 2*s.* 6*d.*

*This work is offered as a slight contribution to a more scientific study
of the Old Testament Scriptures. The author aims at completeness,
independence, and originality, and constantly endeavours to keep
philology distinct from exegesis, to explain the form without pro-
nouncing on the matter. Saad Yah's Arabic Version in the Bod-*

Ieian has been referred to, while Walton and Buxtorf have been carefully consulted. The philological works of German critics, especially Ewald and Delitsch, have been anxiously and repeatedly studied. The Academy *calls the work "a valuable contribution to the more scientific study of the Old Testament."*

Choice Notes on the Four Gospels, drawn from
Old and New Sources.   Crown 8vo.   4s. 6d. each Vol.   (St. Matthew and St. Mark in one Vol. price 9s.).

These Notes are selected from the Rev. Prebendary Ford's Illustrations of the Four Gospels, the choice being chiefly confined to those of a more simple and practical character. The plan followed is to go over the Gospels verse by verse, and introduce the remarks, mostly meditative and practical, of one or more noted divines, on the verses selected for illustration. The names of the writers from whom the remarks are taken are invariably appended to the extracts, and amongst others to be met with, are the following:—J. Ford, Bonaventura, William Law, Pascal, Austin, Dr. Donne, Bonnell, Flavel, Bishop Hall, Dr. John Scott, Thomas Scott, R. Cecil, St. Ambrose, Bengel, Bishop Reynolds, J. H. Newman, George Herbert, Bishop Jewel, Jeremy Taylor, Cardinal Bellarmine, Quarles, St. Augustine, Archbishop Trench, Archbishop Leighton, Lord Bacon, Dr. Pusey, St. Chrysostom, Dr. Arnold, Thomas Fuller. Thus the selection is made in a catholic spirit, and the reader will find it a safe and useful companion in his meditations.

Church.—SERMONS PREACHED BEFORE the UNI-
VERSITY OF OXFORD. By the very Rev. R. W. CHURCH, M.A., Dean of St. Paul's.   Second Edition.   Crown 8vo.   4s. 6d.

Sermons on the relations between Christianity and the ideas and facts of modern civilized society. The subjects of the various discourses are:—"The Gifts of Civilization," "Christ's Words and Christian Society," "Christ's Example," and "Civilization and Religion." "Thoughtful and masterly . . . We regard these sermons as a landmark in religious thought. They help us to understand the latent strength of a Christianity that is assailed on all sides."— Spectator.

Clay.—THE POWER OF THE KEYS. Sermons preached in Coventry. By the Rev. W. L. CLAY, M.A. Fcap. 8vo. 3s. 6d.

In this work an attempt is made to shew in what sense, and to what extent, the power of the Keys can be exercised by the layman, the Church, and the priest respectively. The Church Review *says the sermons are "in many respects of unusual merit."*

Clergyman's Self-Examination concerning the

APOSTLES' CREED. Extra fcap. 8vo. 1s. 6d.

"These Confessions have been written by a clergyman for his own use. They speak of his own unbelief. Possibly they may help some of his brethren, who wish to judge themselves that they may not be ashamed before the Judge of all the earth." He takes each clause of the Creed and examines it in the light of common sense, in order to obtain its real meaning; searching at the same time his own heart to discover to what extent he really believes the statements so frequently uttered by him. Not only is it calculated to afford material aid to a proper understanding of the Creed, but will also be found extremely useful as a manual of devotion.

Collects of the Church of England. With a beauti-

fully Coloured Floral Design to each Collect, and Illuminated Cover. Crown 8vo. 12s. Also kept in various styles of morocco.

In this edition of the Church Collects, the paper is thick and handsome, and the type large and beautiful, each Collect, with a few exceptions, being printed on a separate page. The distinctive characteristic of this edition is the coloured floral design which accompanies each Collect, and which is generally emblematical of the character of the day or saint to which it is assigned; the flowers which have been selected are such as are likely to be in bloom on the day to which the Collect belongs. From the variety of plants elected and the faithfulness of the illustrations to nature, the volume should form an instructive and interesting companion to all devout Christians, who are likely to find their devotions assisted and guided by having thus brought before them the flowers in their seasons, God's beautiful and never-failing gifts to men. The

Preface explains the allusions and the table of contents gives both the popular and scientific name of each plant. There are at least one hundred separate plants figured. "Carefully, indeed livingly drawn and daintily coloured," says the Pall Mall Gazette. *The* Guardian *thinks it "a successful attempt to associate in a natural and unforced manner the flowers of our fields and gardens with the course of the Christian year."*

Cotton.—Works by the late GEORGE EDWARD LYNCH COTTON, D.D., Bishop of Calcutta :—

SERMONS PREACHED TO ENGLISH CONGREGA-TIONS IN INDIA. Crown 8vo. 7s. 6d.

These Sermons are selected from those which were preached between the years 1863 *and* 1866 *to English congregations under the varied circumstances of place and season which an Indian Bishop encounters. "The sermons are models of what sermons should be, not only on account of their practical teachings, but also with regard to the singular felicity with which they are adapted to times, places, and circumstances."*—Spectator.

EXPOSITORY SERMONS ON THE EPISTLES FOR THE SUNDAYS OF THE CHRISTIAN YEAR. Two Vols. Crown 8vo. 15s.

These two volumes contain in all fifty-seven Sermons. They were all preached at various stations throughout India, and from the nature of the circumstances which called them forth, the varied subjects of which they treat are dealt with in such a manner as is likely to prove acceptable to Christians in general. Each sermon, furnishes some account of the context and general scope of the epistle for the day, with a careful paraphrase of it, and with an explanation of any important difficulties occurring in it ; and in conclusion, draws out the main truths or precepts of the epistle. The Preface contains some sensible remarks on "Complaints against Modern Sermons," "Expository Preaching," "Plan of the Sermon," and other topics.

Cure.—THE SEVEN WORDS OF CHRIST ON THE
CROSS. Sermons preached at St. George's, Bloomsbury. By
the Rev. E. CAPEL CURE, M.A. Fcap. 8vo. 3s. 6d.

*These seven Sermons were preached at St. George's, Bloomsbury,
during the season of Lent, each having for its text one of the seven
last sayings of Christ while He hung on the Cross, as they are recorded in the following places:—(1) Luke xxiii. 34; (2) Luke
xxiii. 43; (3) John xix. 26; (4) Matthew xxvii. 46; (5) John
xix. 28; (6) John xix. 30; (7) Luke xxiii. 46. Of these Sermons
the* John Bull *says, "They are earnest and practical;" the* Nonconformist, *"The Sermons are beautiful, tender, and instructive;"
and the* Spectator *calls them "A set of really good Sermons."*

Curteis.—DISSENT in its RELATION to the CHURCH
OF ENGLAND. Eight Lectures preached before the University
of Oxford, in the year 1871, on the foundation of the late Rev.
John Bampton, M.A., Canon of Salisbury. By GEORGE HERBERT
CURTEIS, M.A., late Fellow and Sub-Rector of Exeter College ;
Principal of the Lichfield Theological College, and Prebendary of
Lichfield Cathedral; Rector of Turweston, Bucks. 8vo. 14s.

*In these Bampton Lectures the Author has endeavoured to accomplish
three things:—I. To shew those who are in despair at the present
divided aspect of Christendom, that from the Apostles' time downwards there has never been an age of the Church without similar
internal conflicts ; that if well managed, these dissensions may be
kept within bounds, and made to minister to the life and movement
of the whole polity; but if ill-managed, they are always liable to
become a wasting fever instead of a healthy warmth. II. To
present materials by which Churchmen might be aided in forming
an intelligent and candid judgment as to what precisely these dis-
senting denominations really are ; what it is they do, and what
they claim to teach ; and why it is they are now combining to bring
the Church of England, if possible, to the ground. III. To point
out some few indications of the wonderful and every way deplorable
misapprehensions which have clothed the Church of England to
their eyes in colours absolutely foreign to her true character ; have
ascrsbed to her doctrines absolutely contrary to her meaning ; and
have interpreted her customs in a way repellant to the Christian
Common-sense of her own people.*

Davies.—Works by the Rev. J. LLEWELYN DAVIES, M.A., Rector of Christ Church, St. Marylebone, etc. :—

THE WORK OF CHRIST ; or, the World Reconciled to God. With a Preface on the Atonement Controversy. Fcap. 8vo. 6s.

The reader will here find, amongst others, sermons on " The forgive-ness of sins," " Christ dying for men," " Sacrifice," " The Ex-ample of Christ," " The Baptism of Christ," " The Temptation of Christ," "Love, Divine and Human," " Creation by the Word," " Holy Seasons," and " The Coming of the Son of Man." The Preface is devoted to shewing that certain popular theories of the Atonement are opposed to the moral sense of mankind, and are not imposed on Christians by statements either in the Old or New Testaments.

SERMONS on the MANIFESTATION OF THE SON OF GOD. With a Preface addressed to Laymen on the present Position of the Clergy of the Church of England ; and an Ap-pendix on the Testimony of Scripture and the Church as to the possibility of Pardon in the Future State. Fcap. 8vo. 6s. 6d.

The Preface to this work is mainly occupied with the distinction between the essential and non-essential elements of the Christian faith, proving that the central religious controversy of the day relates, not, as many suppose, to such questions as the Inspiration of Scripture, but to the profounder question, whether the Son of God actually has been manifested in the person of Jesus of Nazareth. The grounds on which the Christian bases his faith are also examined. In the Appendix the testimony of the Bible and the Anglican formularies as to the possibility of pardon in the future state is investigated. The sermons, of which the body of the work is composed, treat of the great principles revealed in the words and acts of Jesus. " This volume, both in its substance, prefix, and suffix, represents the noblest type of theology now preached in the English Church."—Spectator.

Davies (Rev. J. Llewelyn)—*continued.*

BAPTISM, CONFIRMATION, AND THE LORD'S SUPPER, as Interpreted by their Outward Signs. Three Expository Addresses for Parochial use. Fcap. 8vo., limp cloth. 1*s.* 6*d.*

The method adapted in these addresses is to set forth the natural and historical meaning of the signs of the two Sacraments and of Confirmation, and thus to arrive at the spiritual realities which they symbolize. The work touches on all the principal elements of a Christian man's faith.

THE EPISTLES of ST. PAUL TO THE EPHESIANS, THE COLOSSIANS, and PHILEMON. With Introductions and Notes, and an Essay on the Traces of Foreign Elements in the Theology of these Epistles. 8vo. 7*s.* 6*d.*

*The Author believes the Epistles to the Ephesians and Colossians to be specially adapted to the wants of the present age. The chief aim, therefore, of the translations and notes in the present volume is simply to bring out as accurately as possible the apostle's meaning. The General Introduction, treats mainly of the time and circumstances in which Paul is believed to have written these Epistles. To each Epistle there is a special critical introduction. The Essay "On the Traces of Foreign elements in the Doctrine of these Epistles" discusses the question how far the ideas in the Epistles which resemble gnostical systems are to be found in books and traditions to which St. Paul and his contemporaries had access. "A valuable contribution to the literature of the Pauline Epistles."—*Freeman.

MORALITY ACCORDING TO THE SACRAMENT OF THE LORD'S SUPPER. Crown 8vo. 3*s.* 6*d.*

These discourses were preached before the University of Cambridge. They form a continuous exposition, and are directed mainly against the two-fold danger which at present threatens the Church—the tendency, on the one hand, to regard Morality as independent of Religion, and, on the other, to ignore the fact that Religion finds its proper sphere and criterion in the moral life.

Davies (Rev. J. Llewelyn)—*continued.*

THE GOSPEL and MODERN LIFE. Sermons on some of the Difficulties of the Present Day, with a Preface on a Recent Phase of Deism. Extra fcap. 8vo. 6*s.*

*The "recent phase of Deism" examined in the preface to this volume is that professed by the "Pall Mall Gazette"—that in the sphere of Religion there are one or two "probable suppositions," but nothing more. The writer starts with an assumption that mankind are under a Divine discipline, and in the light of this conviction passes under review the leading religious problems which perplex thoughtful minds of the present day. Amongst other subjects examined are—"Christ and Modern Knowledge," "Humanity and the Trinity," "Nature," "Religion," "Conscience," "Human Corruption," and "Human Holiness." "There is probably no writer in the Church fairer or more thoroughly worth listening to than Mr. Llewellyn Davies, and this book will do more than sustain his already high reputation."—*Globe.

De Teissier.—Works by G. F. DE TEISSIER, B.D.:—

VILLAGE SERMONS, FIRST SERIES. Crown 8vo. 9*s.*

This volume contains fifty-four short Sermons, embracing many subjects of practical importance to all Christians. The Guardian says they are "a little too scholarlike in style for a country village, but sound and practical." The following are a few of the titles of the Sermons:—"Death of the Prince Consort;" "Particular Providence;" "The Suffering Christ;" "Charity the Crown of Christianity;" "On Self-Deceit;" "On Hypocrisy;" "Christ Risen;" "The Comfort of Religion;" "Good Neighbourhood;" "The Return of Spring;" "A Harvest Sermon;" "Heart-Religion."

VILLAGE SERMONS, SECOND SERIES. Crown 8vo. 8*s.* 6*d.*

"This second volume of Parochial Sermons is given to the public in the humble hope that it may afford many reasonable thoughts for such as are Mourners in Zion." There are in all fifty-two Sermons embracing a wide variety of subjects connected with Christian faith and practice.

De Teissier (G. F.)—*continued.*

THE HOUSE OF PRAYER; or, a Practical Exposition of the Order for Morning and Evening Prayer in the Church of England. 18mo. extra cloth. 4s. 6d.

"There is in these addresses to the Christian reader," says the Introduction, an attempt to set forth the devotional *spirit of our Church in her daily forms of Morning and Evening Prayer, by shewing how all the parts of them may have a just bearing upon Christian practice, and so may have a deep influence upon the conduct of all our honest worshippers, under every possible relation and circumstance of life." "For a certain devout tenderness of feeling and religious earnestness of purpose, this little book of Mr. De Teissier's is really noteworthy; and it is a book which grows upon you very much when you read it."*—Literary Churchman.

Ecce Homo. A SURVEY OF THE LIFE AND WORK OF JESUS CHRIST. 23rd Thousand. Crown 8vo. 6s.

It is needless to say anything in recommendation of a book so widely known, and whose striking merit has been recognised by men and periodicals of all varieties of opinion. The following are a few selections from the very favourable notices with which the press has received it. "A very original and remarkable book, full of striking thought and delicate perception; a book which has realised with wonderful vigour and freshness the historical magnitude of Christ's work, and which here and there gives us readings of the finest kind of the probable motive of His individual words and actions."— Spectator. *He bates not a jot of Christ's pretensions. Miracles he insists upon as an integral part of the history. With a generous-minded sceptic this book may lead him on to give earnest and persistent attention to Christianity. The best and most established believer will find it adding some fresh buttresses to his faith. Finally it traces the working of the great principles of Christian charity through all the ramifications of character and action."—* Literary Churchman. *If we have not misunderstood him, we have before us a writer who has a right to claim deference from those who think deepest and know most."*—Guardian.

2

Farrar.—Works by the Rev. F. W. FARRAR, M.A., F.R.S., Head Master of Marlborough College, and Hon. Chaplain to the Queen :—

THE FALL OF MAN, AND OTHER SERMONS. Second and Cheaper Edition. Extra fcap. 8vo. 4*s.* 6*d.*

This volume contains twenty Sermons. No attempt is made in these sermons to develope a system of doctrine. In each discourse some one aspect of truth is taken up, the chief object being to point out its bearings on practical religious life. The Nonconformist *says of these Sermons,—"Mr. Farrar's Sermons are almost perfect specimens of one type of Sermons, which we may concisely call beautiful. The style of expression is beautiful—there is beauty in the thoughts, the illustrations, the allusions—they are expressive of genuinely beautiful perceptions and feelings." The* British Quarterly *says,—"Ability, eloquence, scholarship, and practical usefulness, are in these Sermons combined in a very unusual degree."*

THE WITNESS OF HISTORY TO CHRIST. Being the Hulsean Lectures for 1870. New Edition. Crown 8vo. 5*s.*

In these Lectures, Mr. Farrar endeavours to grapple with the most recent manifestations of infidelity, and endeavours to prove the divinity of Christ and the supernatural origin of Christianity on rational grounds, and by an appeal to the origin and progress of the Christian Religion itself. The copious notes contain many references which will be found of great use to the enquiring student. The following are the subjects of the Five Lectures:—I. "The Antecedent Credibility of the Miraculous." II. "The Adequacy of the Gospel Records." III. "The Victories of Christianity." IV. "Christianity and the Individual." V. "Christianity and the Race." The subjects of the four Appendices are:—A. "The Diversity of Christian Evidences." B. "Confucius." C. "Buddha." D. "Comte." "Here," the Standard *says, "we have eloquence combined with abundant information on all points of importance, both as regards theology and classical accuracy. This renders the book one of lasting value."*

SEEKERS AFTER GOD. The Lives of Seneca, Epictetus, and Marcus Aurelius. *See* SUNDAY LIBRARY at end of Catalogue.

Fellowship: LETTERS ADDRESSED TO MY SISTER MOURNERS. Fcap. 8vo. cloth gilt.   3s. 6d.

The Seven Letters contained in this little volume are written by one who has herself been shrouded in the darkest shadow of affliction consequent on being bereaved of one in whom her whole life was built up. In these Letters she tells her own sorrowful tale in unaffected, tender, touching words, which cannot but appeal to all who are placed in a similar comfortless position. She does not attempt to preach or to aggravate the sorrow and sense of loss of mourners by administering advice which they cannot take, or quoting texts and sentiments calculated only to irritate. She speaks of her loss and consequent grief in such a way as only a genuine mourner can; of the well-meant but aggravating comfort and useless advice admininistered her by her many comforters, and shews her fellow-mourners by what means, in course of soothing time, she got consolation and arrived at calmness and resignation. "A beautiful little volume, written with genuine feeling, good taste, and a right appreciation of the teaching of Scripture relative to sorrow and suffering."—Nonconformist. *"A very touching, and at the same time a very sensible book. It breathes throughout the truest Christian spirit."*—Contemporary Review.

Forbes.—THE VOICE OF GOD IN THE PSALMS. By GRANVILLE FORBES, Rector of Broughton.   Cr. 8vo.   6s. 6d.

This volume contains a connected series of twenty Sermons, divided into three parts, the two first parts being Introductory. Part I. treats of the "Ground of Faith," and consists of four Sermons on "Faith in God," "God's Voice within us," "Faith in God the Ground of Faith in the Bible," and "God's Voice in the Bible." Part II. treats of " The Voice of God in the Law and the Prophets," on which there are four Sermons; and Part III., occupying the greater part of the volume, deals with " The Voice of God in the Psalms," and consists of twelve Sermons. The last Sermon is on " The Voice of God in History." The Literary Churchman *says these Sermons are "characterized throughout by a strong realisation of the Providence and Fatherhood of God, and by their vivid apprehension of the Voice of God within man as answering to and accepting the Revelation of God to Man."*

Gifford.—THE GLORY OF GOD IN MAN. By E. H. GIFFORD, D.D. Fcap. 8vo., cloth. 3*s*. 6*d*.

This is a connected sequence of four Sermons which treat of "The Unrighteousness of Man," "The Righteousness of God," "Life in Christ," and "The Love of the Spirit." Notes are appended in which the sentiments of various authors on the statements made are quoted or referred to. "The sermons are short, thoughtful, and earnest discussions of the weighty matter involved in the subjects of them."—Journal of Sacred Literature.

Golden Treasury Psalter. *See* p. 50.

Hardwick.—Works by the Ven. ARCHDEACON HARDWICK : CHRIST AND OTHER MASTERS. A Historical Inquiry into some of the Chief Parallelisms and Contrasts between Christianity and the Religious Systems of the Ancient World. New Edition, revised, and a Prefatory Memoir by the Rev. FRANCIS PROCTER, M.A. Two vols. crown 8vo. 15*s*.

After several introductory chapters dealing with the religious tendencies of the present age, the unity of the human race, and the characteristics of Religion under the Old Testament, the Author proceeds to consider the Religions of India, China, America, Oceanica, Egypt, and Medo-Persia. The history and characteristics of these Religions are examined, and an effort is made to bring out the points of difference and affinity between them and Christianity. The object is to establish the perfect adaptation of the latter faith to human nature in all its phases and at all times. "The plan of the work is boldly and almost nobly conceived. . . We commend the work to the perusal of all those who take interest in the study of ancient mythology, without losing their reverence for the supreme authority of the oracles of the living God."—Christian Observer.

A HISTORY OF THE CHRISTIAN CHURCH. Middle Age. From Gregory the Great to the Excommunication of Luther, Edited by WILLIAM STUBBS, M.A., Regius Professor of Modern History in the University of Oxford. With Four Maps constructed for this work by A. KEITH JOHNSTON. Third Edition. Crown 8vo. 10*s*. 6*d*.

Although the ground-plan of this treatise coincides in many points

Hardwick (Archd.)—*continued.*

with that of the colossal work of Schröckh, yet in arranging the materials a very different course has frequently been pursued. With regard to his opinions the late author avowed distinctly that he construed history with the specific prepossessions of an Englishman and a member of the English Church. The reader is constantly referred to the authorities, both original and critical, on which the statements are founded. For this edition Professor Stubbs has carefully revised both text and notes, making such corrections of facts, dates, and the like as the results of recent research warrant. The doctrinal, historical, and generally speculative views of the late author have been preserved intact. "As a Manual for the student of ecclesiastical history in the Middle Ages, we know no English work which can be compared to Mr. Hardwick's book." —Guardian.

A HISTORY of the CHRISTIAN CHURCH DURING THE REFORMATION. New Edition, revised by Professor STUBBS. [*In the Press.*

This volume is intended as a sequel and companion to the "History of the Christian Church during the Middle Age." The author's earnest wish has been to give the reader a trustworthy version of those stirring incidents which mark the Reformation period, without relinquishing his former claim to characterise peculiar systems, persons, and events according to the shades and colours they assume, when contemplated from an English point of view, and by a member of the Church of England.

Hervey.—THE GENEALOGIES OF OUR LORD AND SAVIOUR JESUS CHRIST, as contained in the Gospels of St. Matthew and St. Luke, reconciled with each other, and shown to be in harmony with the true Chronology of the Times. By Lord ARTHUR HERVEY, Bishop of Bath and Wells. 8vo. 10s. 6d.

The difficulties and importance of the subject are first stated, the three main points of inquiry being clearly brought out. The Author then proceeds to shew that the genealogies of St. Matthew's and St. Luke's Gospels are both genealogies of Joseph, and examines the principle on which they are framed. In the following chapters the remaining aspects of the subject are exhaustively investigated.

Hymni Ecclesiæ.—Fcap. 8vo.   7s. 6d.

A selection of Latin Hymns of the Mediæval Church, containing selections from the Paris Breviary, and the Breviaries of Rome, Salisbury, and York.   The selection is confined to such holy days and seasons as are recognised by the Church of England, and to special events or things recorded in Scripture.   This collection was edited by Dr. Newman while he lived at Oxford.

Kempis, Thos. A. — DE IMITATIONE CHRISTI.

LIBRI IV.   Borders in the Ancient Style, after Holbein, Durer, and other Old Masters, containing Dances of Death, Acts of Mercy, Emblems, and a variety of curious ornamentations.   In white cloth, extra gilt.   7s. 6d.

The original Latin text has been here faithfully reproduced.   The Spectator *says of this edition, it " has many solid merits, and is perfect in its way."   While the* Athenæum *says, " The whole work is admirable; some of the figure compositions have extraordinary merit."*

Kingsley.—Works by the Rev. CHARLES KINGSLEY, M.A.,

Rector of Eversley, and Canon of Chester.   (For other Works by the same author, *see* HISTORICAL and BELLES LETTRES CATALOGUES).

The high merits of Mr. Kingsley's Sermons are acknowledged. Whether preached to the rustic audience of a village Church or to the princely congregation of the Chapel Royal, these Sermons are invariably characterized by intense earnestness and magnanimity, combined with genuine charity and winning tenderness; the style is always clear, simple, and unaffectedly natural, abounding in beautiful illustration, the fruit of a rich fancy and a cultivated taste.   They are emphatically practical.

THE WATER OF LIFE, AND OTHER SERMONS.

Second Edition.   Fcap. 8vo.   3s. 6d.

This volume contains twenty-one Sermons preached at various places —Westminster Abbey, Chapel Royal, before the Queen at Windsor,

Kingsley (Rev. C.)—*continued.*

etc. The following are a few of the titles:—"The Water of Life;" "The Wages of Sin;" "The Battle of Life;" "Ruth;" "Friendship, or David and Jonathan;" "Progress;" "Faith;" "The Meteor Shower" (1866); "Cholera" (1866); "The God of Nature."

VILLAGE SERMONS. Seventh Edition. Fcap. 8vo. 3s. 6d.

The following are a few of the titles of these Sermons:—"God's World;" "Religion not Godliness;" "Self-Destruction;" "Hell on Earth;" "Noah's Justice;" "Our Father in Heaven;" "The Transfiguration;" "The Crucifixion;" "The Resurrection;" "Improvement;" "On Books;" "The Courage of the Saviour."

THE GOSPEL OF THE PENTATEUCH. Second Edition. Fcap. 8vo. 3s. 6d.

This volume consists of eighteen Sermons on passages taken from the Pentateuch. They are dedicated to Dean Stanley out of gratitude for his Lectures on the Jewish Church, under the influence and in the spirit of which they were written. "With your book in my hand," Mr. Kingsley says in his Preface, "I have tried to write a few plain Sermons, telling plain people what they will find in the Pentateuch. I have told them that they will find in the Bible, and in no other ancient book, that living working God, whom their reason and conscience demand; and that they will find that He is none other than Jesus Christ our Lord."

GOOD NEWS OF GOD. Fourth Edition. Fcap. 8vo. 3s. 6d.

This volume contains thirty-nine short Sermons, preached in the ordinary course of the author's parochial ministrations. A few of the titles are—"The Beatific Vision;" "The Life of God;" "The Song of the Three Children;" "Worship;" "De Profundis;" "The Race of Life;" "Heroes and Heroines;" "Music;" "Christ's Boyhood;" "Human Nature;" "True Prudence;" "The Temper of Christ;" "Our Deserts;" "The Loftiness of God."

Kingsley (Rev. C.)—*continued.*

SERMONS FOR THE TIMES. Third Edition. Fcap. 8vo. 3*s*. 6*d*.

Here are twenty-two Sermons, all bearing more or less on the every-day life of the present day, including such subjects as these:— "Fathers and Children;" "A Good Conscience;" "Names;" "Sponsorship;" "Duty and Superstition;" "England's Strength;" "The Lord's Prayer;" "Shame;" "Forgiveness";" The True Gentleman;" "Public Spirit."

TOWN AND COUNTRY SERMONS. Second Edition. Extra fcap. 8vo. 3*s*. 6*d*.

Some of these Sermons were preached before the Queen, and some in the performance of the writer's ordinary parochial duty. There are thirty-nine in all, under such titles as the following:—"How to keep Passion-Week;" "A Soldier's Training;" "Turning-points;" "Work;" "The Rock of Ages;" "The Loftiness of Humility;" "The Central Sun;" "Εν Τουτω Νικα;" "The Eternal Man-hood;" "Hypocrisy;" "The Wrath of Love." Of these Sermons the Nonconformist *says, "They are warm with the fervour of the preacher's own heart, and strong from the force of his own con-victions. There is nowhere an attempt at display, and the clear-ness and simplicity of the style make them suitable for the youngest or most unintelligent of his hearers."*

SERMONS on NATIONAL SUBJECTS. Second Edition. Fcap. 8vo. 3*s*. 6*d*.

THE KING OF THE EARTH, and other Sermons. a Second Series of Sermons on National Subjects. Second Edition. Fcap. 8vo. 3*s*. 6*d*.

The following extract from the Preface to the 2nd Series will explain the preacher's aim in these Sermons:—" I have tried......to pro-claim the Lord Jesus Christ, as the Scriptures, both in their

Kingsley (Rev. C.)—*continued.*

strictest letter and in their general method, from Genesis to Reve-
lation, seem to me to proclaim Him; not merely as the Saviour of
a few elect souls, but as the light and life of every human being
who enters into the world; as the source of all reason, strength,
and virtue in heathen or in Christian; as the King and Ruler of
the whole universe, and of every nation, family, and man on
earth; as the Redeemer of the whole earth and the whole human
race...... His death, as a full, perfect, and sufficient sacrifice,
oblation, and satisfaction for the sins of the whole world, by which
God is reconciled to the whole human race.

DISCIPLINE, AND OTHER SERMONS. Fcp. 8vo. 3*s.* 6*d.*

Herein are twenty-four Sermons preached on various occasions, some
of them of a public nature—at the Volunteer Camp, Wimbledon,
before the Prince of Wales at Sandringham, at Wellington College,
etc.   A few of the titles are—"Discipline" (to Volunteers):
"Prayer and Science;" "False Civilization;" "The End of
Religion;" "The Humanity of God;" "God's World;" "Self-
Help;" "Toleration;" "The Likeness of God."   This volume
the Nonconformist *calls,—"Eminently practical and appropriate*
...... Earnest stirring words."   The Guardian *says,—"There is*
much thought, tenderness, and devoutness of spirit in these Sermons,
and some of them are models both in matter and expression."

DAVID.   FOUR SERMONS: David's Weakness—David's
Strength—David's Anger—David's Deserts. Fcap. 8vo. 2*s.* 6*d.*

These four Sermons were preached before the University of Cam-
bridge, and are specially addressed to young men.   Their titles are,
—"David's Weakness;" "David's Strength;" "David's Anger;"
"David's Deserts."   The Freeman *says—"Every paragraph*
glows with manly energy, delivers straightforward practical truths,
in a vigorous, sometimes even passionate way, and exhibits an
intense sympathy with everything honest, pure, and noble."

Lightfoot.—Works by J. B. LIGHTFOOT, D.D., Hulsean Professor of Divinity in the University of Cambridge; Canon of St. Paul's.

ST. PAUL'S EPISTLE TO THE GALATIANS. A Revised Text, with Introduction, Notes, and Dissertations. Third Edition, revised. 8vo. cloth. 12s.

The subjects treated in the Introduction are—the Galatian people, the Churches of Galatia, the date and genuineness of the Epistle, and its character and contents. The dissertations discuss the question whether the Galatians were Celts or Tartars, and the whole subject of " The Brethren of the Lord," and " St. Paul and the Three." While the Author's object has been to make this commentary generally complete, he has paid special attention to everything relating to St. Paul's personal history and his intercourse with the Apostles and Church of the Circumcision, as it is this feature in the Epistle to the Galatians which has given it an overwhelming interest in recent theological controversy. The Spectator *says "there is no commentator at once of sounder judgment and more liberal than Dr. Lightfoot."*

ST. PAUL'S EPISTLE TO THE PHILIPPIANS. A Revised Text, with Introduction, Notes, and Dissertations. Second Edition. 8vo. 12s.

*The plan of this volume is the same as that of " The Epistle to the Galatians." The Introduction deals with the following subjects : —" St. Paul in Rome," " Order of the Epistles of the Captivity," " The Church of Philippi," "Character and Contents of the Epistle," and its genuineness. The Dissertations are on " The Christian Ministry," " St. Paul and Seneca," and " The Letters of Paul and Seneca." "No commentary in the English language can be compared with it in regard to fulness of information, exact scholarship, and laboured attempts to settle everything about the epistle on a solid foundation."—*Athenæum. *" Its author blends large and varied learning with a style as bright and easy, as telling and artistic, as that of our most accomplished essayists."—*Non-conformist.

Lightfoot (Dr. J. B.)—*continued.*

ST. CLEMENT OF ROME, THE TWO EPISTLES TO THE CORINTHIANS. A Revised Text, with Introduction and Notes. 8vo. 8*s.* 6*d.*

This volume is the first part of a complete edition of the Apostolic Fathers. The Introductions deal with the questions of the genuineness and authenticity of the Epistles, discuss their date and character, and analyse their contents. An account is also given of all the different epistles which bear the name of Clement of Rome. "By far the most copiously annotated edition of St. Clement which we yet possess, and the most convenient in every way for the English reader."—Guardian.

ON A FRESH REVISION OF THE ENGLISH NEW TESTAMENT. Second Edition. Crown 8vo. 6*s.*

The Author begins with a few words on S. Jerome's revision of the Latin Bible, and then goes on to shew in detail the necessity for a fresh revision of the authorized version on the following grounds: —1. *False Readings.* 2. *Artificial distinctions created.* 3. *Real distinctions obliterated.* 4. *Faults of Grammar.* 5. *Faults of Lexicography.* 6. *Treatment of Proper Names, official titles, etc.* 7. *Archaisms, defects in the English, errors of the press, etc. The volume is completed by* (1) *an elaborate appendix on the words* ἐπιούσιος *and* περιούσιος, (2) *a table of passages of Scripture quoted, and* (3) *a general index.* " *The book is marked by careful scholarship, familiarity with the subject, sobriety, and circumspection.*"—Athenæum. " *It abounds with evidence of the most extensive learning, and of a masterly familiarity with the best results of modern Greek scholarship.*"—Standard.

Luckock.—THE TABLES OF STONE. A Course of Sermons preached in All Saints' Church, Cambridge, by H. M. Luckock, M.A., Vicar. Fcap. 8vo. 3*s.* 6*d.*

Sermons illustrative of the great principles of morality, mostly based on texts from the New Testament Scriptures.

Maclaren.—SERMONS PREACHED at MANCHESTER.

By ALEXANDER MACLAREN. Third Edition. Fcap. 8vo. 4*s.* 6*d.*

These Sermons, twenty-four in number, are well known for the freshness and vigour of their thought, and the wealth of imagination they display. They represent no special school, but deal with the broad principles of Christian truth, especially in their bearing on practical, every day life. A few of the titles are:—" The Stone of Stumbling," "Love and Forgiveness," " The Living Dead," "Memory in Another World," "Faith in Christ," "Love and Fear," " The Choice of Wisdom," " The Food of the World."

A SECOND SERIES OF SERMONS. Second Edition.

Fcap. 8vo. 4*s.* 6*d.*

This 2nd Series, consisting of nineteen Sermons, are marked by the same characteristics as the 1st. The Spectator *characterises them as "vigorous in style, full of thought, rich in illustration, and in an unusual degree interesting."*

Maclear.—Works by G. F. MACLEAR, D.D., Head Master of King's College School, and Preacher at the Temple Church :—

A CLASS-BOOK OF OLD TESTAMENT HISTORY.

With Four Maps. Sixth Edition. 18mo. 4*s.* 6*d.*

"The present volume," says the Preface, "forms a Class-Book of Old Testament History from the Earliest Times to those of Ezra and Nehemiah. In its preparation the most recent authorities have been consulted, and wherever it has appeared useful, Notes have been subjoined illustrative of the Text, and, for the sake of more advanced students, references added to larger works. The Index has been so arranged as to form a concise Dictionary of the Persons and Places mentioned in the course of the Narrative." The Maps, prepared by Stanford, materially add to the value and usefulness of the book: they are—1. A Map illustrating the Dispersion of Noah's Descendants. 2. A Map of Canaan, Egypt, and Sinai, to illustrate the Patriarchal History and the Exodus; with Mt. Sinai enlarged. 3. The Holy Land divided among the Twelve Tribes. 4. Solomon's Dominions, the Kingdoms of Judah and Israel, and the Lands of the Captivities. In the Appendix are

Maclear (G. F.)—*continued.*

given a variety of Tables of great interest and utility. The British Quarterly Review *calls it "A careful and elaborate, though brief compendium of all that modern research has done for the illustration of the Old Testament. We know of no work which contains so much important information in so small a compass."*

A CLASS-BOOK OF NEW TESTAMENT HISTORY.
Including the Connexion of the Old and New Testament. Fourth Edition. 18mo. 5s. 6d.

The present volume forms a sequel to the Author's Class-Book of Old Testament History, and continues the narrative to the close of St. Paul's second imprisonment at Rome. It is marked by the same characteristics as the former work, and it is hoped that it may prove at once a useful Class-Book and a convenient companion to the study of the Greek Testament. The work is divided into three Books—I. The Connection between the Old and New Testaments. II. The Gospel History. III. The Apostolic History. In the Appendix are given Chronological Tables, I. Of the Jews under the Empire. II. The Era of the Ptolemies and Seleucidæ. III. Rise of the Herodian Family. IV. The Gospel History. V. The Apostolic History. Appendix VI. is a Table of the Herodian Family. There are five Maps, viz.—1. A Map of the Holy Land to illustrate the Asmonean Period. 2. A Map of the Holy Land to illustrate the New Testament. 3. The Shores of the Sea of Galilee. 4. Jerusalem in the time of our Lord. 5. A Map to illustrate the Apostolic History. The Clerical Journal *says, "It is not often that such an amount of useful and interesting matter on biblical subjects, is found in so convenient and small a compass, as in this well-arranged volume."*

A CLASS-BOOK OF THE CATECHISM OF THE CHURCH OF ENGLAND. Second Edition. 18mo. cloth. 2s. 6d.

The present work is intended as a sequel to the two preceding books. "Like them, it is furnished with notes and references to larger works, and it is hoped that it may be found, especially in the higher

Maclear (G. F.)—*continued.*

forms of our Public Schools, to supply a suitable manual of in-struction in the chief doctrines of our Church, and a useful help in the preparation of Candidates for Confirmation." The Author goes over the Church Catechism clause by clause, and gives all needful explanation and illustration, doctrinal, practical, and historical; the Notes make the work especially valuable to the student and clergyman. After a brief Introduction on the Derivation, Division, and History of the Catechism, the book is divided into five Parts:—I. The Christian Covenant. II. The Creed. III. The Ten Commandments. IV. The Lord's Prayer. V. The Sacraments. Appended are a General Index, an Index of Greek and Latin Words, and an Index of the Words ex-plained throughout the book. The Literary Churchman *says, "It is indeed the work of a scholar and divine, and as such, though extremely simple, it is also extremely instructive. There are few clergy who would not find it useful in preparing candidates for Confirmation; and there are not a few who would find it useful to themselves as well."*

A FIRST CLASS-BOOK OF THE CATECHISM OF THE CHURCH OF ENGLAND, with Scripture Proofs for Junior Classes and Schools. Second Edition. 18mo. 6*d.*

This is an epitome of the larger Class-book, meant for junior students and elementary classes. The book has been carefully condensed, so as to contain clearly and fully, the most important part of the contents of the larger book. Like it the present Manual is sub-divided into five parts, each part into a number of short chapters, one or more of which might form a suitable lesson, and each chapter is subdivided in a number of sections, each with a pro-minent title indicative of its contents. It will be found a valuable Manual to all who are concerned with the religious training of children.

A SHILLING-BOOK of OLD TESTAMENT HISTORY. 18mo. cloth limp. 1*s.*

This Manual bears the same relation to the larger Old Testament

Maclear (G. F.)—*continued.*

History, that the book just mentioned does to the larger work on the Catechism. As in it, the small-type notes have been omitted, and a clear and full epitome given of the larger work. It consists of Ten Books, divided into short chapters, and subdivided into sections, each section treating of a single episode in the history, the title of which is given in bold type. The Map is clearly printed, and not overcrowded with names.

A SHILLING-BOOK of NEW TESTAMENT HISTORY. 18mo. cloth limp. 1s.

This bears the same relation to the larger New Testament History that the work just mentioned has to the large Old Testament History, and is marked by similar characteristics.

THE ORDER OF CONFIRMATION. A Sequel to the Class-Book of the Church Catechism, with Prayers and Collects. 18mo. 3d.

The Order of Confirmation is given in full, after which the Manual is divided into seven brief chapters:—I. " The Meaning of Confirmation." II. " The Origin of Confirmation." III., IV., V. " The Order of Confirmation," treating, (1) of " The Interrogation and Answer," (2) " The Laying on of Hands," (3) " The Prayers and Benediction," VI. " The Holy Communion." Chapter VII. consists of a few suitable Prayers and Collects intended to be used by the candidate during the days of preparation for Confirmation. Valuable references and notes are added. The Manual will be found valuable both by candidates and by clergymen. The Literary Churchman *calls it "An admirable Manual. Thoroughly sound, clear, and complete in its teaching, with some good, clear, personal advice as to Holy Communion, and a good selection of prayers and collects for those preparing for Confirmation."*

Macmillan.—Works by the Rev. HUGH MACMILLAN. (For other Works by the same Author, see CATALOGUE OF TRAVELS and SCIENTIFIC CATALOGUE).

THE TRUE VINE; or, the Analogies of our Lord's Allegory. Second Edition. Globe 8vo. 6s.

This work is not merely an exposition of the fifteenth chapter of St. John's Gospel, but also a general parable of spiritual truth from the world of plants. It describes a few of the points in which the varied realm of vegetable life comes into contact with the higher spiritual realm, and shews how rich a field of promise lies before the analogical mind in this direction. The majority of the analogies are derived from the grape-vine; but the whole range of the vegetable kingdom is laid under contribution for appropriate illustration. Indeed, Mr. Macmillan has brought into his service many of the results of recent scientific and historic research and biblical criticism; as well as the discoveries of travellers ancient and modern. The work will thus be found not only admirably suited for devotional reading, but also full of valuable and varied instruction. The Nonconformist *says, "It abounds in exquisite bits of description, and in striking facts clearly stated." The* British Quarterly *says, "Readers and preachers who are unscientific will find many of his illustrations as valuable as they are beautiful."*

BIBLE TEACHINGS IN NATURE. Sixth Edition. Globe 8vo. 6s.

In this volume the author has endeavoured to shew that the teaching of nature and the teaching of the Bible are directed to the same great end; that the Bible contains the spiritual truths which are necessary to make us wise unto salvation, and the objects and scenes of nature are the pictures by which these truths are illustrated. The first eight chapters describe, as it were, the exterior appearance of nature's temple—the gorgeous, many-coloured curtain hanging before the shrine. The last seven chapters bring us into the interior—the holy place, where is seen the very core of symbolical ordinances. "He has made the world more beautiful to us, and unsealed our ears to voices of praise and messages of love that might

Macmillan (H.)—*continued.*

otherwise have been unheard."—British Quarterly Review. "*Mr. Macmillan has produced a book which may be fitly described as one of the happiest efforts for enlisting physical science in the direct service of religion.*"—Guardian.

THE MINISTRY OF NATURE. Second Edition. Globe 8vo. 6*s.*

Mr. Macmillan believes that nature has a spiritual as well as a material side,—that she exists not only for the natural uses of the body, but also for the sustenance of the life of the soul. This higher ministry, the author believes, explains all the beauty and wonder of the world, which would often be superfluous or extravagant. In this volume of fourteen chapters the Author attempts to interpret Nature on her religious side in accordance with the most recent discoveries of physical science, and to shew how much greater significance is imparted to many passages of Scripture and many doctrines of Christianity when looked at in the light of these discoveries. Instead of regarding Physical Science as antagonistic to Christianity, the Author believes and seeks to shew that every new discovery tends more strongly to prove that Nature and the Bible have One Author. "Whether the reader agree or not with his conclusions, he will acknowledge he is in the presence of an original and thoughtful writer."—Pall Mall Gazette. "*There is no class of educated men and women that will not profit by these essays.*"—Standard.

M'Cosh.—For Works by JAMES McCOSH, LL.D., President of Princeton College, New Jersey, U.S., *see* PHILOSOPHICAL CATALOGUE.

Maurice.—Works by the late Rev. F. DENISON MAURICE, M.A., Professor of Moral Philosophy in the University of Cambridge.

Professor Maurice's Works are recognized as having made a deep impression on modern theology. With whatever subject he dealt he tried to look at it in its bearing on living men and their everyday surroundings, and faced unshrinkingly the difficulties which

3

Maurice (F. D.)—*continued.*

occu̇r to ordinary earnest thinkers in a manner that showed he had intense sympathy with all that concerns humanity. By all who wish to understand the various drifts of thought during the present century, Mr. Maurice's works must be studied. An intimate friend of Mr. Maurice's, one who has carefully studied all his works, and had besides many opportunities of knowing the Author's opinions, in speaking of his so-called "obscurity," ascribes it to "the never-failing assumption that God is really moving, teaching and acting; and that the writer's business is not so much to state something for the reader's benefit, as to apprehend what God is saying or doing." The Spectator *says—"Few of those of our own generation whose names will live in English history or literature have exerted so profound and so permanent an influence as Mr. Maurice."*

THE PATRIARCHS AND LAWGIVERS OF THE OLD TESTAMENT. Third and Cheaper Edition. Crown 8vo. 5*s*.

The Nineteen Discourses contained in this volume were preached in the chapel of Lincoln's Inn during the year 1851. *The texts are taken from the books of Genesis, Exodus, Numbers, Deuteronomy, Joshua, Judges, and Samuel, and involve some of the most interesting biblical topics discussed in recent times. In his Preface to the First Edition, Mr. Maurice endeavours to explain the mission and justify the position of the Church of England against the attacks of Dissenters and others; in his Preface to the Second Edition he comments upon some remarks made by Mr. Mansel on the meaning given by Mr. Maurice to the word 'Eternal.' In the latter Preface the writer says,—"My chief object in preaching and writing upon the Old Testament has been to shew that God has created man in His image; that being so created he is capable of receiving a revelation from God,—of knowing what God is; that without such a revelation he cannot be truly a man; that without such knowledge he cannot become what he is always feeling that he ought to become."*

Maurice (F. D.)—*continued.*

THE PROPHETS AND KINGS OF THE OLD TES-
TAMENT. Third Edition, with new Preface. Crown 8vo.
10s. 6d.

*The previous work brings down Old Testament history to the time of
Samuel. The Sermons contained in the present volume—twenty-
seven in number, coming down to the time of Ezekiel—though they
commence at that point are distinct in their subject and treatment.
Mr. Maurice, in the spirit which animated the compilers of the
Church Lessons, has in these Sermons regarded the Prophets more
as preachers of righteousness than as mere predictors—an aspect
of their lives which, he thinks, has been greatly overlooked in our
day, and than which, there is none we have more need to con-
template. He has found that the Old Testament Prophets, taken
in their simple natural sense, clear up many of the difficulties
which beset us in the daily work of life; make the past intelligible,
the present endurable, and the future real and hopeful. In the
Preface to this Third Edition, Mr. Maurice propounds his views
with regard to the connection of Church and State, with special
reference to the recent disestablishment of the Irish Church, and
the wish in certain quarters to treat the Church of England in the
same way.*

THE GOSPEL OF THE KINGDOM OF HEAVEN.
A Series of Lectures on the Gospel of St. Luke. Crown 8vo. 9s.

*Mr. Maurice, in his Preface to these Twenty-eight Lectures, says,
—"In these Lectures I have endeavoured to ascertain what is told
us respecting the life of Jesus by one of those Evangelists who proclaim Him to be the Christ, who says that He did come from a
Father, that He did baptize with the Holy Spirit, that He did rise
from the dead. I have chosen the one who is most directly connected with the later history of the Church, who was not an Apostle,
who professedly wrote for the use of a man already instructed in
the faith of the Apostles. I have followed the course of the writer's
narrative, not changing it under any pretext. I have adhered to
his phraseology, striving to avoid the substitution of any other for
his." This is necessary on account of the conventional notions*

Maurice (F. D.)—*continued.*

which most people are apt to attach to the words of the Gospels; and in the remainder of his Preface, Mr. Maurice points out some of these conventional notions, 1. *In relation to Miracles.* 2. *On the question, Are the Gospels the announcement of a religion?* 3. *Concerning Eternal Punishment.* 4. *The Authenticity and Inspiration of the Gospels.*

THE GOSPEL OF ST. JOHN. A Series of Discourses. Third and Cheaper Edition. Crown 8vo. 6s.

These Discourses, twenty-eight in number, are of a nature similar to those on the Gospel of St. Luke, and will be found to render valuable assistance to any one anxious to understand the Gospel of the beloved disciple, so different in many respects from those of the other three Evangelists. Appended are eleven notes illustrating various points which occur throughout the discourses, such as, "Baur's Theory of the Gospels;" "On the objections to a Revision of the Scriptures;" "On the Resurrection of the Body and the Judgment-day;" "On the doctrine of the Atonement—Scotch and English Divinity;" "On Corporate Holiness," etc. The Literary Churchman *thus speaks of this volume:—"Thorough honesty, reverence, and deep thought pervade the work, which is every way solid and philosophical, as well as theological, and abounding with suggestions which the patient student may draw out more at length for himself."*

THE EPISTLES OF ST. JOHN. A Series of Lectures on Christian Ethics. Second and Cheaper Edition. Cr. 8vo. 6s.

These Lectures on Christian Ethics were delivered to the students of the Working Men's College, Great Ormond Street, London, on a series of Sunday mornings. There are twenty Lectures in all, founded on various texts taken from the Epistles of St. John, which abound in passages bearing directly on the conduct of life, the duty of men to God and to each other. It will be found that a very complete system of practical morality is developed in this volume, in which the most important points in Ethics are set forth in an unconventional and interesting manner. Mr. Maurice believes that the question in which we are most interested, the question which

Maurice (F. D.)—*continued.*

most affects our studies and our daily lives, is the question, whether there is a foundation for human morality, or whether it is dependent upon the opinions and fashions of different ages and countries. This important question will be found amply and fairly discussed in this volume, which the National Review *calls " Mr. Maurice's most effective and instructive work. He is peculiarly fitted by the constitution of his mind, to throw light on St. John's writings." Appended is a note on "Positivism and its Teacher."*

EXPOSITORY SERMONS ON THE PRAYER-BOOK. The Prayer-book considered especially in reference to the Romish System. Second Edition. Fcap. 8vo. 5*s.* 6*d.*

" There are certain popular notions which," says the Preface, " assume that the Church of England is the result of a compromise; that the Articles embody the opinions of one party to the bargain, the Liturgy those of the other; that every time I put my hand to the former document I proclaim myself in the strictest sense a Protestant, that every time I use the latter I act as a Papist; that in fact, I am neither . . . . In delivering these Sermons [in Lincoln's Inn Chapel in 1848-9], *I endeavoured to tell laymen why I could with a clear heart and conscience ask them to take part with me in this Common Prayer. In publishing them I would address myself with equal earnestness and affection to another class, to the younger part of the clergy, and to those who are preparing for Orders." After an Introductory Sermon, Mr. Maurice goes over the various parts of the Church Service, expounds in eighteen Sermons, their intention and significance, and shews how appropriate they are as expressions of the deepest longings and wants of all classes of men.*

LECTURES ON THE APOCALYPSE, or Book of the Revelation of St. John the Divine. Crown 8vo. 10*s.* 6*d.*

These Twenty-three Lectures on what is generally regarded as the most mysterious Book in the Bible, do not demand that extensive knowledge of ancient or modern history which it is necessary to possess to be able to judge of most modern commentaries on Prophecy. Mr. Maurice, instead of trying to find far-fetched allusions to great historical events in the distant future, endeavours to discover the

Maurice (F. D.)—*continued.*

plain, literal, obvious meaning of the words of the writer, and shews that as a rule these refer to events contemporaneous with or immediately succeeding the time when the book was written. At the same time he shews the applicability of the contents of the book to the circumstances of the present day and of all times. Here, as in his other expositions of Scripture, Mr. Maurice attempts to shew that the Bible authorises us to believe that the Kingdom of Heaven, instead of being some dull Utopia in the far-distant future, is not "far off from any one of us," is indeed in our very midst. "Never," says the Nonconformist, *"has Mr. Maurice been more reverent, more careful for the letter of the Scripture, more discerning of the purpose of the Spirit, or more sober and practical in his teaching, than in this volume on the Apocalypse."*

WHAT IS REVELATION? A Series of Sermons on the Epiphany; to which are added, Letters to a Theological Student on the Bampton Lectures of Mr. Mansel. Crown 8vo. 10s. 6d.

Both Sermons and Letters were called forth by the doctrine maintained by Mr. Mansel in his Bampton Lectures, that Revelation cannot be a direct Manifestation of the Infinite Nature of God. Mr. Maurice maintains the opposite doctrine, and in his Sermons explains why, in spite of the high authorities on the other side, he must still assert the principle which he discovers in the Services of the Church and throughout the Bible. In the Letters to a Student of Theology, he has followed out all Mr. Mansel's Statements and Arguments step by step. The subjects of the Sermons are:—I. The Magians. II. Christ among the Doctors. III. St. Paul at Athens. IV. The Miracles. V. Casting out the Evil Spirit. VI. Christ's Parables. VII. Practice and Speculation. Among the matters discussed in the Letters are:— Sir William Hamilton; Butler; the Atonement and Incarnation; the Criterion of Truth; Philosophy of Consciousness; the Scotch; Prayer; Knowing and Being; the Trinity; Miracles; Kant; Contents and Evidences of the Bible. The Nonconformist *says, "There will be found ample materials to stimulate Christian faith and earnestness, to quicken and give tenderness to charity, and to vivify conceptions of the 'things not seen which are eternal.'"*

Maurice (F. D.)—*continued.*

SEQUEL TO THE INQUIRY, "WHAT IS REVELA-
TION?" Letters in Reply to Mr. Mansel's Examination of
"Strictures on the Bampton Lectures." Crown 8vo. 6s.

This, as the title indicates, was called forth by Mr. Mansel's Ex-
amination of Mr. Maurice's Strictures on his doctrine of the
Infinite.

THEOLOGICAL ESSAYS. Third Edition. Crown 8vo.
10s. 6d.

"The book," says Mr. Maurice, "expresses thoughts which have
been working in my mind for years; the method of it has not been
adopted carelessly; even the composition has undergone frequent
revision." There are seventeen Essays in all, and although meant
primarily for Unitarians, to quote the words of the Clerical
Journal, *"it leaves untouched scarcely any topic which is in agita-*
tion in the religious world; scarcely a moot point between our
various sects; scarcely a plot of debateable ground between Christ-
ians and Infidels, between Romanists and Protestants, between
Socinians and other Christians, between English Churchmen and
Dissenters on both sides. Scarce is there a misgiving, a dif-
ficulty, an aspiration stirring amongst us now,—now, when men
seem in earnest as hardly ever before about religion, and ask and
demand satisfaction with a fearlessness which seems almost awful
when one thinks what is at stake—which is not recognised and
grappled with by Mr. Maurice."

THE DOCTRINE OF SACRIFICE DEDUCED FROM
THE SCRIPTURES. Crown 8vo. 7s. 6d.

Throughout the Nineteen Sermons contained in this volume, Mr.
Maurice expounds the ideas which he has formed of the Doctrine
of Sacrifice, as it is set forth in various parts of the Bible. The
first five Sermons consider various sacrifices referred to in the Old
Testament, while in the remainder the death and resurrection of
Christ are looked at from different points of view. He has "tried
to speak of Sacrifice under every aspect in which the Bible presents
it." In the Dedicatory Letter (occupying fifty pages) to the

Maurice (F. D.)—*continued.*

Members of the Young Men's Christian Association, Mr. Maurice animadverts on an attack made on his opinions and character, by the Rev. Dr. Candlish of Edinburgh, in an address to that Society in Exeter Hall. "The habitual tone," says the Christian Spectator, *"is that of great seriousness and calm,—a seriousness which makes an impression of its own, and a serenity which is only broken by some overpowering feeling forcing itself into expression, and making itself heard in most meaning and stirring words."*

THE RELIGIONS OF THE WORLD, AND THEIR RELATIONS TO CHRISTIANITY. Fourth Edition. Fcap. 8vo. 5*s.*

These Eight Boyle Lectures are divided into two parts, of four Lectures each. In the first part Mr. Maurice examines the great Religious systems which present themselves in the history of the world, with the purpose of inquiring what is their main characteristic principle. The second four Lectures are occupied with a discussion of the questions, "In what relation does Christianity stand to these different faiths? If there be a faith which is meant for mankind, is this the one, or must we look for another?" In the Preface, the most important authorities on the various subjects discussed in the Lectures are referred to, so that the reader may pursue the subject further.

ON THE LORD'S PRAYER. Fourth Edition. Fcap. 8vo. 2*s.* 6*d.*

In these Nine Sermons the successive petitions of the Lord's Prayer are taken up by Mr. Maurice, their significance expounded, and, as was usual with him, connected with the every-day lives, feelings, and aspirations of the men of the present time. They were delivered in the momentous year 1848, *and frequent allusions are made and lessons drawn from the events of that year.*

ON THE SABBATH DAY; the Character of the Warrior, and on the Interpretation of History. Fcap. 8vo. 2*s.* 6*d.*

This volume contains Three Sermons on the Sabbath-day, one of them being in reference to the proposed opening of the Crystal Palace on Sunday—one on the "Character of the Warrior,"

Maurice (F. D.)—*continued.*

suggested by the Death of the Duke of Wellington; the fifth being on "The Divine Interpretation of History," delivered during the Great Exhibition of 1851. *In this last Mr. Maurice points out a few difficulties which, judging from his own experience, he thinks likely to perplex students of history, explaining how the Bible has anticipated and resolved them.*

THE GROUND AND OBJECT OF HOPE FOR MANKIND. Four Sermons preached before the University of Cambridge. Crown 8vo. 3*s.* 6*d.*

In these Four Sermons Mr. Maurice views the subject in four aspects :—I. The Hope of the Missionary. II. The Hope of the Patriot. III. The Hope of the Churchman. IV. The Hope of Man. The Spectator says, "It is impossible to find anywhere deeper teaching than this ;" and the Nonconformist, *"We thank him for the manly, noble, stirring words in these Sermons—words fitted to quicken thoughts, to awaken high aspiration, to stimulate to lives of goodness."*

THE LORD'S PRAYER, THE CREED, AND THE COMMANDMENTS. A Manual for Parents and Schoolmasters. To which is added the Order of the Scriptures. 18mo. cloth limp. 1*s.*

This book is not written for clergymen, as such, but for parents and teachers, who are often either prejudiced against the contents of the Catechism, or regard it peculiarly as the clergyman's book, but, at the same time, have a general notion that a habit of prayer ought to be cultivated, that there are some things which ought to be believed, and some things which ought to be done. It will be found to be peculiarly valuable at the present time, when the question of religious education is occupying so much attention. The book consists of four parts:—I. The Lord's Prayer. II. The Belief (Creed). III. The Commandments. IV. The Scriptures. Each part is divided into days, for each day a petition of the Prayer, a clause of the Creed, a Commandment, or a book or connected group of books of the Bible is taken, and a few words of exhortation, explanation, or reflection given on the sentiment suggested.

Maurice (F. D.)—*continued.*

THE CLAIMS OF THE BIBLE AND OF SCIENCE.

A Correspondence on some Questions respecting the Pentateuch.
Crown 8vo.   4s. 6d.

*This volume consists of a series of Fifteen Letters, the first and last
addressed by a 'Layman' to Mr. Maurice, the intervening thirteen
written by Mr. Maurice himself.   In the Layman's first letter to
Mr. Maurice, immediately called forth by the appearance of Bishop
Colenso's work on the Pentateuch, the writer sets forth some of the
difficulties likely to be suggested to an ordinary thinker and believer
in Christianity, by recent criticisms on the Bible of the class to
which the works of Colenso belong.   Three questions especially he
propounds, to which, he thinks, a layman may naturally at the
present time ask for an answer:—1. Do not our faith in Christ,
and our belief in the four Gospels as a real history, rest on grounds
independent of the results of any critical inquiry into the authorship
of the Pentateuch?   2. May we not continue to read the Pentateuch
as the Word of God, speaking of man and to man, without putting
a forced construction on the plain meaning of the words, and without imposing fetters on the freedom of scientific or critical investigation in any matters which God has given us the power to inquire
into?   3. Is faith in Christ contingent on the proof or disproof of
the existence of certain natural phenomena, which seem not to accord
with the language of the Bible?   Mr. Maurice, in his Thirteen
Letters, takes up these and the other points suggested by the Layman, and endeavours to clear them up and to throw light on the
all-important Biblical controversy generally.*

DIALOGUES ON FAMILY WORSHIP.   Crown 8vo.   6s.

*"The parties in these Dialogues," says the Preface, "are a Clergy-
man who accepts the doctrines of the Church, and a Layman
whose faith in them is nearly gone.   The object of the Dialogues
is not confutation, but the discovery of a ground on which two
Englishmen and two fathers may stand, and on which their
country and their children may stand when their places know
them no more."   Some of the most important doctrines of the
Church are discussed, the whole series of dialogues tending to shew*

Maurice (F. D.)—*continued.*

that men of all shades of belief may look up to and worship God as their common and loving Father. The key-words of the Dialogues are as follow:—I. A Layman's Perplexities. II. A Mother's Faith. III. Male Calvinism. IV. The Regenerate and the Unregenerate. V. The Natural and the Supernatural. VI. The Revelation and the Family of Abraham. VII. The Father and the Son. VIII. Repentance and Conversion. IX. Fathers in God. X. Heathen and Christian Devotion. XI. The Method of Prayer. XII. The Soul and the Spirit.

THE COMMANDMENTS CONSIDERED AS IN-STRUMENTS OF NATIONAL REFORMATION. Crown 8vo. 4s. 6d.

This is a book of practical morality and divinity. It was to some extent occasioned by Dr. Norman Macleod's Speech on the Sabbath, and his views of the Commandments. The author endeavours to shew that the Commandments are now, and ever have been, the great protesters against Presbyteral and Prelatical assumptions, and that if we do not receive them as Commandments of the Lord God spoken to Israel, and spoken to every people under heaven now, we lose the greatest witnesses we possess for national morality and civil freedom.

MORAL AND METAPHYSICAL PHILOSOPHY. Vol. I. Ancient Philosophy from the First to the Thirteenth Centuries. Vol. II. Fourteenth Century and the French Revolution, with a Glimpse into the Nineteenth Century. Two Vols. 8vo. 25s.

This is an edition in two volumes of Professor Maurice's History of Philosophy from the earliest period to the present time. It was formerly issued in a number of separate volumes, and it is believed that all admirers of the author and all students of philosophy will welcome this compact edition. In a long introduction to this edition, in the form of a dialogue, Professor Maurice justifies his own views, and touches upon some of the most important topics of the time.

Maurice (F. D.)—*continued.*

SOCIAL MORALITY. Twenty-one Lectures delivered in the University of Cambridge. Cheaper Edition. [*In the Press.*

In this series of Lectures, Professor Maurice considers, historically and critically, Social Morality in its three main aspects:—I. "The Relations which spring from the Family—Domestic Morality." II. "Relations which subsist among the various constituents of a Nation—National Morality." III. "As it concerns Universal Humanity—Universal Morality." Appended to each series is a chapter on " Worship:" first, "Family Worship;" second, "National Worship;" third, "Universal Worship." "Whilst reading it we are charmed by the freedom from exclusiveness and prejudice, the large charity, the loftiness of thought, the eagerness to recognise and appreciate whatever there is of real worth extant in the world, which animates it from one end to the other. We gain new thoughts and new ways of viewing things, even more, perhaps, from being brought for a time under the influence of so noble and spiritual a mind."—Athenæum.

THE CONSCIENCE: Lectures on Casuistry, delivered in the University of Cambridge. Second and Cheaper Edition. Crown 8vo. 5*s.*

In this series of nine Lectures, Professor Maurice, endeavours to settle what is meant by the word "Conscience," and discusses the most important questions immediately connected with the subject. Taking "Casuistry" in its old sense as being the "study of cases of Conscience," he endeavours to show in what way it may be brought to bear at the present day upon the acts and thoughts of our ordinary existence. He shows that Conscience asks for laws, not rules; for freedom, not chains; for education, not suppression. He has abstained from the use of philosophical terms, and has touched on philosophical systems only when he fancied "they were interfering with the rights and duties of wayfarers." The Saturday Review *says:* " We rise from the perusal of these lectures with a detestation of all that is selfish and mean, and with a living impression that there is such a thing as goodness after all."

Maurice (F. D.)—*continued.*

LECTURES ON THE ECCLESIASTICAL HISTORY
OF THE FIRST AND SECOND CENTURIES. 8vo. 10s. 6d.

The work contains a series of graphic sketches and vivid portraits, bringing forcibly before the reader the life of the early Church in all its main aspects. In the first chapter on "The Jewish Calling," besides expounding his idea of the true nature of a "Church," the author gives a brief sketch of the position and economy of the Jews ; while in the second he points out their relation to "the other Nations." Chapter Third contains a succint account of the various Jewish Sects, while in Chapter Fourth are briefly set forth Mr. Maurice's ideas of the character of Christ and the nature of His mission, and a sketch of events is given up to the Day of Pentecost. The remaining Chapters, extending from the Apostles' personal Ministry to the end of the Second Century, contain sketches of the character and work of all the prominent men in any way connected with the Early Church, accounts of the origin and nature of the various doctrines orthordox and heretical which had their birth during the period, as well as of the planting and early history of the Chief Churches in Asia, Africa and Europe. Besides the Apostles, the work contains characteristic sketches of the lives, position, and influence of Justin Martyr, St. Ignatius, Melito, Polycarp, Marcion, Dionysius of Corinth, Clement of Alexandria, Clement of Rome, Irenaeus, Tertullian, and many others. The three concluding chapters treat of the relations of the Church to the Emperors, the Philosophers, and the Sects.

LEARNING AND WORKING. Six Lectures delivered in Willis's Rooms, London, in June and July, 1854.—THE RELIGION OF ROME, and its Influence on Modern Civilisation. Four Lectures delivered in the Philosophical Institution of Edinburgh, in December, 1854. Crown 8vo. 5s.

In the Dedication and Preface to this volume, Professor Maurice shows that these two sets of Lectures have many points of connection. In the first series of Lectures the author endeavours to explain to such an audience as was likely to meet in Willis's Rooms,

Maurice (F. D.)—*continued.*

the scope and aims of the course of education established at the then recently founded Working Men's College, and at the same time expounds his notions of education in general, the pivot of his system being the truth that Learning and Working are not incompatible. The title to the second series is a sufficient index to their nature.

Moorhouse.—Works by JAMES MOORHOUSE, M.A., Vicar of Paddington :—

SOME MODERN DIFFICULTIES RESPECTING the FACTS OF NATURE AND REVELATION. Fcap. 8vo. 2s. 6d.

The first of these Four Discourses is a systematic reply to the Essay of the Rev. Baden Powell on Christian Evidences in "Essays and Reviews." The fourth Sermon, on "The Resurrection," is in some measure complementary to this, and the two together are intended to furnish a tolerably complete view of modern objections to Revelation. In the second and third Sermons, on the "Temptation" and "Passion," the author has endeavoured "to exhibit the power and wonder of those great facts within the spiritual sphere, which modern theorists have especially sought to discredit." The British Quarterly *says of them,—"The tone of the discussion is able, and throughout conservative of Scriptural truth."*

JACOB. Three Sermons preached before the University of Cambridge in Lent 1870. Extra fcap. 8vo. 3s. 6d.

In these Three Sermons the author endeavours to indicate the course of that Divine training by which the patriarch Jacob was converted from a deceitful and unscrupulous into a pious and self-denying man. In the first Sermon is considered "The Human Subject," or the nature to be trained; in the second "The Divine Power," the power by which that training was effected; and in the third "The Great Change," or the course and form of the training.

Moorhouse (J.)—*continued.*

THE HULSEAN LECTURES FOR 1865. Cr. 8vo. 5*s.*

The following are the subjects of the Four Hulsean Lectures in this volume:—I. "Bearing of Present Controversies on the Doctrine of the Incarnation." II. "How far the Hypothesis of a real Limitation in our Saviour's Human Knowledge is consistent with the Doctrine of His Divinity." III. "The Scriptural Evidence of our Saviour's Sinlessness." IV. "What Kind and Degree of Human Ignorance were left possible to our Lord Jesus Christ by the fact of His Human Sinlessness." The three Sermons which follow elucidate many difficulties which in the Lectures could not be investigated with that degree of care and fulness which was desirable. "Few more valuable works have come into our hands for many years . . . a most fruitful and welcome volume."—Church Review.

O'Brien.—AN ATTEMPT TO EXPLAIN and ESTABLISH THE DOCTRINE OF JUSTIFICATION by FAITH ONLY. By James Thomas O'Brien, D.D., Bishop of Ossory. Third Edition. 8vo. 12*s.*

This work consists of Ten Sermons. The first four treat of the nature and mutual relations of Faith and Justification; the fifth and sixth examine the corruptions of the doctrine of Justification by Faith only, and the objections which have been urged against it. The four concluding sermons deal with the moral effects of Faith. Various Notes are added explanatory of the Author's reasoning.

Palgrave.—HYMNS. By Francis Turner Palgrave. Third Edition, enlarged. 18mo. 1*s.* 6*d.*

This is a collection of twenty original Hymns, which the Literary Churchman *speaks of as "so choice, so perfect, and so refined,— · so tender in feeling, and so scholarly in expression."*

Palmer.—THE BOOK OF PRAISE: From the Best English Hymn Writers. Selected and arranged by Sir Roundell Palmer. With Vignette by Woolner. 18mo. 4*s.* 6*d.*

The present is an attempt to present, under a convenient arrangement, a collection of such examples of a copious and interesting branch of popular literature, as, after several years' study of the subject, have seemed to the Editor most worthy of being separated from the mass to which they belong. It has been the Editor's desire and aim to adhere strictly, in all cases in which it could be ascertained, to the genuine uncorrupted text of the authors themselves. The names of the authors and date of composition of the hymns, when known, are affixed, while notes are added to the volume, giving further details. The Hymns are arranged according to subjects. "There is not room for two opinions as to the value of the 'Book of Praise.'" —Guardian. *"Approaches as nearly as one can conceive to perfection."*—Nonconformist.

BOOK OF PRAISE HYMNAL. *See* end of this Catalogue.

Paul of Tarsus. An Inquiry into the Times and the Gospel of the Apostles of the Gentiles. By a GRADUATE. 8vo. 10*s.* 6*d.*

The Author of this work has attempted, out of the materials which were at his disposal, to construct for himself a sketch of the time in which St. Paul lived, of the religious systems with which he was brought in contact, of the doctrine which he taught, and of the work which he ultimately achieved. The Author's researches have been pursued with independence, candour, and ability, and it is confidently expected that the work will afford considerable assistance towards the solution of the important question,—By what means, and under what pressure, have the dogmas of later Christianity been developed from the Pauline original? "Turn where we will throughout the volume, we find the best fruit of patient inquiry, sound scholarship, logical argument, and fairness of conclusion. No thoughtful reader will rise from its perusal without a real and lasting profit to himself, and a sense of permanent addition to the cause of truth."—Standard.

Prescott.—THE THREEFOLD CORD. Sermons preached before the University of Cambridge. By J. E. PRESCOTT, B.D. Fcap. 8vo. 3*s.* 6*d.*

The title of this volume is derived from the subjects of the first three of these Sermons—Love, Hope, Faith. Their full titles are:—

I. "Christ the Bringer of Peace—Love." II. "Christ the Reno-vator—Hope." III. "Christ the Light—Faith." The fourth, an Assize Sermon, is on "The Divinity of Justice." The Sermons are an attempt to shew that Christian theology is sufficient for the wants of the present day. The Notes throughout the volume direct the reader to valuable sources of information. The Churchman *says the volume "is evidently the production of a scholar. Eloquent and striking passages abound throughout."*

Procter.—A HISTORY OF THE BOOK OF COMMON
PRAYER: With a Rationale of its Offices. By Francis Procter, M.A. Tenth Edition, revised and enlarged. Crown 8vo. 10s. 6d.

The fact that in fifteen years nine editions of this volume have been called for, shews that such a work was wanted, and that to a large extent Mr. Procter's book has supplied the want. "In the course of the last thirty years," the author says, "the whole subject has been investigated by divines of great learning, and it was mainly with a view of epitomizing their extensive publications, and correcting by their help sundry traditional errors or misconceptions, that the present volume was put together." The Second Part is occupied with an account of "The Sources and Rationale of the Offices." The Athenæum *says:—"The origin of every part of the Prayer-book has been diligently investigated,—and there are few questions or facts connected with it which are not either sufficiently explained, or so referred to, that persons interested may work out the truth for themselves."*

Procter and Maclear.—AN ELEMENTARY INTRO-
DUCTION TO THE BOOK OF COMMON PRAYER. Fourth Edition, Re-arranged and Supplemented by an Explanation of the Morning and Evening Prayer and the Litany. By F. Procter, M.A. and G. F. Maclear, D.D. 18mo. 2s. 6d.

This book has the same object and follows the same plan as the Manuals already noticed under Mr. Maclear's name. Each book is subdivided into chapters and sections. In Book I. is given a detailed History of the Book of Common Prayer down to the

Attempted Revision in the Reign of William III. Book II., consisting of four Parts, treats in order the various parts of the Prayer Book. Valuable Notes, etymological, historical, and critical, are given throughout the book, while the Appendix contains several articles of much interest and importance. Appended is a General Index and an Index of Words explained in the Notes. The Literary Churchman *characterizes it as "by far the completest and most satisfactory book of its kind we know. We wish it were in the hands of every schoolboy and every schoolmaster in the kingdom."*

Psalms of David CHRONOLOGICALLY ARRANGED.

An Amended Version, with Historical Introductions and Explanatory Notes. By FOUR FRIENDS. Second and Cheaper Edition, much enlarged. Crown 8vo. 8s. 6d.

One of the chief designs of the Editors, in preparing this volume, was to restore the Psalter as far as possible to the order in which the Psalms were written. They give the division of each Psalm into strophes, and of each strophe into the lines which composed it, and amend the errors of translation. In accomplishing this work they have mainly followed the guidance of Professor Henry Ewald. A Supplement contains the chief specimens of Hebrew Lyric poetry not included in the Book of Psalms. The Spectator *calls it "One of the most instructive and valuable books that have been published for many years."*

Golden Treasury Psalter.—THE STUDENT'S EDITION.

Being an Edition with briefer Notes of the above. 18mo. 3s. 6d.

This volume will be found to meet the requirements of those who wish for a smaller edition of the larger work, at a lower price for family use, and for the use of younger pupils in Public Schools. The short notes which are appended to the volume will, it is hoped, suffice to make the meaning intelligible throughout. The aim of this edition is simply to put the reader as far as possible in possession of the plain meaning of the writer. "It is a gem," the Nonconformist *says.*

Ramsay.—THE CATECHISER'S MANUAL; or, the Church Catechism Illustrated and Explained, for the Use of Clergymen, Schoolmasters, and Teachers. By ARTHUR RAMSAY, M.A. Second Edition. 18mo. 1*s.* 6*d.*

This Manual, which is in the form of question and answer, is intended to afford full assistance both to learners and teachers, to candidates for Confirmation as well as to clergymen, in the understanding of the Church Catechism, and of all the matters referred to therein. It is divided into seven chapters:—I. "The Church Catechism," in which the meaning and object of the Catechism is explained, as well as the significance and object of Confirmation. II. The various parts of the Catechism are analysed and explained. III. The Creeds—the Apostles', the Nicene, and the Athanasian. IV. The Apostles' Creed. V. The Commandments. VI. The Lord's Prayer. VII. The Sacraments. The English Journal of Education says,—"This is by far the best Manual on the Catechism we have met with, adapted not only for the use of the national schoolmaster, but also for the clergyman and the tutor.

Rays of Sunlight for Dark Days. A Book of Selections for the Suffering. With a Preface by C. J. VAUGHAN, D.D. 18mo. Fifth Edition. 3*s.* 6*d.* Also in morocco, old style.

Dr. Vaughan says in the Preface, after speaking of the general run of Books of Comfort for Mourners, "It is because I think that the little volume now offered to the Christian sufferer is one of greater wisdom and of deeper experience, that I have readily consented to the request that I would introduce it by a few words of Preface." The book consists of a series of very brief extracts from a great variety of authors, in prose and poetry, suited to the many moods of a mourning or suffering mind. "Mostly gems of the first water."—Clerical Journal.

Reynolds.—NOTES OF THE CHRISTIAN LIFE. A Selection of Sermons by HENRY ROBERT REYNOLDS, B.A., President of Cheshunt College, and Fellow of University College, London. Crown 8vo. 7*s.* 6*d.*

This work may be taken as representative of the mode of thought and

*feeling which is most popular amongst the freer and more cultivated
Nonconformists. "The reader throughout," says the* Patriot,
*"feels himself in the grasp of an earnest and careful thinker."
"It is long," says the* Nonconformist, *"since we have met with
any published sermons better calculated than these to stimulate
devout thought, and to bring home to the soul the reality of a
spiritual life."*

Roberts.—DISCUSSIONS ON THE GOSPELS. By the
Rev. ALEXANDER ROBERTS, D.D. Second Edition, revised and
enlarged. 8vo. 16s.

> *This volume is divided into two parts. Part I. "On the Language
> employed by our Lord and His Disciples," in which the author
> endeavours to prove that Greek was the language usually employed
> by Christ Himself, in opposition to the common belief that Our
> Lord spoke Aramæan. Part II. is occupied with a discussion
> "On the Original Language of St. Matthew's Gospel," and on
> "The Origin and Authenticity of the Gospels." The author pro-
> pounds some novel views on the points discussed, the result of
> long and deep study and research. The volume abounds in valu-
> able Notes, and in the Second Part is a chapter bearing chiefly
> on the proper authenticity of the Gospels as recently challenged
> by M. Renan. "The author brings the valuable qualifications of
> learning, temper, and an independent judgment. . . . It is but bare
> justice to affirm that his arguments render it [his proposition]
> extremely probable."*—Daily News. *"This volume is of intense
> interest to every Biblical student. It enters a field of inquiry
> hitherto untrodden."*—British Standard.

Robertson.—PASTORAL COUNSELS. Being Chapters
on Practical and Devotional Subjects. By the late JOHN ROBERT-
SON, D.D. Third Edition, with a Preface by the Author of
"The Recreations of a Country Parson." Extra fcap. 8vo. 6s.

> *These Sermons are the free utterances of a strong and independent
> thinker. He does not depart from the essential doctrines of his
> Church, but he expounds them in a spirit of the widest charity, and
> always having most prominently in view the requirements of prac-
> tical life. "The sermons are admirable specimens of a practical,
> earnest, and instructive style of pulpit teaching."*—Nonconformist.

Rowsell.—MAN'S LABOUR AND GOD'S HARVEST.
Sermons preached before the University of Cambridge in Lent,
1861. Fcap. 8vo. 3s.

*This volume contains Five Sermons, the general drift of which is
indicated by the title.* "*We strongly recommend this little volume
to young men, and especially to those who are contemplating working for Christ in Holy Orders.*"—Literary Churchman. "*Mr.
Rowsell's Sermons must, we feel sure, have touched the heart of
many a Cambridge Undergraduate, and are deserving of a wide
general circulation.*"—The Ecclesiastic.

Sanday.—THE AUTHORSHIP AND HISTORICAL
CHARACTER OF THE FOURTH GOSPEL, considered in
reference to the Contents of the Gospel itself. A Critical Essay.
By WILLIAM SANDAY, M.A., Fellow of Trinity College, Oxford.
Crown 8vo. 8s. 6d.

*The object of this Essay is critical and nothing more. The Author
attempts to apply faithfully and persistently to the contents of the
much disputed fourth Gospel that scientific method which has been
so successful in other directions.* "*The facts of religion,*" *the
Author believes,* "*(i. e. the documents, the history of religious
bodies, &c.) are as much facts as the lie of a coal-bed or the formation of a coral-reef.*" *It is believed that the work will prove of
value to theologians, as well as to all who take an interest in the
subject of which it treats.*

Sergeant.—SERMONS. By the Rev. E. W. SERGEANT,
M.A., Balliol College, Oxford ; Assistant Master at Westminster
College. Fcap. 8vo. 2s. 6d.

*This volume contains Nine Sermons on a variety of topics, preached
by the author at various times and to various classes of hearers.
The First Sermon is on Free Inquiry.*

Smith.—PROPHECY A PREPARATION FOR CHRIST.
Eight Lectures preached before the University of Oxford, being the
Bampton Lectures for 1869. By R. PAYNE SMITH, D.D., Dean
of Canterbury. Second and Cheaper Edition. Crown 8vo. 6s.

The author's object in these Lectures is to shew that there exists in the

Old Testament an element, which no criticism on naturalistic principles can either account for or explain away: that element is Prophecy. The author endeavours to prove that its force does not consist merely in its predictions. The Bible describes man's first estate of innocency, his fall, and the promise given by God of his restoration. Virtually the promise meant that God would give man a true religion; and the author asserts that Christianity is the sole religion on earth that fulfils the conditions necessary to constitute a true religion. God has pledged His own attributes in its behalf; this pledge He has given in miracle and prophecy. The author endeavours to shew the reality of that portion of the proof founded on prophecy. "These Lectures overflow with solid learning."—Record.

Smith.—CHRISTIAN FAITH. Sermons preached before the University of Cambridge. By W. SAUMAREZ SMITH, M.A., Principal of St. Aidan's College, Birkenhead. Fcap. 8vo. 3s. 6d.

The first two sermons in this volume have special reference to the Person of Christ; the next two are concerned with the inner life of Christians; and the last speaks of the outward development of Christian faith. "Appropriate and earnest sermons, suited to the practical exhortation of an educated congregation."—Guardian.

Stanley.—Works by the Very Rev. A. P. STANLEY, D.D., Dean of Westminster.

THE ATHANASIAN CREED, with a Preface on the General Recommendations of the RITUAL COMMISSION. Cr. 8vo. 2s.

The object of the work is not so much to urge the omission or change of the Athanasian Creed, as to shew that such a relaxation ought to give offence to no reasonable or religious mind. With this view, the Dean of Westminster discusses in succession—(1) the Authorship of the Creed, (2) its Internal Characteristics, (3) the Peculiarities of its Use in the Church of England, (4) its Advantages and Disadvantages, (5) its various Interpretations, and (6) the Judgment passed upon it by the Ritual Commission. In conclusion, Dr. Stanley maintains that the use of the Athanasian

Stanley (Dean)—*continued.*

Creed should no longer be made compulsory. "*Dr. Stanley puts with admirable force the objections which may be made to the Creed ; equally admirable, we think, in his statement of its advantages.*"— Spectator.

THE NATIONAL THANKSGIVING. Sermons preached in Westminster Abbey. Second Edition. Crown 8vo. 2*s.* 6*d.*

These Sermons are (1) "*Death and Life,*" *preached December* 10, 1871 ; (2) "*The Trumpet of Patmos,*" *December* 17, 1871 ; (3) "*The Day of Thanksgiving,*" *March* 3, 1872. *It is hoped that these Sermons may recall, in some degree, the serious reflections connected with the Prince of Wales's illness, which, if the nation is true to itself, ought not to perish with the moment. The proceeds of the publication will be devoted to the Fund for the Restoration of St. Paul's Cathedral.* "*In point of fervour and polish by far the best specimens in print of Dean Stanley's eloquent style.*"—Standard.

Sunday Library. See end of this Catalogue.

Swainson.—Works by C. A. SWAINSON, D.D., Canon of Chichester :—

THE CREEDS OF THE CHURCH IN THEIR RE-LATIONS TO HOLY SCRIPTURE and the CONSCIENCE OF THE CHRISTIAN. 8vo. cloth. 9*s.*

The Lectures which compose this volume discuss, amongst others, the following subjects: "*Faith in God,*" "*Exercise of our Reason,*" "*Origin and Authority of Creeds,*" *and* "*Private Judgment, its use and exercise.*" "*Treating of abstruse points of Scripture, he applies them so forcibly to Christian duty and practice as to prove eminently serviceable to the Church.*"—John Bull.

THE AUTHORITY OF THE NEW TESTAMENT, and other LECTURES, delivered before the University of Cambridge. 8vo. cloth. 12*s.*

The first series of Lectures in this work is on "*The Words spoken by the Apostles of Jesus,*" "*The Inspiration of God's Servants,*"

" The Human Character of the Inspired Writers," and " The Divine Character of the Word written." The second embraces Lectures on " Sin as Imperfection," " Sin as Self-will," "Whatsoever is not of Faith is Sin," " Christ the Saviour," and " The Blood of the New Covenant." The third is on "Christians One Body in Christ," " The One Body the Spouse of Christ," " Christ's Prayer for Unity," " Our Reconciliation should be manifested in common Worship," and "Ambassadors for Christ." "All the grave and awful questions associated with human sinfulness and the Divine plan of redemption are discussed with minute and painstaking care, and in the Appendix all the passages of Scripture referring to them are marshalled and critically reviewed."— Wesleyan Times.

Taylor.—THE RESTORATION OF BELIEF. New and Revised Edition. By ISAAC TAYLOR, Esq. Crown 8vo. 8s. 6d.

The earlier chapters are occupied with an examination of the primitive history of the Christian Religion, and its relation to the Roman government; and here, as well as in the remainder of the work, the author shews the bearing of that history on some of the difficult and interesting questions which have recently been claiming the attention of all earnest men. The book will be found to contain a clear and full statement of the case as it at present stands in behalf of Christianity. The last chapter of this New Edition treats of " The Present Position of the Argument concerning Christianity," with special reference to M. Renan's Vie de Jésus. *The* Journal of Sacred Literature *says,—" The current of thought which runs through this book is calm and clear, its tone is earnest, its manner courteous. The author has carefully studied the successive problems which he so ably handles."*

Temple.—SERMONS PREACHED IN THE CHAPEL of RUGBY SCHOOL. By F. TEMPLE, D.D., Bishop of Exeter. New and Cheaper Edition. Extra fcap. 8vo. 4s. 6d.

This volume contains Thirty-five Sermons on topics more or less intimately connected with every-day life. The following are a few of the subjects discoursed upon:—"Love and Duty;" "Coming to Christ;" "Great Men;" "Faith;" " Doubts;" " Scruples:"

Temple (F., D.D.)—*continued.*

"Original Sin;" "Friendship;" "Helping Others;" "The Discipline of Temptation;" "Strength a Duty;" "Worldliness;" "Ill Temper;" "The Burial of the Past." The Critic *speaks of them thus:—"We trust that the tender affectionate spirit of practical Christianity which runs through every page of the volume will have its due effect. . . . desiring to rouse the youthful hearers to a sense of duty, and to arm them against the perils and dangers of the world against which they are so soon to battle."*

A SECOND SERIES OF SERMONS PREACHED IN THE CHAPEL OF RUGBY SCHOOL. Extra fcap. 8vo. 6s.

This Second Series of Forty-two brief, pointed, practical Sermons, on topics intimately connected with the every-day life of young and old, will be acceptable to all who are acquainted with the First Series. The following are a few of the subjects treated of:—"Disobedience," "Almsgiving," "The Unknown Guidance of God," "Apathy one of our Trials," "High Aims in Leaders," "Doing our Best," "The Use of Knowledge," "Use of Observances," "Martha and Mary," "John the Baptist," "Severity before Mercy," "Even Mistakes Punished," "Morality and Religion," "Children," "Action the Test of Spiritual Life," "Self-Respect," "Too Late," "The Tercentenary."

A THIRD SERIES OF SERMONS PREACHED IN RUGBY SCHOOL CHAPEL IN 1867—1869. Extra fcap. 8vo. 6s.

This third series of Bishop Temple's Rugby Sermons, contains thirty-six brief discourses, characterized by "a penetrating and direct practicalness, informed by a rare intuitive sympathy with boy-nature; its keen perception of reality and earnestness, its equally keen sympathy with what is noblest in sentiment and feelings." The volume includes the "Good-bye" sermon preached on his leaving Rugby to enter on the office he now holds.

Thring.—Works by Rev. EDWARD THRING, M.A.

SERMONS DELIVERED AT UPPINGHAM SCHOOL.
Crown 8vo. 5*s.*

*In this volume are contained Forty-seven brief Sermons, all on
subjects more or less intimately connected with Public-school life.
"These Sermons," the author says, "are sent into the world as
parts of a system, and as exponents, in some degree, of the experience of working men, that it is possible to have a free and
manly school-life, complete in all its parts, neither lost in a crowd,
nor shut up in a prison, nor reared in a hot-bed."—"We desire
very highly to commend these capital Sermons which treat of a boy's
life and trials in a thoroughly practical way and with great
simplicity and impressiveness.   They deserve to be classed with the
best of their kind."*—Literary Churchman.

THOUGHTS ON LIFE-SCIENCE.   New Edition, enlarged and revised.   Crown 8vo.   7*s.* 6*d.*

*In this volume are discussed in a familiar manner some of the most
interesting problems between Science and Religion, Reason and
Feeling.   "Learning and Science," says the Author, "are claiming
the right of building up and pulling down everything, especially
the latter.   It has seemed to me no useless task to look steadily at
what has happened, to take stock as it were of man's gains, and to
endeavour amidst new circumstances to arrive at some rational
estimate of the bearings of things, so that the limits of what is possible at all events may be clearly marked out for ordinary readers.
.... This book is an endeavour to bring out some of the main
facts of the world."*

Tracts for Priests and People.   By VARIOUS
WRITERS.

THE FIRST SERIES.   Crown 8vo.   8*s.*
THE SECOND SERIES.   Crown 8vo.   8*s.*
The whole Series of Fifteen Tracts may be had separately, price
One Shilling each.

*A series of papers written after the excitement aroused by the publica-
tion of "Essays and Reviews" had somewhat abated, and designed,*

by the exposition of positive truth, to meet the religious difficulties of honest inquirers. Amongst the writers are Mr. Thomas Hughes, Professor Maurice, the Rev. J. Llewellyn Davies, and Mr. J. M. Ludlow.

Trench.—Works by R. CHENEVIX TRENCH, D.D., Archbishop of Dublin. (For other Works by the same author, *see* BIOGRAPHICAL, BELLES LETTRES, and LINGUISTIC CATALOGUES).

Archbishop Trench is well known as a writer who has the happy faculty of being able to take with discrimination the results of the highest criticism and scholarship, and present them in such a shape as will be not only valuable to scholars, but interesting, intelligible, and of the greatest use even to the ordinary reader. It is generally acknowledged that few men have been more successful in bringing out the less obvious meanings of the New Testament, or done more for the popular yet scholarly exposition of the Bible generally.

NOTES ON THE PARABLES OF OUR LORD. Eleventh Edition. 8vo. 12s.

This work has taken its place as a standard exposition and interpretation of Christ's Parables. The book is prefaced by an Introductory Essay in four chapters:—I. On the definition of the Parable. II. On Teaching by Parables. III. On the Interpretation of the Parables. IV. On other Parables besides those in the Scriptures. The author then proceeds to take up the Parables one by one, and by the aid of philology, history, antiquities, and the researches of travellers, shew forth the significance, beauty, and applicability of each, concluding with what he deems its true moral interpretation. In the numerous Notes are many valuable references, illustrative quotations, critical and philological annotations, etc., and appended to the volume is a classified list of fifty-six works on the Parables.

NOTES ON THE MIRACLES OF OUR LORD. Ninth Edition. 8vo. 12s.

In the 'Preliminary Essay' to this work, all the momentous and interesting questions that have been raised in connection with

Trench—*continued.*

Miracles, are discussed with considerable fulness, and the author's usual candour and learning. The Essay consists of six chapters : —I. On the Names of Miracles, i. e. *the Greek words by which they are designated in the New Testament. II. The Miracles and Nature—What is the difference between a Miracle and any event in the ordinary course of Nature? III. The Authority of Miracles—Is the Miracle to command absolute obedience? IV. The Evangelical, compared with the other cycles of Miracles. V. The Assaults on the Miracles*—1. *The Jewish.* 2. *The Heathen (Celsus etc.).* 3. *The Pantheistic (Spinosa etc.).* 4. *The Sceptical (Hume).* 5. *The Miracles only relatively miraculous (Schleiermacher).* 6. *The Rationalistic (Paulus).* 7. *The Historico-Critical (Woolston, Strauss). VI. The Apologetic Worth of the Miracles. The author then treats the separate Miracles as he does the Parables.*

SYNONYMS OF THE NEW TESTAMENT. New Edition, enlarged. 8vo. cloth. 12*s.*

The study of synonyms in any language is valuable as a discipline for training the mind to close and accurate habits of thought ; more especially is this the case in Greek—" a language spoken by a people of the finest and subtlest intellect ; who saw distinctions where others saw none ; who divided out to different words what others often were content to huddle confusedly under a common term. . . . Where is it so desirable that we should miss nothing, that we should lose no finer intention of the writer, as in those words which are the vehicles of the very mind of God Himself?" This work is recognised as a valuable companion to every student of the New Testament in the original. This, the Seventh Edition, has been carefully revised, and a considerable number of new synonyms added. Appended is an Index to the Synonyms, and an Index to many other words alluded to or explained throughout the work. "He is," the Athenæum *says, " a guide in this department of knowledge to whom his readers may intrust themselves with confidence. His sober judgment and sound sense are barriers against the misleading influence of arbitrary hypotheses."*

Trench—*continued.*

ON THE AUTHORIZED VERSION OF THE NEW TESTAMENT. Second Edition. 8vo. 7s.

Archbishop Trench's familiarity with the New Testament makes him peculiarly fitted to estimate the value of the present translation, and to give directions as to how a new one should be proceeded with. After some Introductory Remarks, in which the propriety of a revision is briefly discussed, the whole question of the merits of the present version is gone into in detail, in eleven chapters. Appended is a chronological list of works bearing on the subject, an Index of the principal Texts considered, an Index of Greek Words, and an Index of other Words referred to throughout the book.

STUDIES IN THE GOSPELS. Second Edition. 8vo. 10s. 6d.

This book is published under the conviction that the assertion often made is untrue,—viz. that the Gospels are in the main plain and easy, and that all the chief difficulties of the New Testament are to be found in the Epistles. These "Studies," sixteen in number, are the fruit of a much larger scheme, and each Study deals with some important episode mentioned in the Gospels, in a critical, philosophical, and practical manner. Many learned references and quotations are added to the Notes. Among the subjects treated are:—The Temptation; Christ and the Samaritan Woman; The Three Aspirants; The Transfiguration; Zacchæus; The True Vine; The Penitent Malefactor; Christ and the Two Disciples on the way to Emmaus.

COMMENTARY ON THE EPISTLES to the SEVEN CHURCHES IN ASIA. Third Edition, revised. 8vo. 8s. 6d.

Bengel was wont above all things to recommend the study of these Epistles to youthful ministers of Christ's Word and Sacraments; and, as the author says in his Preface, the number of aspects in which they present themselves to us as full of interest, is extraordinary. They are full of interest to the student of ecclesiastical history; possess a strong attraction for those who occupy them-

Trench—*continued.*

selves with questions of pure exegesis, from the fact of their con-taining so many unsolved problems of interpretation; their purely theological interest is great; their practical interest in their bearing on the whole pastoral and ministerial work is extreme; and finally, there is about these Epistles a striking originality, an entire unlikeness, in some points at least, to anything else in Scripture. The present work consists of an Introduction, being a commentary on Rev. i. 4—20, a detailed examination of each of the Seven Epistles, in all its bearings, and an Excursus on the Historico-Prophetical Interpretation of the Epistles.

THE SERMON ON THE MOUNT. An Exposition drawn from the writings of St. Augustine, with an Essay on his merits as an Interpreter of Holy Scripture. Third Edition, enlarged. 8vo. 10*s.* 6*d.*

The first half of the present work consists of a dissertation in eight chapters on "Augustine as an Interpreter of Scripture," the titles of the several chapters being as follow:—I. Augustine's General Views of Scripture and its Interpretation. II. The External Helps for the Interpretation of Scripture possessed by Augustine. III. Augustine's Principles and Canons of Interpretation. IV. Augustine's Allegorical Interpretation of Scripture. V. Illustrations of Augustine's Skill as an Interpreter of Scripture. VI. Augustine on John the Baptist and on St. Stephen. VII. Augustine on the Epistle to the Romans. VIII. Miscellaneous Examples of Augustine's Interpretation of Scripture. The latter half of the work consists of Augustine's Exposition of the Sermon on the Mount, not however a mere series of quotations from Augustine, but a connected account of his sentiments on the various passages of that Sermon, interspersed with criticisms by Archbishop Trench.

SERMONS PREACHED in WESTMINSTER ABBEY. Second Edition. 8vo. 10*s.* 6*d.*

These Sermons embrace a wide variety of topics, and are thoroughly practical, earnest, and evangelical, and simple in style. The following are a few of the subjects:—"Tercentenary Celebration

Trench—*continued.*

of Queen Elizabeth's Accession;" "Conviction and Conversion;" "The Incredulity of Thomas;" "The Angels' Hymn;" "Counting the Cost;" "The Holy Trinity in Relation to our Prayers;" "On the Death of General Havelock;" "Christ Weeping over Jerusalem;" "Walking with Christ in White."

SHIPWRECKS OF FAITH. Three Sermons preached before the University of Cambridge in May, 1867. Fcap. 8vo. 2s. 6d.

These Sermons are especially addressed to young men. The subjects are "Balaam," "Saul," and "Judas Iscariot," three of the mournfullest lives recorded in Scripture, "for the greatness of their vocation, and their disastrous falling short of the same, for the utter defeat of their lives, for the shipwreck of everything which they made." These lives are set forth as beacon-lights, "to warn us off from perilous reefs and quicksands, which have been the destruction of many, and which might only too easily be ours." The John Bull *says, "they are, like all he writes, affectionate and earnest discourses."*

Tudor.—The DECALOGUE VIEWED as the CHRISTIAN'S LAW. With Special Reference to the Questions and Wants of the Times. By the Rev. RICH. TUDOR, B.A. Crown 8vo. 10s. 6d.

The author's aim is to bring out the Christian sense of the Decalogue in its application to existing needs and questions. The work will be found to occupy ground which no other single work has hitherto filled. It is divided into Two Parts, the First Part consisting of three lectures on "Duty," and the Second Part of twelve lectures on the Ten Commandments. The Guardian *says of it, "His volume throughout is an outspoken and sound exposition of Christian morality, based deeply upon true foundations, set forth systematically, and forcibly and plainly expressed—as good a specimen of what pulpit lectures ought to be as is often to be found." The* Westminster Review *says, "There is an earnestness in his purpose and evidently a sincere endeavour to apply the words of Scripture to present needs."*

Tulloch.—THE CHRIST OF THE GOSPELS AND THE CHRIST OF MODERN CRITICISM. Lectures on M. RENAN's "Vie de Jésus." By JOHN TULLOCH, D.D., Principal of the College of St. Mary, in the University of St. Andrew's. Extra fcap. 8vo. 4s. 6d.

While Dr. Tulloch does not hesitate to grapple boldly with the statements and theories of Renan, he does so in a spirit of perfect fairness and courtesy, eschewing all personalities and sinister insinuations as to motives and sincerity. The work will be found to be a fair and full statement, in Dr. Tulloch's eloquent style, of the case as it stands against Renan's theory. "Amongst direct answers," says the Reader, *"to M. Renan, this volume will not be easily surpassed. . . The style is animated, pointed, and scholarly; the tone fair and appreciative; the philosophy intelligent and cautious; the Christianity liberal, reverent, and hearty."*

Vaughan.—Works by CHARLES J. VAUGHAN, D.D., Master of the Temple :—

Dr. Vaughan's genuine sympathy with the difficulties, sorrows and struggles of all classes of his fellow-men, his thorough disinterestedness, and his high views of life have been acknowledged by critics of all creeds. No sermons can be more applicable to the ever-recurring ills, bodily, mental, and spiritual, that flesh is heir to. His commentaries and expository lectures are those of a faithful evangelical, but at the same time liberal-minded interpreter of what he believes to be the Word of God.

CHRIST SATISFYING THE INSTINCTS OF HUMANITY. Eight Lectures delivered in the Temple Church. Extra fcp. 8vo. 3s. 6d.

The object of these Sermons is to exhibit the spiritual wants of human nature, and to prove that all of them receive full satisfaction in Christ. The various instincts which He is shewn to meet are those of Truth, Reverence, Perfection, Liberty, Courage, Sympathy, Sacrifice, and Unity. "We are convinced that there are congregations, in number unmistakeably increasing, to whom such Essays as these, full of thought and learning, are infinitely more beneficial, for they are more acceptable, than the recognised type of sermons." —John Bull.

Vaughan (Dr. C. J.)—*continued.*

MEMORIALS OF HARROW SUNDAYS. A Selection of Sermons preached in Harrow School Chapel. With a View of the Chapel. Fourth Edition. Crown 8vo. 10s. 6d.

While these Sermons deal with subjects that in a peculiar way concern the young, and in a manner that cannot fail to attract their attention and influence their conduct, they are in every respect applicable to people of all ages. "Discussing," says the John Bull, *"those forms of evil and impediments to duty which peculiarly beset the young, Dr. Vaughan has, with singular tact, blended deep thought and analytical investigation of principles with interesting earnestness and eloquent simplicity." The* Nonconformist *says "the volume is a precious one for family reading, and for the hand of the thoughtful boy or young man entering life."*

THE BOOK AND THE LIFE, and other Sermons, preached before the University of Cambridge. New Edition. Fcap. 8vo. 4s. 6d.

These Sermons are all of a thoroughly practical nature, and some of them are especially adapted to those who are in a state of anxious doubt. "They meet," the Freeman *says, "in what appears to us to be the one true method, the scepticism and indifference to religious truth which are almost sure to trouble young men who read and think. In short, we know no book more likely to do the young and inquiring good, or to help them to gain that tone of mind wanting which they may doubt and ask for ever, because always doubting and asking in vain."*

TWELVE DISCOURSES on SUBJECTS CONNECTED WITH THE LITURGY and WORSHIP of the CHURCH OF ENGLAND. Fcap. 8vo. 6s.

Four of these discourses were published in 1860, *in a work entitled* Revision of the Liturgy; *four others have appeared in the form of separate sermons, delivered on various occasions, and published at the time by request; and four are new. All will be found to*

5

Vaughan (Dr. C. J.)—*continued.*

fall strictly under the present title, reviewing the chief matters suggested by the Church Liturgy. The Appendix contains two articles,—one on "Subscription and Scruples," the other on the "Rubric and the Burial Service." The Press *characterises the volume as "eminently wise and temperate."*

LESSONS OF LIFE AND GODLINESS. A Selection of Sermons preached in the Parish Church of Doncaster. Fourth and Cheaper Edition. Fcap. 8vo. 3s. 6d.

This volume consists of Nineteen Sermons, mostly on subjects connected with the every-day walk and conversation of Christians. They bear such titles as "The Talebearer," "Features of Charity," "The Danger of Relapse," "The Secret Life and the Outward," "Family Prayer," "Zeal without Consistency," "The Gospel an Incentive to Industry in Business," "Use and Abuse of the World." The Spectator *styles them "earnest and human. They are adapted to every class and order in the social system, and will be read with wakeful interest by all who seek to amend whatever may be amiss in their natural disposition or in their acquired habits."*

WORDS FROM THE GOSPELS. A Second Selection of Sermons preached in the Parish Church of Doncaster. Second Edition. Fcap. 8vo. 4s. 6d.

In this volume are Twenty-two Sermons on subjects taken from one or other of the four Gospels. The Nonconformist *characterises these Sermons as "of practical earnestness, of a thoughtfulness that penetrates the common conditions and experiences of life, and brings the truths and examples of Scripture to bear on them with singular force, and of a style that owes its real elegance to the simplicity and directness which have fine culture for their roots. . . . A book than which few could give more holy pleasantness and solemn purpose to their Sabbath evenings at home."*

Vaughan (Dr. C. J.)—*continued.*

LESSONS OF THE CROSS AND PASSION. Six
Lectures delivered in Hereford Cathedral during the Week before
Easter, 1869. Fcap. 8vo. 2*s.* 6*d.*

*This volume contains Six Sermons on subjects mainly connected with
the death and passion of Christ. The titles of the Sermons are:—
I. "Too Late" (Matt. xxvi. 45). II. "The Divine Sacrifice and
the Human Priesthood." III. "Love not the World." IV.
"The Moral Glory of Christ." V. "Christ made perfect through
Suffering." VI. "Death the Remedy of Christ's Loneliness."
"This little volume," the* Nonconformist *says, "exhibits all his
best characteristics. Elevated, calm, and clear, the Sermons owe
much to their force, and yet they seem literally to owe nothing to it.
They are studied, but their grace is the grace of perfect simplicity."*

LIFE'S WORK AND GOD'S DISCIPLINE. Three
Sermons. Fcap. 8vo. cloth. 2*s.* 6*d.*

*The Three Sermons contained in this volume have a oneness of aim
indicated by the title, and are on the following subjects:—I. "The
Work burned and the Workmen saved." II. "The Individual
Hiring." III. "The Remedial Discipline of Disease and Death."*

THE WHOLESOME WORDS OF JESUS CHRIST.
Four Sermons preached before the University of Cambridge in
November 1866. Second Edition. Fcap. 8vo. cloth. 3*s.* 6*d.*

*Dr. Vaughan uses the word "Wholesome" here in its literal and
original sense, the sense in which St. Paul uses it, as meaning*
healthy, sound, conducing to right living; *and in these Sermons
he points out and illustrates several of the "wholesome" characteristics of the Gospel,—the Words of Christ. The subjects of these
Sermons are as follow:—I. "Naturalness and Spirituality of
Revelation—Grandeur and Self-Control—Truthfulness and Tenderness." II. "Universality and Individuality of Christ's Gospel."
III. "Oblivions and Ambitions of the Life of Grace." IV.
"Regrets and Preparations of Human Life." The* John Bull
*says this volume is "replete with all the author's well-known
vigour of thought and richness of expression."*

Vaughan (Dr. C. J.)—*continued.*

FOES OF FAITH. Sermons preached before the University of Cambridge in November 1868. Fcap. 8vo. 3s. 6d.

*The "Foes of Faith" preached against in these Four Sermons are:—
I. "Unreality." II. "Indolence." III. "Irreverence." IV.
"Inconsistency,"—"Foes," says the author, "which must be manfully fought against by all who would be finally admitted into that holy communion and fellowship which is, for time and eternity,* the blessed company of all faithful people." *"They are written," the* London Review *says, "with culture and elegance, and exhibit the thoughtful earnestness, piety, and good sense of their author."*

LECTURES ON THE EPISTLE to the PHILIPPIANS. Second Edition. Crown 8vo. 7s. 6d.

Each Lecture is prefaced by a literal translation from the Greek of the paragraph which forms its subject, contains first a minute explanation of the passage on which it is based, and then a practical application of the verse or clause selected as its text. The Press *speaks of these Lectures thus:—"Replete with good sense and practical religious advice... The language of the Apostle assumes a practical significance, which it seldom wears in the eyes of any ordinary reader, and Dr. Vaughan's listeners would feel themselves placed in the position of men receiving inspired instruction on the ordinary business of life. We can scarcely praise this plan too highly."*

LECTURES ON THE REVELATION OF ST. JOHN. Third and Cheaper Edition. Two Vols. Extra fcap. 8vo. 9s.

In this the Third Edition of these Lectures, the literal translations of the passages expounded will be found interwoven in the body of the Lectures themselves. In attempting to expound this most-hard-to-understand Book, Dr. Vaughan, while taking from others what assistance he required, has not adhered to any particular school of interpretation, but has endeavoured to shew forth the significance of this Revelation by the help of his strong common

Vaughan (Dr. C. J.)—*continued.*

sense, critical acumen, scholarship, and reverent spirit. "*Dr. Vaughan's Sermons,*" *the* Spectator *says,* "*are the most practical discourses on the Apocalypse with which we are acquainted.*" *Prefixed is a Synopsis of the Book of Revelation, and appended is an Index of passages illustrating the language of the Book.*

EPIPHANY, LENT, AND EASTER. A Selection of Expository Sermons. Third Edition. Crown 8vo. 10s. 6d.

The first eighteen of these Sermons were preached during the seasons of 1860, *indicated in the title, and are practical expositions of passages taken from the lessons of the days on which they were delivered. The last eight Sermons were added to the Second Edition. As in the case of the Lectures on Philippians, each Lecture is prefaced with a careful and literal rendering of the original of the passage of which the Lecture is an exposition.* The Nonconformist *says that* "*in simplicity, dignity, close adherence to the words of Scripture, insight into 'the mind of the Spirit,' and practical thoughtfulness, they are models of that species of pulpit instruction to which they belong.*"

THE EPISTLES OF ST. PAUL. For English Readers. PART I., containing the FIRST EPISTLE TO THE THESSALONIANS. Second Edition. 8vo. 1s. 6d. Each Epistle will be published separately in its chronological order.

It is the object of this work to enable English readers, unacquainted with Greek, to enter with intelligence into the meaning, connection, and phraseology of the writings of the great Apostle. (1) *Each Epistle will be prefaced by an Introduction containing information as to the circumstances, design, and order of its composition.* (2) *The Authorized English Version occupies the foremost place in each page.* (3) *Beside it, in smaller type, is a literal English Version, made from the original Greek.* (4) *A free paraphrase stands below, in which it is attempted to express the sense and connection of the Epistle.* (5) *The Notes include both doctrinal explanation and verbal illustration; occasionally a brief word of application has been introduced.*

Vaughan (Dr. C. J.)—continued.

ST. PAUL'S EPISTLE TO THE ROMANS. The Greek Text, with English Notes. Third Edition, greatly enlarged. Crown 8vo. 7s. 6d.

This volume contains the Greek Text of the Epistle to the Romans as settled by the Rev. B. F. Westcott, D.D., for his complete recension of the Text of the New Testament. Appended to the text are copious critical and exegetical Notes, the result, of almost eighteen years' study on the part of the author. The "Index of Words illustrated or explained in the Notes" will be found, in some considerable degree, an Index to the Epistles as a whole. "I have desired," the author says, "to catch and to represent the meaning of each passage and of the whole, without deriving it from any secondary source. One of my principal endeavours has been, to trace through the New Testament the uses of the more remarkable words or phrases which occur in the Epistle, arranging them, where the case required it, under their various modifications of sense." Prefixed to the volume is a discourse on "St. Paul's Conversion and Doctrine," suggested by some recent publications on St. Paul's theological standing. In the Preface to the Third Edition, which has been almost entirely rewritten, among other things, is a Synopsis of the contents of the Epistle. The Guardian says of the work,— "For educated young men his commentary seems to fill a gap hitherto unfilled. . . As a whole, Dr. Vaughan appears to us to have given to the world a valuable book of original and careful and earnest thought bestowed on the accomplishment of a work which will be of much service and which is much needed."

THE CHURCH OF THE FIRST DAYS.

Series I. The Church of Jerusalem. Second Edition.
   "   II. The Church of the Gentiles. Second Edition.
   "   III. The Church of the World. Second Edition.
Fcap. 8vo. cloth. 4s. 6d. each.

The work is in three volumes:—I. "The Church of Jerusalem," extending from the 1st to the 8th chapter (inclusive) of the Acts. II. "The Church of the Gentiles," from the 9th to the 16th chapter. III. "The Church of the World," from the 17th to the 28th chapter. Where necessary, the Authorized Version has been

Vaughan (Dr. C. J.)—*continued.*

departed from, and a new literal translation taken as the basis of exposition. All possible topographical and historical light has been brought to bear on the subject; and while thoroughly practical in their aim, these Lectures will be found to afford a fair notion of the history and condition of the Primitive Church. The British Quarterly *says,—" These Sermons are worthy of all praise, and are models of pulpit teaching."*

COUNSELS for YOUNG STUDENTS. Three Sermons preached before the University of Cambridge at the Opening of the Academical Year 1870-71. Fcap. 8vo. 2s. 6d.

The titles of the Three Sermons contained in this volume are:—I. "The Great Decision." II. "The House and the Builder." III. "The Prayer and the Counter-Prayer." They all bear pointedly, earnestly, and sympathisingly upon the conduct and pursuits of young students and young men generally, to counsel whom, Dr. Vaughan's qualifications and aptitude are well known.

NOTES FOR LECTURES ON CONFIRMATION, with suitable Prayers. Eighth Edition. Fcap. 8vo. 1s. 6d.

In preparation for the Confirmation held in Harrow School Chapel, Dr. Vaughan was in the habit of printing week by week, and distributing among the Candidates, somewhat full notes of the Lecture he purposed to deliver to them, together with a form of Prayer adapted to the particular subject. He has collected these weekly Notes and Prayers into this little volume, in the hope that it may assist the labours of those who are engaged in preparing Candidates for Confirmation, and who find it difficult to lay their hand upon any one book of suitable instruction. The Press *says the work "commends itself at once by its simplicity and by its logical arrangement. . . . While points of doctrine, as they arise, are not lost sight of, the principal stress is laid on the preparation of the heart rather than the head."*

THE TWO GREAT TEMPTATIONS. The Temptation of Man, and the Temptation of Christ. Lectures delivered in the Temple Church, Lent 1872. Extra fcap. 8vo. 3s. 6d.

Vaughan.—Works by DAVID J. VAUGHAN, M.A., Vicar of St. Martin's, Leicester :—

SERMONS PREACHED IN ST. JOHN'S CHURCH, LEICESTER, during the Years 1855 and 1856. Crown 8vo. 5s. 6d.

These Twenty-five Sermons embrace a great variety of topics, all of the highest interest, are thoroughly practical in their nature, and calculated to give a hopeful view of life as seen in the light shed upon it by Christianity.

SERMONS on the RESURRECTION. With a Preface. Fcap. 8vo. 3s.

In the Preface to this work, the author expounds and endeavours to justify his view of the Atonement, shewing it to be more reasonable and scriptural than the ordinary doctrine. There are Seven Sermons in all, bearing the following titles :—I. "The Fellowship of Christ's Sufferings." II. "Christ the Resurrection and the Life." III. "Christ our Passover." IV. "Christ the Shepherd." V. "The True Light which lighteth every man." VI. "The City of God, and the Light thereof." VII. "Christ going to the Father, and the Way to the Father."

CHRISTIAN EVIDENCES AND THE BIBLE. New Edition, revised and enlarged. Fcap. 8vo. cloth. 5s. 6d.

The main object of this series of Twelve Sermons is to shew, that, quite irrespective of any theory as to the nature of the Bible and the special inspiration of its authors, there is good and sufficient reason for believing that Jesus Christ is the Son of God, who reveals and reconciles men to the Father. The author thinks that the true and solid rock, upon which the Church really stands and ought consciously to stand, is simply the confession that "Jesus is the Christ, the Son of the living God." The Preface to this, the Second Edition, consists of an "Analysis of the Nature of Scientific Truth,"—the nature of the evidence which is universally held to be sound and conclusive. In the Sermons themselves the Internal and External Evidences of Christianity and cognate subjects are

Vaughan (D. J.)—*continued.*

discussed, and throughout the volume are several long notes on points occurring in the text. Appended is a short Essay on "The Nature and Sphere of Law."—"*This little volume,*" the Spectator says, "*is a model of that honest and reverent criticism of the Bible which is not only right, but the duty of English clergymen in such times as these to put forth from the pulpit.*"

Venn.—ON SOME OF THE CHARACTERISTICS OF

BELIEF, Scientific and Religious. Being the Hulsean Lectures for 1869. By the Rev. J. VENN, M.A. 8vo. 6s. 6d.

These discourses are intended to illustrate, explain, and work out into some of their consequences, certain characteristics by which the attainment of religious belief is prominently distinguished from the attainment of belief upon most other subjects. The first Lecture is an attempt to explain what is the nature of the logical foothold for differences of opinion among men; to shew what there is in the constitution of the evidence which makes it possible for these differences to commence and persist. The second meets the question, What is the criterion of truth? How are we to decide which of the varying but honest judgments on the same subject is right and which wrong? The third and fourth Lectures are devoted to working out into several of their consequences the characteristics of evidence on religious subjects which were explained and illustrated in the first.

Warington.—THE WEEK OF CREATION; OR, THE

COSMOGONY OF GENESIS CONSIDERED IN ITS RELATION TO MODERN SCIENCE. By GEORGE WARINGTON, Author of "The Historic Character of the Pentateuch Vindicated." Crown 8vo. 4s. 6d.

The greater part of this work is taken up with the teaching of the Cosmogony. Its purpose is also investigated, and a chapter is devoted to the consideration of the passage in which the difficulties occur. "A very able vindication of the Mosaic Cosmogony by a writer who unites the advantages of a critical knowledge of the Hebrew text and of distinguished scientific attainments."—Spectator.

Westcott.—Works by BROOKE FOSS WESTCOTT, D.D., Regius Professor of Divinity in the University of Cambridge; Canon of Peterborough :—

The London Quarterly, *speaking of Mr. Westcott, says,—" To a learning and accuracy which command respect and confidence, he unites what are not always to be found in union with these qualities, the no less valuable faculties of lucid arrangement and graceful and facile expression."*

AN INTRODUCTION TO THE STUDY OF THE GOSPELS. Fourth Edition. Crown 8vo. 10s. 6d.

The author's chief object in this work has been to shew that there is a true mean between the idea of a formal harmonization of the Gospels and the abandonment of their absolute truth. After an Introduction on the General Effects of the course of Modern Philosophy on the popular views of Christianity, he proceeds to determine in what way the principles therein indicated may be applied to the study of the Gospels. The treatise is divided into eight Chapters :—I. The Preparation for the Gospel. II. The Jewish Doctrine of the Messiah. III. The Origin of the Gospels. IV. The Characteristics of the Gospels. V. The Gospel of St. John. VI. and VII. The Differences in detail and of arrangement in the Synoptic Evangelists. VIII. The Difficulties of the Gospels. The Appendices contain much valuable subsidiary matter.

A GENERAL SURVEY OF THE HISTORY OF THE CANON OF THE NEW TESTAMENT DURING THE FIRST FOUR CENTURIES. Third Edition, revised. Crown 8vo. 10s. 6d.

The object of this treatise is to deal with the New Testament as a whole, and that on purely historical grounds. The separate books of which it is composed are considered not individually, but as claiming to be parts of the apostolic heritage of Christians. The Author has thus endeavoured to connect the history of the New Testament Canon with the growth and consolidation of the Catholic

Westcott (Dr. B. F.)—*continued.*

Church, and to point out the relation existing between the amount of evidence for the authenticity of its component parts and the whole mass of Christian literature. "The treatise," says the British Quarterly, *"is a scholarly performance, learned, dispassionate, discriminating, worthy of his subject and of the present state of Christian literature in relation to it."*

THE BIBLE IN THE CHURCH. A Popular Account of the Collection and Reception of the Holy Scriptures in the Christian Churches. Third Edition. 18mo. 4s. 6d.

The present volume has been written under the impression that a History of the whole Bible, and not of the New Testament only, would be required, if those unfamiliar with the subject were to be enabled to learn in what manner and with what consent the collection of Holy Scriptures was first made and then enlarged and finally closed by the Church. Though the work is intended to be simple and popular in its method, the author, for this very reason, has aimed at the strictest accuracy. The History of the Bible is brought down to the 16th *century, and the Appendix contains two articles,—I. "On the History of the Canon of the Old Testament before the Christian Era." II. "On the Contents of the most ancient MSS. of the Christian Bible." The* Literary Churchman *says, "Mr. Westcott's account of the 'Canon' is* true history *in the very highest sense."*

A GENERAL VIEW OF THE HISTORY OF THE ENGLISH BIBLE. Crown 8vo. 10s. 6d.

In the Introduction the author notices briefly the earliest vernacular versions of the Bible, especially those in Anglo-Saxon. Chapter I. is occupied with an account of the Manuscript English Bible from the 14th *century downwards; and in Chapter II. is narrated, with many interesting personal and other details, the External History of the Printed Bible. In Chapter III. is set forth the Internal History of the English Bible, shewing to what extent the various English Translations were independent, and to what*

Westcott (Dr. B. F.)—*continued.*

extent the translators were indebted to earlier English and foreign versions. In the Appendices, among other interesting and valuable matter, will be found "Specimens of the Earlier and Later Wycliffite Versions;" "Chronological List of Bibles;" "An Examination of Mr. Froude's History of the English Bible." The Pall Mall Gazette *calls the work "A brief, scholarly, and, to a great extent, an original contribution to theological literature."*

THE CHRISTIAN LIFE, MANIFOLD AND ONE.
Six Sermons preached in Peterborough Cathedral. Crown 8vo. 2s. 6d.

The Six Sermons contained in this volume are the first preached by the author as a Canon of Peterborough Cathedral. The subjects are:—I. "Life consecrated by the Ascension." II. "Many Gifts, One Spirit." III. "The Gospel of the Resurrection." IV. "Sufficiency of God." V. "Action the Test of Faith." VI. "Progress from the Confession of God." The Nonconformist *calls them "Beautiful discourses, singularly devout and tender."*

THE GOSPEL OF THE RESURRECTION. Thoughts
on its Relation to Reason and History. New Edition. Fcap. 8vo. 4s. 6d.

The present Essay is an endeavour to consider some of the elementary truths of Christianity, as a miraculous Revelation, from the side of History and Reason. The author endeavours to shew that a devout belief in the Life of Christ is quite compatible with a broad view of the course of human progress and a frank trust in the laws of our own minds. After a "Statement of the Question," and an Introduction on "Ideas of God, Nature, Miracles," Chapter I. treats of "The Resurrection and History;" Chapter II. "The Resurrection and Man;" Chapter III. "The Resurrection and the Church."—" We owe," the Patriot *says, "Mr. Westcott a very great debt of gratitude for his very able little treatise, so faithful to the great truths which are so precious to us, so catholic and spiritual in its conceptions of these truths, and, moreover, so philosophical in analysis, organism, and presentation."*

Wilkins.—THE LIGHT OF THE WORLD. An Essay, by A. S. WILKINS, M.A., Professor of Latin in Owens College, Manchester. Second Edition. Crown 8vo. 3*s.* 6*d.*

This is the Hulsean Prize Essay for 1869. *The subject proposed by the Trustees was, "The Distinctive Features of Christian as compared with Pagan Ethics." This the author treats in six chapters:—I. "The Object and Scope of the Discussion." II. and III. "Pagan Ethics—their Historical Development," and their Greatest Perfection." IV. V. and VI. "Christian Ethics —their Method," their Perfection," and their Power." The author has tried to show that the Christian ethics so far transcend the ethics of any or all of the Pagan systems in method, in purity and in power, as to compel us to assume for them an origin, differing in kind from the origin of any purely human system. "It would be difficult to praise too highly the spirit, the burden, the conclusions, or the scholarly finish of this beautiful Essay."*—British Quarterly Review.

Wilson.—RELIGIO CHEMICI. With a Vignette beautifully engraved after a Design by Sir NOEL PATON. By GEORGE WILSON, M.D. Crown 8vo. 8*s.* 6*d.*

"George Wilson," says the Preface to this volume, "had it in his heart for many years to write a book corresponding to the Religio Medici of Sir Thomas Browne, with the title Religio Chemici. Several of the Essays in this volume were intended to form chapters of it, but the health and leisure necessary to carry out his plans were never attainable, and thus fragments only of the designed work exist. These fragments, however, being in most cases like finished gems waiting to be set, some of them are now given in a collected form to his friends and the public." The Contents of the volume are:—"Chemistry and Natural Theology." "The Chemistry of the Stars; an Argument touching the Stars and their Inhabitants." "Chemical Final Causes; as illustrated by the presence of Phosphorus, Nitrogen, and Iron in the Higher Sentient Organisms." "Robert Boyle." "Wollaston." "Life and Discoveries of Dalton." "Thoughts on the Resurrection; an Address to Medical Students."—"A more fascinating volume," the Spectator *says, "has seldom fallen into our hands."*

Wilson.—THE BIBLE STUDENT'S GUIDE TO THE MORE CORRECT UNDERSTANDING of the ENGLISH TRANSLATION OF THE OLD TESTAMENT, BY REFERENCE TO THE ORIGINAL HEBREW. By WILLIAM WILSON, D.D., Canon of Winchester. Second Edition, carefully revised. 4to. 25*s*.

" The author believes that the present work is the nearest approach to a complete Concordance of every word in the original that has yet been made: and as a Concordance, it may be found of great use to the Bible student, while at the same time it serves the important object of furnishing the means of comparing synonymous words, and of eliciting their precise and distinctive meaning. The knowledge of the Hebrew language is not absolutely necessary to the profitable use of the work ; and it is believed that many devout and accurate students of the Bible, entirely unacquainted with it, will derive great advantage from frequent reference to these pages."   Introductory to the body of the work, the author gives a sketch of the Construction of Hebrew.   The plan of the work is simple : every word occurring in the English Version is arranged alphabetically, and under it is given the Hebrew word or words, with a full explanation of their meaning, of which it is meant to be a translation, and a complete list of the passages where it occurs.   Following the general work is a complete Hebrew and English Index, which is, in effect, a Hebrew-English Dictionary. Appended are copious examples of the Figure Paronomasia, which occurs so frequently in the Bible.

Worship (The) of God and Fellowship among Men. Sermons on Public Worship. By Professor MAURICE, and others. Fcap. 8vo. 3*s*. 6*d*.

This volume consists of Six Sermons preached by various clergymen, and although not addressed specially to any class, were suggested by recent efforts to bring the members of the Working Class to our Churches.   The preachers were—Professor Maurice, I. "Preaching, a Call to Worship." II. "The Bible, a Revelation of the Beginning and End of Worship."   Rev. T. J. Rowsell, "Common Prayer, the Method of Worship."   Rev. J. Ll. Davies,

*I. "Baptism, an Admission to the Privilege of Worship." II.
"The Sabbath Day, the Refreshment of Worship." Rev. D. J.
Vaughan, " The Lord's Supper, the most Sacred Bond of Worship."
" They are very suggestive to those who may have to prepare sermons,
and well calculated to be lent amongst the more thoughtful parish-
ioners."*—Literary Churchman.

Yonge (Charlotte M.)—SCRIPTURE READINGS for
SCHOOLS AND FAMILIES. By CHARLOTTE M. YONGE,
Author of "The Heir of Redclyffe." Globe 8vo. 1s. 6d. With
Comments. 3s. 6d.
A SECOND SERIES. From Joshua to Solomon. Extra fcap. 8vo.
1s. 6d. With Comments. 3s. 6d.

*Actual need has led the author to endeavour to prepare a reading book
convenient for study with children, containing the very words of
the Bible, with only a few expedient omissions, and arranged in
Lessons of such length as by experience she has found to suit with
children's ordinary power of accurate attentive interest. The verse
form has been retained because of its convenience for children reading
in class, and as more resembling their Bibles ; but the poetical
portions have been given in their lines. When Psalms or portions
from the Prophets illustrate or fall in with the narrative, they are
given in their chronological sequence. The Scripture portion, with
a very few notes explanatory of mere words, is bound up apart to
be used by children, while the same is also supplied with a brief
comment, the purpose of which is either to assist the teacher in
explaining the lesson, or to be used by more advanced young people
to whom it may not be possible to give access to the authorities whence
it has been taken. Professor Huxley at a meeting of the London
School-board, particularly mentioned the Selection made by Miss
Yonge, as an example of how selections might be made for School
reading. " Her Comments are models of their kind."*—Literary
Churchman.

In crown 8vo. cloth extra, Illustrated, price 4*s*. 6*d*. each Volume ; also
kept in morocco and calf bindings at moderate prices, and in
Ornamental Boxes containing Four Vols., 21*s*. each.

MACMILLAN'S SUNDAY LIBRARY.

A Series of Original Works by Eminent Authors.

The projectors of the Sunday Library *feel that there is a want of
books of a kind that will be welcome in many Households for reading
on Sundays, and will be in accordance with earnest convictions as to
the nature of the "Sabbath Day."*

*Sunday should contain the theory, the collective view, of our work-day
lives; and these work-days should be the Sunday in action. Our
Sunday Books, therefore, ought to do more than afford abstract subjects of meditation; they should exercise a living power, by bringing
us into direct contact with all that is true and noble in human nature
and human life, and by shewing us the life of Christ as the central
truth of humanity.*

*For Sunday reading, therefore, we need not only history, but history in
its relation to Christianity; not only biography, but the lives of men
who have consciously promoted the Christian religion—Christian
heroes in art, in science, in divinity, and in social action. The
history of Christianity, permanent and progressive, is also the history
of civilization, and from the growth of the latter we may be strengthened
in the faith that the former will ultimately prevail throughout the
whole world.*

*The Publishers have secured the co-operation of very eminent writers,
a list of whom, with the works they undertake, is herewith given.*

THE FOLLOWING VOLUMES ARE NOW READY:—

The Pupils of St. John the Divine.—By CHARLOTTE M. YONGE, Author of "The Heir of Redclyffe."

The author first gives a full sketch of the life and work of the Apostle himself, drawing the material from all the most trustworthy authorities, sacred and profane; then follow the lives of his immediate disciples, Ignatius, Quadratus, Polycarp, and others; which are succeeded by the lives of many of their pupils. The author then proceeds to sketch from their foundation the history of the many churches planted or superintended by St. John and his pupils, both in the East and West. In the last chapter is given an account of the present aspect of the Churches of St. John,—the Seven Churches of Asia mentioned in Revelations; *also those of Athens, of Nîmes, of Lyons, and others in the West. Throughout the volume, much of early Church History is necessarily introduced, and details are given of the many persecutions to which Christianity was subjected during its struggling infancy. "Young and old will be equally refreshed and taught by these pages, in which nothing is dull, and nothing is far-fetched."*—Churchman.

The Hermits.—By CANON KINGSLEY.

In the Introduction to this volume, Mr. Kingsley shews that early hermit-life was a natural outcome of the corrupt condition of Roman society, "which was no place for honest men,"— "where but to think was to be full of sorrow and leaden-eyed despair." The hermits "were a school of philosophers who altered the whole current of human thought; their influence is being felt around us in many a puzzle—educational, social, and political ;" these lives afford a "key to many a lock, which just now refuses to be tampered with or burst open." The volume contains the lives of some of the most remarkable early Egyptian, Syrian, Persian, and Western hermits. The lives are mostly translations from the original biographies ; "the reader will thus be able to see the men as wholes, to judge of their merits and defects."—"It is from first to last a production full of interest, written with a liberal appreciation of what is

6

memorable for good in the lives of the Hermits, and with a wise forbearance towards legends which may be due to the ignorance, and, no doubt, also to the strong faith of the early chroniclers."—London Review.

Seekers after God.—By the Rev. F. W. FARRAR, M.A., F.R.S., Head Master of Marlborough College.

In this volume the author seeks to record the lives, and gives copious samples of the almost Christ-like utterances of, with perhaps the exception of Socrates, " the best and holiest characters presented to us in the records of antiquity." They are Seneca, Epictetus, and Marcus Aurelius, most appropriately called "Seekers after God," seeing that "amid infinite difficulties and surrounded by a corrupt society, they devoted themselves to the earnest search after those truths which might best make their lives ' beautiful before God.'" The reader will learn from this volume in what kind of atmosphere the influences of Christianity were forced to work. Many details are also given which afford an insight into Roman life and manners, the kind of education bestowed on Roman youth, and the characteristics of the chief systems of ancient philosophy. The volume contains portraits of Aurelius, Seneca, and Antoninus Pius. "We can heartily recommend it as healthy in tone, instructive, interesting, mentally and spiritually stimulating and nutritious."—Nonconformist.

England's Antiphon.—By GEORGE MACDONALD.

This volume deals chiefly with the lyric or song-form of English religious poetry, other kinds, however, being not infrequently introduced. The author has sought to trace the course of our religious poetry from the 13th to the 19th centuries, from before Chaucer to Tennyson. He endeavours to accomplish his object by selecting the men who have produced the finest religious poetry, setting forth the circumstances in which they were placed, characterising the men themselves, critically estimating their productions, and giving ample specimens of their best religious lyrics, and quotations from larger poems, illustrating the religious feeling of the poets or their times. Thus the volume, besides providing a concert of the sweetest and purest music, will be found to exhibit the beliefs held and aspirations cherished by many of the noblest, purest, and most richly endowed minds during the last 600 years. —"Dr. Macdonald has very successfully endeavoured to bring together in his little book a whole series of the sweet singers of England, and makes them raise, one after the other, their voices in praise of God."—Guardian.

Great Christians of France: ST. LOUIS and CALVIN. By M. GUIZOT.

From among French Catholics, M. Guizot has, in this volume, selected Louis, King of France in the 13th century, and among Protestants, Calvin the Reformer in the 16th century, "as two earnest and illustrious representatives of the Christian faith and life, as well as of the loftiest thought and purest morality of their country and generation." In setting forth with considerable fulness the lives of these prominent and representative Christian men, M. Guizot necessarily introduces much of the political and religious history of the periods during which they lived. "A very interesting book," says the Guardian.

Christian Singers of Germany. — By CATHERINE WINKWORTH.

In this volume the authoress gives an account of the principal hymn-writers of Germany from the 9th to the 19th century, introducing ample (altogether about 120 translations) specimens from their best productions. In the translations, while the English is perfectly idiomatic and harmonious, the characteristic differences of the poems have been carefully imitated, and the general style and metre retained. The book is divided into chapters, the writers noticed and the hymns quoted in each chapter, being representative of an epoch in the religious life of Germany. In thus tracing the course of German hymnology, the authoress is necessarily "brought into contact with those great movements which have stirred the life of the people."—*"Miss Winkworth's volume of this series is, according to our view, the choicest production of her pen."* —British Quarterly Review.

Apostles of Mediæval Europe.—By the Rev. G. F. MACLEAR, D.D., Head Master of King's College School, London.

In two Introductory Chapters the author notices some of the chief characteristics of the mediæval period itself; gives a graphic sketch of the devastated state of Europe at the beginning of that period, and an interesting account of the religions of the three great groups of vigorous barbarians—the Celts, the Teutons, and the Sclaves—who had, wave after wave, overflowed its surface. He then proceeds to sketch the lives and work of the chief of the courageous men who devoted themselves to the stupendous task of their conversion and civilization, during a period extending from the 5th to the 13th century; such as St. Patrick, St. Columba, St. Columbanus, St. Augustine of Canterbury, St. Boniface, St. Olaf, St. Cyril, Raymond Sull, and others. In narrating the lives of these men, many glimpses are given into the political, social, and religious life of Europe during the Middle Ages, and many interesting and instructive incidents are introduced. "Mr. Maclear will have done a great work if his admirable little volume shall help to break up the dense ignorance which is still prevailing among people at large."—Literary Churchman.

Alfred the Great.—By THOMAS HUGHES, M.P., Author of "Tom Brown's School Days."

"The time is come when we English can no longer stand by as interested spectators only, but in which every one of our institutions will be sifted with rigour, and will have to shew cause for its existence. . . . As a help in this search, this life of the typical English King is here offered." After two Introductory Chapters, one on Kings and Kingship, and another depicting the condition of Wessex when Alfred became its ruler, the author proceeds to set forth the life and work of this great prince, shewing how he

conducted himself in all the relations of life. In the last chapter the author shews the bearing which Christianity has on the kingship and government of the nations and people of the world in which we live. Besides other illustrations in the volume, a Map of England is prefixed, shewing its divisions about 1000 A.D., *as well as at the present time.* "*Mr. Hughes has indeed written a good book, bright and readable we need hardly say, and of a very considerable historical value.*"—Spectator.

Nations Around.—By Miss A. KEARY.

This volume contains many details concerning the social and political life, the religion, the superstitions, the literature, the architecture, the commerce, the industry, of the Nations around Palestine, an acquaintance with which is necessary in order to a clear and full understanding of the history of the Hebrew people. The authoress has brought to her aid all the most recent investigations into the early history of these nations, referring frequently to the fruitful excavations which have brought to light the ruins and hieroglyphic writings of many of their buried cities. "*Miss Keary has skilfully availed herself of the opportunity to write a pleasing and instructive book.*"—Guardian. "*A valuable and interesting volume.*" —Illustrated Times.

St. Anselm.—By the Very Rev. R. W. CHURCH, M.A., Dean of St. Paul's.

In this biography of St. Anselm, while the story of his life as a man, a Christian, a clergyman, and a politician, is told impartially and fully, much light is shed on the ecclesiastical and political history of the time during which he lived, and on the internal economy of the monastic establishments of the period. Of the worthiness of St. Anselm to have his life recorded, Mr. Church says, "*It would not be easy to find one who so joined the largeness and daring of a powerful and inquiring intellect, with the graces and sweetness and unselfishness of the most loveable of friends, and with the fortitude, clear-sightedness, and dauntless*

firmness of a hero, forced into a hero's career in spite of himself."
The author has drawn his materials from contemporary biographers
and chroniclers, while at the same time he has consulted the best
recent authors who have treated of the man and his time. "*It is*
a sketch by the hand of a master, with every line marked by taste,
learning, and real apprehension of the subject." — Pall Mall
Gazette.

Francis of Assisi.—By Mrs. OLIPHANT.

The life of this saint, the founder of the Franciscan order, and one of
the most remarkable men of his time, illustrates some of the chief
characteristics of the religious life of the Middle Ages. Mrs.
Oliphant, in an Introduction, gives a slight sketch of the political
and religious condition of Europe in the 13th *century, in order to*
shew that the kind of life adopted by St. Francis was a natural
result of the influences by which he was surrounded. In the sub-
sequent biography much information is given concerning the mis-
sionary labours of the saint and his companions, as well as con-
cerning the religious and monastic life of the time. Many graphic
details are introduced from the saint's contemporary biographers,
which shew forth the prevalent beliefs of the period; and abundant
samples are given of St. Francis's own sayings, as well as a few
specimens of his simple tender hymns. "*We are grateful to Mrs.*
Oliphant for a book of much interest and pathetic beauty, a book
which none can read without being the better for it."—John Bull.

Pioneers and Founders; or, Recent Workers in the
Mission Field. By CHARLOTTE M. YONGE, Author of "The
Heir of Redclyffe." With Frontispiece, and Vignette Portrait of
BISHOP HEBER.

The author has endeavoured in these narratives to bring together such
of the more distinguished Missionaries of the English and American
Nations as might best illustrate the character and growth of
Mission-work in the last two centuries. The object has been to
throw together such biographies as are most complete, most illus-

trative, and have been found most inciting to stir up others— representative lives, as far as possible. The missionaries whose biographies are here given, are—John Eliot, the Apostle of the Red Indians; David Brainerd, the Enthusiast; Christian F. Schwartz, the Councillor of Tanjore; Henry Martyn, the Scholar-Missionary; William Carey and Joshua Marshman, the Serampore Missionaries; the Judson Family; the Bishops of Calcutta,—Thomas Middleton, Reginald Heber, Daniel Wilson; Samuel Marsden, the Australian Chaplain and Friend of the Maori; John Williams, the Martyr of Erromango; Allen Gardener, the Sailor Martyr; Charles Frederick Mackenzie, the Martyr of Zambesi. "Likely to be one of the most popular of the 'Sunday Library' volumes."—Literary Churchman.

THE "BOOK OF PRAISE" HYMNAL,

COMPILED AND ARRANGED BY

SIR ROUNDELL PALMER,

In the following four forms :—

A. Beautifully printed in Royal 32mo., limp cloth, price 6d.

B.   ,,   ,,   Small 18mo., larger type, cloth limp, 1s.

C. Same edition on fine paper, cloth, 1s. 6d.

Also an edition with Music, selected, harmonized, and composed by **JOHN HULLAH**, in square 18mo., cloth, 3s. 6d.

The large acceptance which has been given to " The Book of Praise" by all classes of Christian people encourages the Publishers in entertaining the hope that this Hymnal, which is mainly selected from it, may be extensively used in Congregations, and in some degree at least meet the desires of those who seek uniformity in common worship as a means towards that unity which pious souls yearn after, and which our Lord prayed for in behalf of his Church. " The office of a hymn is not to teach controversial Theology, but to give the voice of song to practical religion. No doubt, to do this, it must embody sound doctrine ; but it ought to do so, not after the manner of the schools, but with the breadth, freedom, and simplicity of the Fountain-head." On this principle has Sir R. Palmer proceeded in the preparation of this book.

The arrangement adopted is the following :—

PART I. *consists of Hymns arranged according to the subjects of the Creed—"God the Creator," "Christ Incarnate," "Christ Crucified," "Christ Risen," "Christ Ascended," "Christ's Kingdom and Judgment," etc.*

PART II. *comprises Hymns arranged according to the subjects of the Lord's Prayer.*

PART III. *Hymns for natural and sacred seasons.*

There are 320 Hymns in all.

CAMBRIDGE :—PRINTED BY J. PALMER.

www.ingramcontent.com/pod-product-compliance
Lightning Source LLC
Chambersburg PA
CBHW030825110726

47900CB00006B/1750